THE TRANSFORMING MOMENT

p. 49

D1025730

THE
TRANSFORMING
➤ MOMENT

SECOND EDITION

James E. Loder

HELMERS & HOWARD

COLORADO SPRINGS

Acknowledgment is made for the permission of Alfred A. Knopf, Inc., to reprint "The Curtains in the House of the Metaphysician" from *The Collected Poems of Wallace Stevens*, copyright 1923 and renewed 1951 by Wallace Stevens.

© 1989 by James E. Loder.

Second edition.

Published by Helmers & Howard, Publishers, Inc.
P.O. Box 7407, Colorado Springs, CO 80933 USA,
by arrangement with Harper & Row, Publishers Inc.

First edition (hardbound) published in 1981 by Harper & Row.

All rights reserved. No part of this book may be reproduced in any form or by any electronic or mechanical means, including information storage and retrieval systems, without permission in writing from the publisher, except by a reviewer, who may quote brief passages in a review.

Library of Congress Cataloging-in-Publication Data

Loder, James Edwin.
      The transforming moment / James E. Loder. — 2nd ed.
        p.   cm.
      Includes bibliographical references.
      ISBN 0-939443-17-1
        1. Christianity—Psychology.   2. Knowledge, Theory of
(Religion)   3. Experience (Religion)   I. Title.
      BR110.L625   1989
      248.2—dc20

Printed in the United States of America.

CONTENTS

PREFACE TO THE
SECOND EDITION

➤ AS THE SECOND edition of this book appears we will be entering the 1990s, almost a decade after the book was first written. The needs it was addressing in the early 1980s are if anything more urgent and timely now. Thus for any continuing influence this book may have, I am grateful that a second edition has now been made available.

Those needs may be related to four types of concern which are at issue throughout the discussion of the book. The first and uppermost concern is to understand the relationship between the human spirit and the Holy Spirit in a way that takes account of the human sciences (particularly psychology in the developmental and psychoanalytic traditions) as well the theology of the Holy Spirit (particularly in the Reformed theological tradition).

The second concern is to bring this understanding to bear on particular individuals and situations in which spiritual conflict is explicitly or tacitly the key issue. Since originally theological ideas about the human and Holy Spirit arose from just such situations, it is necessary that any new understanding be able to illuminate similar situations. Thus, the second concern is essentially hermeneutical: it is to show how reciprocity between understanding and situation can, indeed, issue in fresh insight and healing.

The third concern, implied in the first two, is for the interdisciplinary methodology that pertains between theology and the human sciences, and guides the unfolding of the relationship between human and Holy Spirit in varied contexts of thought and experience. This methodology may be characterized briefly as transformational and analogical. A transformational pattern which characterizes both spirits is the constructive basis for the analogy, but the human spirit must itself undergo transformation if it is to indwell the Holy Spirit in conformation with Christ. This methodology is potentially applicable to a wide range of contexts in which the human spirit is at work to generate new life and meanings, but its use is perhaps nowhere more trenchant and penetrating than in the study of human development. Since it is from the development of personality over the course of a lifetime that all other issues of thought, knowledge, and experience emerge, a major portion of the book is devoted to human development as a context for relating psychological and theological understandings.

The fourth concern is to reinvest theological language concerning the knowledge of God and life in the Spirit with tangible substance and experience. Since that language originated in the convergence between the life of God and human experience, its power to draw hidden dimensions out of common experience—to say nothing of its unique capacity to interpret convictional experiences—is immense. However, it can only perform that task if it is deeply related to scientific understandings and existential dimensions of human experience. Thus the reciprocity between the language of the theological tradition and human experience in this book is intended to address not only specific situations but also to counter dualistic tendencies in modern culture, which tend both to deracinate theological language in its concern for human existence and to impoverish our scientific understandings of what it means to be human in the context of transcendence.

Alongside these needs which the book originally addressed are new needs that have arisen from its readers. First, there has been a request for an overview of the argument that will lead the reader into the text with some anticipation of what is to come. To meet this need an introductory chapter has been added in which a missing note from Kierkegaard's journals sets the stage.

A second need is for a more "reader friendly" text. Since this is an interdisciplinary study, many of the terms having technical significance in one discipline may not be familiar to persons from other disciplines. In any case, for a book with the above concerns, technical terminology should be made understandable to any intelligent reader. To that end a glossary has been included in this second edition, not only for those interested in a more careful and informed reading of the text, but also for those interested in consulting outside texts which might be used to illuminate this one.

A third need has to do with the reader's personal appropriation of the material in the main body of the text. To overcome the sense of an abrupt ending to the first edition, an epilogue has been added. This is presented in the hope of encouraging further reflection and meditation on the main themes of the book in light of certain scriptural and theological events and images, out of which much of the book was originally generated.

I am grateful to Helmers and Howard for their suggestions and direction in preparing these last three additions. In particular, Kathy Yanni and Don Simpson have been extremely encouraging and attentive to the development of the text for this edition. Throughout my years at Princeton Seminary and at the Center of Theological Inquiry, Dr. James I. McCord has been a continual strength, inspiration, and unfailing resource. This book owes a great deal to his encouragement. I am also grateful for many informative and supportive conversations with Professor T. F. Torrance both in Princeton and Edinburgh, where he was a most gracious host. In this connection I am indebted to Princeton Seminary, which gave me a grant to do research at New College, Edinburgh. I must also express a debt of gratitude to the late Harold Nebelsick, whose personal warmth, theological and scientific scholarship, and generosity of mind were a continual inspiration during our days together at the Center of Theological Inquiry. Most unexpectedly gracious has been the immense help and friendship of Professor Jim Neidhardt, a physicist at the New Jersey Institute of Technology. His efforts in bringing this second edition to completion have been invaluable. There are too many others to mention by name, but I want to thank my students at Princeton Seminary for their insightful and critical reading of the book and for their specific contributions to this second edition. Finally, I must express my abiding gratitude to my wife and family, without whose support and shared life in the Spirit of Christ this book would never have been conceived, much less carried into a second edition.

PREFACE TO
THE FIRST EDITION

➢ WIDESPREAD ENTHUSIASM FOR spiritual experience arose phoenix-like out of the religious ashes of the 1960s. It has continued to flourish for ten years, and we are now entering the 1980s. Greatly encouraged by the "electronic church," Americans continue to grow in their enthusiasm for spiritual phenomena, mystical experiences, charismatic manifestations, neopentecostalism, and spiritual renewal movements. All these religious expressions have moved into the mainline denominations of Christianity, and their influence is spreading through this country and the world. In view of the various distortions of personality and social behavior that so often accompany such matters, this flourishing of ecstasies could be quite alarming. However, members of these groups, including Roman Catholics, Protestants, Pentecostals, and independent sects, claim more committed Christian lives, better physical and emotional health, economic security, and stronger family ties. In many instances, they can cite empirical studies to prove they did not "make it up." Spirit-directed counseling for emotionally disturbed people is gaining more highly trained leadership and a major following. Yet we can all cite instances of split churches and split personalities that have sanctioned destruction in the name of visions, ecstasies, new powers, healings, and so on.

How shall we tell the difference between subjective intoxication and the Divine Presence? And if it is Divine Presence, what then?

This era of spirituality requires a new way of thinking—thinking that not only is informed by theological and clinical approaches but also interprets transforming moments in their own right. Transforming moments need to be recognized as sources of new knowledge about God, self, and the world, and as generating the quality and strength of life that can deal creatively with the sense of nothingness shrouding the extremities and pervading the mainstream of modern living. Accordingly, this book explores an approach to convictional experiences, or experiences of potentially convicting significance, with the aim of bringing them into a perspective where they can be examined, unpacked, and interpreted, both for insight into God's action in the world and for informing our response to what he is doing.

The approach of this book explicitly deals with conviction in terms of Christian theology and the human sciences. Because none of these disciplines alone is sufficient, a genuinely interdisciplinary approach must be found that keeps faith with its parent disciplines while breaking fresh ground, particularly in relation to spiritual matters, My approach is a viewpoint to contemplate; it is not an attempt to say what God must be doing but a way of viewing his action with respect to our contemporary religious consciousness.

Moments of transforming significance radically reopen the question of reality for the person who experiences them. Coming to terms with a new sense of reality is a multidimensional struggle; this is where the study begins (Chapter 1). A coherent theory that is theologically and behaviorally adequate for viewing this question will be transformational (Chapter 2), four-dimensional (Chapter 3), and Christocentric (Chapter 4). Each of these characteristics is grounded in the structures and dynamics of human development (Chapters 5 and 6). The consequent theoretical viewpoint, integral as it is to Christian faith and human development, brings certain guidelines into focus. By these guidelines, situations of transforming significance may be opened up, assessed, and interpreted for their contribution to life in Christ (Chapter 7). I hope this approach and its conclusions will be helpful to many who are encountered by overpowering, life-changing moments but who do not know where to go from there.

My line of indebtedness extends far beyond the reach of this preface. However, I am especially grateful to the Center for Theological Inquiry for a grant that enabled me to spend time at Oxford

University consulting with Professor John Macquarrie, who very helpfully read and commented on the first full manuscript draft. I am grateful to many of my faculty colleagues who worked with me on key parts of this book or who have supported me in other ways. In this connection, I should mention especially David Willis and D. Campbell Wyckoff. Also, I must express my gratitude to the Reverend Sandra Murphy, who first boldly undertook to put my lecture notes into typed form, and I will mention as a group the long series of secretaries who have followed her effort with revisions of revisions. This book is dedicated to my students and counselees, who through their struggles have taught me so much.

Last, but surely not least, I am most grateful to my wife, who patiently and tirelessly edited nearly all of these pages, and to my entire family, who have heard many of these ideas discussed at great length with patience and insight, and have participated with me in that deeply mysterious, immensely gracious, and ever-faithful reality, the Holy Spirit of God.

INTRODUCTION

➤ THE AIM OF this book is to set forth a patterned process that describes the inner generative source of knowledge on several different levels of human experience. That pattern characterizes—though does not exhaust—the nature of the human spirit, and in a very different but analogical way it also characterizes the work of the Holy Spirit in human experience.

This introduction begins with a paradigm case in which much of the overall argument is contained and some is directly stated. This approach is to invite personal as well as intellectual participation on the part of the reader and to suggest that even if every point is not fully understood step by step, the sense of the whole should be permitted to illuminate the parts.

THE GENERATIVITY OF THE HUMAN SPIRIT

On May 19, 1838 at 10:30 A.M. a licentious university student, age 25, whose life had been plagued by a family curse, an ethos of death, a father whose Christianity was austere and guilt-ridden, and the unremitting dialectical powers of his own genius, recorded the following experience:

There is such a thing as an *indescribable joy* which glows through us as unaccountably as the Apostle's outburst is unexpected: "Rejoice, and

1

again I say, Rejoice!"—not a joy over this or that, but full jubilation "with hearts, and souls, and voices": "I rejoice over my joy, of, in, by, at, on, through, with my joy"— a heavenly refrain which cuts short, as it were, our ordinary song; a joy which cools and refreshes like a breeze, a gust of the trade wind which blows from the Grove of Mamre to the eternal mansion.[1]

When I went to the Royal Library of Denmark in Copenhagen to read this account in Søren Kierkegaard's own hand, I found that it had been neatly excised from the page by some razor sharp instrument. At first I was frustrated and angry, ready with righteous indignation to condemn the one who stole the blessing. But then I caught myself in a wry smile. How befitting Kierkegaardian irony this situation was. He was, after all, the master of indirect communication. His life's passion, like that of Socrates (though with a very different idea of the truth), was to provoke and to explore the inner contradictions in his readers, but then to vanish so his reader might find her or his own unique stance before the Truth. It was almost as if he had cut it out himself to make sure that the experience, important and decisive as it might be in its own right, become transparent to the reality it embodied. Thus, the reader's experience of it could then be as unique to him or her as this account was for Kierkegaard himself.

THE LOGIC OF TRANSFORMATION

We will return to Kierkegaard's journal, but first note that in my secondary response to the excision is evidence that the generative sources of human intelligence abhor a vacuum. Beneath our educated and scholarly ways of knowing, another dynamic moves to explore "the deep things of the person," and to generate from hidden resources new, and sometimes powerful, insights that transform the horizons of intelligibility. Already in my brief experience at the Royal Library, that underlying generativity had created something out of the nothing I had found. Kierkegaard called this generative *dunamis* the human spirit.

Much more must be said about this dynamic, but here let me introduce the human spirit, the uninvited guest in every meaningful knowing event and the dynamic that unobtrusively directs and shapes them all. This dynamic can be characterized as a coherent pattern of knowing which draws into a differentiated whole the many splintered

---

1. Walter Lowrie, *A Short Life of Kierkegaard* (Garden City, N.J.: Doubleday Anchor Books, 1961), p. 100.

ways we are taught to think. Although this pattern does not emphasize cognitive behavior, its power to shape cognition is familiar to us
in acts of creativity and scientific discovery. It is not predominantly a
passionate, Dionysian way of knowing, but it is profoundly evident in
the intuitive and affective ways we know each other in acts of love and
compassion. It does not stress either the transcendent self or the
immanent self at the expense of the other, but tends to accentuate the
dual unity of the self by holding transcendence and immanence
together and apart at the same time (as discussed in Chapter 3).

Essential to the spirit's nature is its wind-like quality; it often takes
us by surprise and leads us where we would not otherwise go. Its
deeper characteristic, however, is its integrity in driving toward
meaning and wholeness in every complex and variegated context.
Thus, in an understanding of the spirit, continuity and discontinuity
must be combined in a patterned process that does justice to both in
the context of a single act or event. This study proposes to show how
they are combined in what will be called the logic of transformation.

The steps of this logic are as follows:

(1) *Conflict-in-context.* In a given context, the deep movement of
the human spirit begins in restless incoherence, dichotomy, or frag-
mented situations (such as documents missing from the Royal Library) which defy our elemental longings for coherence. The spirit's
movement is "deep" because often the basic incoherence is more
unconscious than conscious. Furthermore, the generative powers of
the spirit are not sufficiently engaged until unconscious resources
become involved in resolving the incoherence.

(2) *Interlude for scanning.* Whether conscious or unconscious, the
spirit in the psyche cannot rest with incoherence. Although much of
human activity, intellectual as well as experiential, is random and
inconsistent, the inner drive toward consistency and the resolution of
dissonance is a persistent force in psychic life. Thus once a conflict is
engaged, the spirit begins the search for resolution. It scans inward
and outward for relevant possibilities and prototypes beyond the
frame of the problem (or beyond the empty rectangle in the middle of
that page of Kierkegaard's journal) that can overcome the discrepan-
cies which are not consistent with the integrity of our research or of
our souls.

(3) *Insight felt with intuitive force.* Sooner or later the ingenuity of
the spirit will surprise and often delight us with a constructive
resolution that reconstellates the elements of the incoherence and
creates a new, more comprehensive context of meaning. This new

context transforms the previously conflicted elements or frames of reference, yet without distorting their integrity. (Thus the absence of the document is, in a larger and appropriate frame of reference, more Kierkegaardian than its presence would have been).

(4) *Release and repatterning.* It is a basic principle of the spirit that energy is invested in and bound by the incoherence, holding on to the conflicted elements so as to effect, if possible, a transformation. Consequently, when the constructive resolution appears, there is a release of energy bound up with the conflict. This "aha" (wry smile), "Eureka," or "Hosanna" effect is not an incidental byproduct of an otherwise clear-cut logical sequence; it is the usually necessary but not sufficient evidence that the resolution fits. Energy is now available for testing and repatterning the original situation in light of the new resolution.

(5) *Interpretation and verification.* In keeping with this drive toward completion of continuity, the spirit eventually seeks confirmation and verification by interpreting the insight back into the incoherence to see whether its conditions have been met. (The requirements of indirect communication are met in the empty rectangle on the journal page.) Finally, the resolution must be submitted to a public test (such as putting it in print).

These five steps, in their systemic interconnectedness, constitute the logic of transformation inherent in the human spirit. Here it is important to understand that transformation is not merely a synonym for positive change. Rather it occurs whenever, within a given frame of reference or experience, hidden orders of coherence and meaning emerge to alter the axioms of the given frame and reorder its elements accordingly.

The pattern described above is easily recognized in common acts of constructive experience (as I have illustrated with the missing document), in acts of scientific discovery, and in creative work in the arts or literature. However, in such examples the human spirit is operating largely under the agency of the human ego, which does not itself undergo transformation. Let us suppose that the conflicted situation, vacuum, or void was endemic to the ego itself. Then, would this patterned process still pertain? The basic answer of this study will be "yes," but in such cases the logic of transformation is transposed to the level of divine action. In this the Holy Spirit as *Spiritus Creator,* whose mission begins and ends in the inner life of God, transforms the human ego—and by implication, then, all human transformations which issue from the ego are themselves transformed.

THE TRANSFORMING POWER OF *SPIRITUS CREATOR*

To illustrate this transformation, return to Kierkegaard's description of indescribable joy.[2] Note first that he himself did not explicitly connect this stunning moment to anything past or future. In fact he does not refer to it anywhere else except here in his journals. However, through the lenses of his life and authorship, it can be seen as a highly condensed, transfigured resolution of conflicted forces which lie behind the immense influence of this solitary individual.

This account is an in-breaking insight coming upon young Søren before he himself was fully aware of the depth of his own conflicts. It represents what he would later call a "transparent" grounding in "the Power that posits the self" (*Sickness Unto Death*), and proleptically this anticipates a transformation of all registers of behavior that issue from the self—particularly imagination, which yields to "transparency" or imageless images; reason, which yields to the *supra rationem* expressed in "Absolute Paradox"; and passion, which becomes "the happy passion of faith."

Specifically, the journal entry is extremely rich in imagery, but this is mainly an account in which imagery is inherently insufficient. Like Paul's experience (2 Cor. 12:4) when he was "caught up into paradise and heard unspeakable words . . . ," Søren's experience essentially exceeds all language or metaphor. Although Kierkegaard was not a mystic, this is very like a direct knowledge of God in the classical mystical tradition. The transparency relationship of the human self to the Divine Presence temporarily bursts the limits of the imagination, but imagination recoils and images rush like a torrent into the pure light of the transparency as one shields one's eyes when surprised by a sudden burst of sunlight. Imagination, Kierkegaard later wrote, is the faculty *instar omnium* (for all other faculties), but it never supersedes transparency.

What the imagination does accomplish, however, is illuminating. The dominant theme is the rush of joy, expressed as the "glow" of light to which one awakens. To place himself somehow in this joy, Kierkegaard identifies with St. Paul, and joy, like light, pulsates back and forth through his soul, "over . . . of, in, by, at, on, through, with. . . ." Each additional preposition catches some new facet of the

---

2. The following account of Kierkegaard's experience is schematized for the sake of illustration. The deeper and more complex issues which such experiences raise regarding one's existence before God over the course of a lifetime are necessarily postponed for fuller treatment in the main text of this book.

ineffable Source, and then, as if each preposition were still not enough, it is immediately superseded by a new surge of illumination. Then glowing joy shifts to singing, and song gives way to a breeze that cools and refreshes. From the glow that bursts with joy to the breeze that cools, a full range of ecstatic experience is covered. Clearly, this experience is not a product of Kierkegaard's imagination: it is an ineffable experience for which his imagination tries to provide a cognitive shape that will unite conscious and unconscious in a new horizon of meaning for a radically transformed personal existence.

The crowning image alluding to Abraham transforms the depth of unconscious despair in Kierkegaard and metaphorically unites him to the transcendent holiness of God. Thus, the One who comes to young Søren is the One (in three) who comes to Abraham in Genesis 18:1 — "The Lord appeared to him by the Oaks of Mamre, as he sat in the tent door in the heat of the day." The fundamental incoherence that lies behind this master image in Kierkegaard is the personally devastating relationship that Søren had with his father, and the alienation they both had from God. This was a desperate separation which both took extremely seriously, and it was the curse under which they lived.[3] The reference to Abraham puts this and Søren's recent reconciliation to his father in startling new focus as follows.

On Søren's twenty-fifth birthday, just two weeks before this experience, his father, a very old eighty-two, confessed the sins of his youth (his cursing of God and his sensuality) to his son. He asked his forgiveness for them and for all the negative consequences they had brought on the family. Walter Lowrie writes that Søren must have been horrified to discover that his own apostasy and sensuality "had exactly repeated the experience of his father."[4] This brought him to himself, and when father and son had forgiven and blessed each other, Søren could return home. This is the most significant human occasion behind the higher order, spiritual reconciliation, which his experience of joy displays.

As a human reconciliation, it is immensely satisfying, as in the joy between Cordelia and King Lear when they are reconciled (a parallel to which Kierkegaard refers), but it is at the same time theologically and existentially deficient. The power of the Spirit under which this experience occurs negates all the negations of human kinship; the human bloodline must be negated and transformed into the blood of

---

3. Referring to the prevailing significance of this curse, Kierkegaard's elder brother Peter said in his later years, "This is our father's story *and ours*."
4. Lowrie, *A Short Life of Kierkegaard*, p. 101.

Christ if eternal death is to be overcome. Young Søren had to be transformed from an illegitimate child of the flesh, Ishmael, to the child of promise and of God, Isaac. The message of the cooling "trade wind" was that this had been accomplished. Less than two months after this indescribable experience, Søren went to confession to prepare himself for receiving Communion. When he took Communion, he went alone without his father or his brother, an ordained clergyman. On August 8 of that same year, his father died.

By the transformative power of the Holy Spirit (note that the "trade wind" is Søren's addition to Genesis 18), the double conflict between father and son, and between them both and God, was resolved in a stunning moment of participation in the joyful holiness of God. The biblical image that transforms kinship and alienation into reconciliation to God is aged Abraham, who runs from his tent in the heat of the day to receive from God the promise of the son who will be conceived in Sarah's womb. Thus an aged father of eighty-two reaching out to his estranged son becomes young Søren's prototype for the master image of Abraham, in whom the father-son relationship is transfigured into a relationship constituted and sustained not by kinship but by grace alone. This God made plain to Abraham on Mt. Moriah many years later, and Kierkegaard later dramatically restated the point in his famous "Panegyric on Abraham" in *Fear and Trembling*, all in anticipation of Calvary.[5]

If Lowrie was correct, the experience of inexpressible joy "was . . . super real, and it preoccupied him all his life long."[6] If the joy here is Kierkegaard's "Hosanna," then verification and confirmation can be found in his "prodigious authorship," which has been perpetuated around the globe from West to East and portrayed in every medium of the modern world from literature and drama to television and film. Most profoundly, of course, he altered the course of modern philosophy and theology though he had no institutional connections in church or university to promote his thought. It should not be forgotten, however, that his own assessment of his influence, which knowledge of subsequent history would not have changed, was that he "was just a little bit of spice."

Finally, Kierkegaard's identification with St. Paul is not incidental. For him, his authorship was in the last analysis like St. Paul's gospel,

---

5. The Abraham-Isaac relationship is a long-standing multivalent image in Kierkegaard's relation to his father. What is described here is the preeminent, positive turn it takes in making Kierkegaard, like Isaac (as prototype of Jesus), one whose relations to God and to his father are sustained only by grace.
6. Lowrie, *A Short Life of Kierkegaard*, p. 103.

from God alone (Gal. 1:12). Although there were human prototypes, he "did not receive it from man, nor was [he] taught it, but it came through a revelation of Jesus Christ." For those aware of Kierkegaardian stereotypes, it comes as an irony that joy, not melancholy; relationship, not individualism; transparent union with God, not despairing alienation; have generated this incredible authorship.

Of course, this is only to suggest for the case of Søren Kierkegaard some of the aspects of human existence that are taken up in the power of the Creator Spirit and transformed through an experience of indescribable joy. Clearly we have just begun to explore the dimensions of the dynamic reality that lies behind such convictional experience as this, the gracious complementarity between the human spirit and the Holy Spirit, and the impact they may have upon individual and corporate life. These matters will be taken up in the following chapters.

For the moment we return to the larger significance of the fact that this section of Kierkegaard's journals was missing from the Royal Library. Its absence is parabolic, since in the end we will not be able to imagine the depth and magnitude of the reality to which even the best images of the most profound minds are pointing us. All understanding and models must finally become transparent and vanish. Then, in death to all else, each one may appear face to face before the One who always comes from the other side of ultimate human emptiness.

Sometimes one must be thrown into such a confrontation, and here is where this book begins.

One

CONVICTION
BEYOND REASON

A BEGINNING EVENT

➤ ON SATURDAY, SEPTEMBER 2, 1970, my wife, two daughters, and I
set forth on a brief trip from our home in Princeton, New Jersey, to
Quebec, Canada. The day was lifted from a travel poster. The sun
glistened on the green, wooded hills lining the highway, and a gentle
breeze from the east rippled the grass and pushed wispy clouds across
a bright blue sky. The setting was in stark contrast to the scene that
follows, although quite in keeping with its ultimate significance.

About 4:30 P.M. we were heading north on the throughway near
Kingston, New York, when we saw a middle-aged woman standing
near a disabled car. Gingerly waving a white glove, she stood danger-
ously near the constant stream of rocketing traffic. Alarmed at her
precarious stance, and her apparent incapacity to implement the
standard methods of getting help, we pulled off the road to offer
assistance.[1]

I parked our camper about fifteen feet in front of her car and
emerged to discover nothing more demanding than a flat tire on the
left front wheel. While I tried to make a wobbly jack work on the

---

1. The Kingston newspaper carried a story about the following accident, calling me a
"good Samaritan"; but I was quite unaccustomed to stopping, because in my view
standardized procedures for getting help were already a differentiated version of the
good Samaritan. Thus I started on this venture more out of alarm and duty than out of
any special compassion.

rusting Oldsmobile, my wife, Arlene, went to speak with the woman and her traveling companion. They chatted as they stood by watching my frustrated efforts.

The jack wouldn't lock into the chassis on the left front side, so I moved over to the right wheel, hoping for clues. Just as I knelt in front of the right front fender, there was an ear-splitting screech of brakes. A sixty-four-year-old man who had "never had an accident in his life" had gone to sleep at that precise point on the throughway. Braking only for an instant, he rammed the Olds from behind and shoved it over on top of me. I had heard, seen, and felt it coming; I kept my legs pushing from under the car to keep my head and shoulders ahead of the bumper as the body of the car ground me forward through the gravel. The next impact was the Olds smashing into the rear of our camper. This came, fortunately, on the left side of the Olds, and it stopped at an angle with enough room for my head and shoulders to rest to the right of the point of impact.

I later learned that my right thumb had been torn off at the first joint, five ribs were broken, the left lung was bleeding, and my skin was gouged and scraped from head to foot. In spite of these injuries, I never lost consciousness, although some shock reaction apparently numbed the pain. Trapped with the front of the Olds on my chest, I called for help.

Because the two women who had been traveling together had also been injured in the collision, there was no one to help but my wife. Arlene is a slight woman, barely over five feet tall. With her hands under the bumper, she prayed, "In the name of Jesus Christ, in the name of Jesus Christ. . . ." Recounting this event later, she said that when her strength in the heaving effort began to give way, she partially lost consciousness for a few seconds; when she was able to refocus her attention, she was surprised to see that the car had been lifted. As the medical record shows, she broke a vertebra in this effort, but she did not notice it at the time and, with treatment, recovered full use of her back about three months later.

As I roused myself from under the car, a steady surge of life was rushing through me, carrying with it two solid assurances. First, I knew how deeply I felt love for those around me, especially my family. My two daughters sat crying on the embankment, and a deep love reached out of me toward them. The second assurance was that this disaster had a purpose. These were the words with which I repeatedly tried to reassure my wife and children: "Don't worry; this has a purpose."

Walking from the car to the embankment, I never felt more conscious of the life that poured through me, nor more aware that this life was not my own. My well-being came from beyond my natural strength, and I lay down on the grass mostly because I thought I ought to. When our three-year-old daughter, Tami, came to sit on my broken chest, I was able to comfort her with a story.

My state of being was not strictly controlled by adrenalin. The adrenalin activated aggression toward the driver who had caused the collision, but the flow of life in me was both a stronger and quieter force, so that the thought of retaliation was subdued. By far, the most significant and memorable effect was not the pain, nor the anger, but the gracious nature of the life I was experiencing.

The state troopers and a corps of others stopped to help and stare. A clergyman wanted to give me pastoral care. An elderly gentleman leaned on his cane to inquire whether I would be all right. The physician's hands trembled as she checked my eyes for concussion. To me, life was never in doubt because I was being lived, it seemed, by a life not my own. I was very much in my body, but life was pouring into me from a gracious source beyond the power of that accident to damage or destroy me.

When the ambulance arrived, I moved over to the stretcher. Arlene refused to leave the scene until the trooper promised to find my thumb. With resigned determination, he set about the search, while the ambulance left for the hospital. I was still being sustained in my physical strength and in my spirit.

At the hospital, it was not the medical staff, grateful as I was for them, but the crucifixes—in the lobby and in the patients' rooms—that provided a total account of my condition. In that cruciform image of Christ, the combination of physical pain and the assurance of a life greater than death gave objective expression and meaning to the sense of promise and transcendence that lived within the midst of my suffering.

The ordeal in the x-ray department was physically debilitating; I was beginning to feel cold, and my hands looked a little blue. My physical strength declined as the pain increased. Nevertheless, the enduring essentials of love and purpose remained. In the hallway, the trooper appeared with the thumb fragment too dirty to be reattached. Showing my wife the x-rays of a bleeding lung, the surgeon said they would round off the thumb quickly so that I could go into oxygen as soon as possible. "That thumb won't do him any good if he's dead," he added tersely.

When Arlene called her father, a clergyman near Chicago, she found him at church, praying with a number of friends from his congregation. "We'll *all* pray for him right now," was his reply. I didn't know that several people were praying for me just about the time I entered surgery (it was about 9 P.M. Kingston time); but I knew that the power of life from beyond me once again rushed into my body. Moreover, my sense was that the power was not impersonal, but was emanating from the center of Another's awareness — an awareness that positively, even joyfully, intended my well-being. Even as I entertained that intuition, the physical pain decreased. Down in the waiting room, my older daughter Kim suddenly stopped crying, turned to her mother, and said, "I know Daddy is going to be all right."

In contrast to my immediate exhilaration, I could see as I entered surgery the tired, solemn faces of the surgical staff waiting for what they must have thought would be another grim life-against-death struggle, in which they would valiantly play their part for life. I found humor on the tip of my tongue and began to assure them that I was soon going to be well. It did not seem inappropriate in that joyful Presence to invite the staff to join me in a hymn of praise before the surgery began. Probably wondering if I had gone into shock, the staff remained quiet as I sang a few bars of "Fairest Lord Jesus" alone. Nevertheless, the atmosphere of the room seemed to quicken, the humor became contagious even in the aseptic surroundings, and, before long, the personnel were smiling and laughing with me, passing on information about surgical procedures and practice. The Jewish surgeon and I enjoyed discussing portions of the Hebrew scriptures as he rounded off and sewed up my thumb. To corroborate with visible evidence what had been going on invisibly in that room, my bluish skin was turning pink, and the bleeding in my lung had ceased. The plan to send me into oxygen was canceled.

Two days after the accident, a telling remark was made by the head surgeon on this case. Canceling plans to perform skin grafts on damaged areas of my back, he remarked, "A good surgeon knows when to get out of the way and let God do the healing." Thus he summarized from his own viewpoint how I had lived through an otherwise very factual matter contained in police reports, medical records, insurance claims, and newspaper accounts. Fact and meaning had combined to compose a convicting experience.

Many things could be noted in the aftermath of this experience. Later we found in my wife's notes, taken down in prayer several days before, a saying that greatly puzzled her at the time. The words that had come to her were, "Take the cup I have prepared for you." This, of course, raises the question of theodicy; namely, how can a good God allow the presence of evil, as in this and other more disastrous events? I tend to agree with those who say theodicy is presumptuous, but we all ask this question, so I will discuss it further when I take up the issue of the void and its many faces in human experience (Chapter 3).

As to the two women who were hurt in the accident, they recovered after a period in the hospital, and we continued to stay in touch with them for some time, even exchanging Christmas gifts. I could never reach the driver of the car that hit us. He left the hospital after a brief examination, unhurt, and did not answer his phone. We took minimum insurance benefits from this accident because it meant so much to us in other ways. Our lawyer understood this but insisted that we take some reparation for damages; what we did receive, we gave to the church.

Some months later, I visited the church that had so promptly prayed for me. Rising during the worship service to say a few words of appreciation, I found myself unable to speak, too overcome by the gratitude I felt. I stood in silence before a smiling and receptive congregation who nevertheless perceived in the silence my inexpressible thanksgiving to the God we all worshipped.

Although I resisted the implications of this experience for over two years, the eventual consequence was that I had to act on the growing internal necessity to identify myself with the ministry of the church and to complete the ordination proceedings, which I had held in reservation for several years. This became a matter of conscience, not derived from any moral sense of obligation or abstract principles, but in the sense of knowing within oneself the necessary direction of one's integrity.

I do not want to leave the impression that this episode had only positive implications. Convictional experience should not be taken as valid because everything came out all right; the pragmatic test is more dramatic, but it is no more true than those in which one comes under conviction through loss and death. More about this later.

This episode, in fact, raised countless new questions, disturbed several personal relationships, and forced me to reenvision the spiritual center of my vocation—not an easy matter when one is already teaching in a theological seminary. It undoubtedly presented me with the reality to which I have had to be true and from which I have departed only with a keen sense of having violated my own soul. I had been and am convicted.

QUESTIONING CONVICTION

The word "convict" and its cognates are intended to mean what the Latin root, *convinco*, suggests: "to overcome, to conquer, to refute."[2] Speaking of "conviction" draws on judicial imagery and declares that that one is thoroughly convinced; the case is incontestable; the conviction will stand as part of a permanent record. In this imagery three axes of conviction are evident: the Convictor, the convicted person, and the endurance through time of the convictional relationship between them. Speaking of "experience" in relation to conviction means that the convicted person is compelled to reopen the question of reality in light of the presumed nature of the Convictor and the convictional relationship. The way in which "convictional experience" discloses reality and calls for new interpretations is the focus of my attention here.

Now, you might first wish to ask if I have reported my experience fully and accurately. Then, if you were satisfied on that account, but there remained some explanatory gap, you might insist, "Is it not necessary to assume that the gap will eventually be closed by as-yet-unknown natural causes? There is nothing more remarkable here than some unexplained connections." In this way, you might seek to dismiss as largely imaginary what I have told you as a remarkably convincing experience.

I do believe I have reported accurately, although many details and further aspects could be added and developed; however, it seems to me that the more important question is, "What really happened?" or "Is this a *true* story in the deepest sense?" Elaborated, this question would be, "What is the presumed reality by which you determine the truth or falsity of this experience? Then, how does it fit or not fit that reality?" We have to raise the issue this way not only for this experience but for countless other accounts just like it that fall victim to unexamined "realities" and end up confused and troublesome half-truths for the people involved. Summarily, the experiences we want eventually to understand in *Christian* terms are precisely those that reopen the question of reality because the subject of the experience has been convicted by a Spiritual Presence far greater than the subject him- or herself.[3]

2. My use of the term *conviction* is in some debt to Willem Zuurdeeg's *An Analytical Philosophy of Religion*, but my emphasis is more upon the experience designated by the word than on the placing of *conviction* as a term in the philosophy of religion.
3. This way of formulating the essence of the phenomenon is partly indebted to Sir Alister Hardy's wording in *The Spiritual Nature of Man* (Oxford, England: Oxford

As you will see, insisting on examining the question of one's presumed reality makes it necessary for us to understand a great deal more before we can understand and assess any of these experiences in particular. It may seem that such a circumspect approach will take us too far afield, but it is precisely the inclination to make a quick assessment on the basis of an unexamined reality that usually deprives these experiences of what they want to tell us. They are rich in meaning and implications for our participation in the Christian faith. Consequently, they must be set in an appropriately broad and rich context if their truth is to become evident. Thus, I will turn now to several of those larger contexts; some are helpful, some are not, and some are both.

TWO PROMINENT MISUNDERSTANDINGS

There are two basic ways to misunderstand such experiences, or more properly, two ways in which a partial understanding may easily be taken for the whole. The first misunderstanding we owe to psychology and its cognate disciplines, ranging from physiology, on the one hand, to sociology, on the other. For convenience, we will refer to these as the "human sciences." The human sciences affect our reaction to such stories on two levels.

On the experiential level, many of us resort to unreflective rituals of denial, using popularized phrases and partially grasped notions (stress reaction, hysteria, shock, and so on) handed down by the human sciences to dismiss or disdain such accounts as unreflectively as possible. A typical case is a man who commuted to work every day by train. At the train station one morning, he suddenly slipped and was caught between train and platform. Screaming in pain and crying out for help, he promised God he would "do anything" if he could be saved; and so he was, by a couple of alert students who pulled him free. Later, recovering from the episode in the hospital, he at first denied that he had made any such promise, and then, pushed to honesty, he consigned his cry to mere desperation.

Is it possible that he was closer to the fundamental reality of his existence while being crushed in pain against the platform than he was

---

University Press, 1969). I am asking a different sort of question, focusing more on the issue of "reality." This does not suggest that I am interested *only* in that particular sort of experience in which the subject him- or herself raises the reality question. Rather, any of the experiences Hardy has catalogued may serve to reopen the question for someone else and so are grist for this discussion.

reclining in that hospital bed? Most of us will consider that possibility only as briefly as it takes to mention it. In any case, he exorcised the whole matter and resumed his usual routine after being dismissed from the hospital. This, I suggest, is common and tends to occur whether the experience is extraordinarily violent, ecstatic, deeply mystical, or some combination of these. It does not have to be painful for us to want it dismissed, just inexplicable. Thus popular realism bolstered by snippets of insight from the human sciences exerts a powerful repressive force against such experiences. Because most of us do not like to be reminded of times when, in our waking hours, we have even briefly lost control of our lives, we tend to give as little afterthought to these experiences as we can.

On the academic level, there have been many recountings, classifications, and reinterpretations of experiences in which people have been directly or indirectly brought under the influence of a spiritual power beyond themselves. From William James, James Leuba, Edwin Starbuck, George A. Coe, and others down to the more contemporary psychoanalytic school (Sigmund Freud, his circle, and his followers), the so-called "third force" school (Abraham Maslow), and the psychosocial approach (Milton Rokeach, Andrew Greeley, Charles Glock, and Rodney Stark), these experiences have been carefully studied by a variety of methods. Most recently Sir Alister Hardy, a noted Oxford zoologist, has set up a classification scheme of ninety-two categories by which he proposes to study these experiences as natural phenomena.[4]

My purpose is not to rehash all this material but to point out that almost without exception it has concentrated on description, classification, and the general question of *how* people believe or come to belief. The human sciences have given considerably less attention to *what* people believe and the power that content may have in determining the truth of a crisis situation in which some degree of conviction occurs. This is ironic because, of course, it is *what* the human scientist believes regarding empirical reality, inductive reasoning, and falsifiability that determines *how* he or she understands and values such experiences. That is, the presumed reality of the human sciences becomes normative for those experiences that to the experiencer are disclosing a reality of a related but distinctly different order. Thus, analysis and interpretation by the human sciences is implicitly circular—that is, cut off from new knowledge just at the crucial point

4. Hardy, *The Spiritual Nature of Man.*

where the experiencer him- or herself is breaking into a new order of reality. It must be said that human scientists such as Alister Hardy who study these experiences with earnest care admit they cannot get at the essence of the matter but want to go as far as they can with their methods. Nevertheless, the irony pertains: if the *what* determines the *how* for the human scientist, can he or she overlook or bypass the way *what* determines *how* for the convicted person?

I will say more in the following sections about the traps in the inductive approach. Here it needs only to be noted that convictional experiences challenge the assumptional world of the human sciences. They are essentially beyond naturalistic study and should be recognized and accepted as such, except where personality disintegration is being imposed by the experience. Then, of course, a return to the assumptional world of the human sciences is most likely to be progress for the health of the personality involved. I am aware that this claim and the exception raise many questions about normality, disintegration, and the ecstatic, all of which I will deal with in the following pages. Here I only want to point out the irony implicit in the human sciences' effort to investigate a phenomenon that in its own right challenges the major assumptions on which the human sciences work. Of course, partial understandings or distorting reductionisms are the most frequent outcomes.

Pointing out the irony is important not merely as a matter of argument but also because people who have these experiences are often awed by "science" or "what the studies show," and, looking at one or two studies, they take moments of profound conviction to be temporary insanity or evidence that they are unstable personalities. In fact, of course, the studies generally give evidence to the contrary; the human sciences within and among themselves generally agree on the relative health or health-producing effects of these experiences. All that the studies show is surely relevant and important in its own right, but even what they indicate about health still does not answer our basic question. If we are to get at the *truth* of the matter, we must push through the irony.

Suppose that in such moments one is not diminished or disordered but *more* fully oneself than ever before. Suppose that such a moment reopens the whole question of reality. What then? Wouldn't an outsider's insistence on an empirical reality or some standard of collective agreement be so clearly wide of the mark as to be painfully humorous? One does not have to be in a state of personal disintegration to reopen this question with sustained conviction; one only needs to be prepared to challenge the assumptional worlds of those who would otherwise repress the reality question. This, then, is the question: "How can we know the truth of these experiences when they challenge the realities presumed by ordinary thought and experience? How can we think about such exceptional experiences when they transcend the horizons within which ordinary ways of thinking are contained, and in that transcendence convince us of who we most truly are? How can we think the unthinkable without losing the essence of what the unthinkable has conveyed to us?"

We must be cautious here. Such a question runs the risk of suggesting that life is best understood and lived most truly only at its extremities. This would be an unfortunate implication, because most of life is surely not lived in constant encounter with its boundaries, and, if we meet God in times of extremity, that surely does not limit the Divine Presence to that dimension of human life. Rather, by focusing on these extreme situations, I am suggesting—as will be evident in Chapter 4—that God's Presence can be discovered at the center of life all the more vividly, all the more precisely, because of his appearance at the extremity.

The second misunderstanding we owe to theology. Surely the human sciences are not designed to deal with extraordinary experience in terms that make it convincing to the experiencer. They are designed to exorcise the demons of the extraordinary for the sake of sustaining and controlling day-to-day life. Yet often theology, which should be the language of conviction, has also had trouble with such experiences. They are too subjective for those preoccupied with rigorous demands for theological thinking, and more unique and particularized than can be coped with by highly generalized theological systems.

It is this tendency in much of modern theology to discredit convictional experiences that is partly responsible for their repression among both clergy and laity. The effect of this repression manifests itself, for example, within the United Presbyterian Church, U.S.A., a mainline denomination of which I am a member. It stresses theology, a cognitive, confessional orientation to faith, and academically trained clergy; as a result, it generally appeals to the middle and upper social strata of society. An open conversation about convicting experiences and their significance for life and faith is the exception among Presbyterians. Yet a recent survey showed that 80 percent of our clergy and approximately half of our lay constituency have had such experiences. The theological repression of that experience has generated a deep, untapped convictional unconscious among Presbyterians, and, on the basis of other research,[5] I would suspect among other churches as well.

Those who do not suffer repression often fall into the opposite extreme. An anti-intellectual rush of enthusiastic clichés marks some whose personal experiences have taken on canonical significance. This is not in itself to disqualify them or their experiences, but it is another symptom, at the opposite extreme, of the fact that theology has not been able to supply understanding, comprehension, and an adequate language for what takes place in these convicting moments of transformation.

Nevertheless, there are important theological observations to be made. These experiences may be understood under a category of biblical theology such as "signs of the presence of the Kingdom of God." This is a helpful category, because it prevents the experiences themselves from being worshipped and points to God of whose Kingdom they are signs. Moreover, relegated to the status of "signs" they are prevented from being strictly private experiences, granting personal powers and divine privileges to the convicted person. This strips away some of the narcissism that accumulates around these events and confirms the experience as belonging not preeminently to an individual but to all who have eyes to see. Just as the miracles of the New Testament are designed as a witness for whoever might see them as such, so these accounts are designed to point away from the experience itself and toward the Spiritual Presence of Jesus, the Christ.

Theologically we may also speak of such experiences as "conversions" in which a person converts from paganism to Christianity. This certainly applies in some cases but does not apply to many, my own case included. It does not describe the occurrence of such experiences in people who are already converted. Moreover, "conversion" has acquired the connotation of "emotionalism" and only recently is it finding its way back into contemporary theological thinking. A better term may be "metanoia," the notion used by H. Richard Niebuhr to describe the "permanent revolution" or the ongoing transformation of human life under divine initiative: "God's self-disclosure is that permanent revolution in our religious life by which all religious truths are painfully transformed and all religious behavior transfigured by repentance and new faith."[6]

---

5. Especially see A. Greeley's *Sociology of the Paranormal* (Beverly Hills, Calif.: Sage, 1975).

6. H. Richard Niebuhr, *The Meaning of Revelation* (New York: Macmillan, 1941), p. 133.

This concept is surely helpful because it places those experiences in the larger context of what God is doing in the world to transform all things. Indeed, it is just the ongoing revolution or transformation that makes us restless with theological reflection that is preoccupied with standoffish warnings about such experiences not being misused or misinterpreted in light of the historical church's self-understanding. Metanoia means that God's self-disclosure should repeatedly transfigure theological thinking itself. In relation to the cases at hand, theological reflection needs to press into the issues posed by convicting experience and to avoid drifting toward a guild mentality. Otherwise theology implicitly undermines its own reason for being, and much of its important positive direction will be lost.

Metanoia is a helpful but insufficient theme. It establishes theological legitimation for attempting to think about these experiences, painfully if need be, but it does not give sufficient constructive theological guidelines beyond legitimation. For instance, how will the detailed content of these experiences be analyzed, and how will the process of one's participation in such experience be interpreted with respect to the process implicit in the notion of metanoia? Metanoia sets the theological ground work, but the actual stuff and dynamics of these experiences remain largely untouched by theological hands.

Theology, in contrast to the human sciences, has concentrated on *what* to believe and has paid relatively less attention to *how* one comes to believe what is theologically sound. Most of the theological answers to *how* have either been subtly turned into questions of *what* or they have been relegated to the Holy Spirit. However, of all doctrines central to Christianity, that one is the most ill-defined, fraught with mystery, and lost in confusion. *How* the Holy Spirit teaches, comforts, afflicts, and leads into "all truth" is largely a theological blank. Yet, notice—it has substance enough to be threatening. If one claims to have had an experience of the Holy Spirit, he or she is immediately suspected of becoming theologically unsound. This sort of threat and suspicion is a case of ignorance controlling orthodoxy and indicates a state of affairs that ought not to continue.

This brief account of two misunderstandings can be summarized thus: The human sciences have the advantage of specificity and concreteness. They also stress predominantly the *process* aspect of knowing implicit in such experiences. But they are unconscious or "forgetful" of the ultimate grounds on which their observations are made, and consequently they ignore the ultimate significance and fundamental reality claims that are essential to such experiences.

The understandings of theology, on the other hand, have the advantage of focusing attention predominantly on content and on the ultimate ground and significance of such experiences. Yet, lacking specificity and concreteness, they do not afford sufficient basis for interpretation regarding the particulars of these experiences, nor is there concreteness or specificity about process; that is, how does one participate via such experiences in the ultimate ground theology affirms?

This situation calls not just for a dialogue or synthesis, valuable as these may be in their own right, but for a new understanding of knowing commensurate with the nature of convictional experience. Because these experiences are so dependent on multifaceted input from a vast universe of possibilities coming into sharp focus in a dramatic or striking way, it seems appropriate to think of the knowing that takes place here as "event." Knowing as event will become the full focus of attention in the next chapter.

Such a view of knowing, if it is not to mean everything and nothing, will depend in part on a new theory of error. The theory of error to be developed does not pretend to eliminate all other theories simply by making a new emphasis, nor is it presumed that what we will call "new" has never been mentioned before. Indeed, the emphasis I want to make is ancient, but it has not been sufficiently stressed as error, especially where other disciplinary studies including the human sciences have been involved. To introduce this view of knowing and the sort of error it imposes on knowing generally, I turn to a familiar transforming event in the New Testament.

THE DAMASCUS EVENT

A brilliant light from heaven threw the venomous Saul into the dust of the Damascus Road; it was for him a transforming moment of truth. More than any other account in the New Testament, this one makes it clear that the transforming moment must be taken seriously. Four references to this episode (three in Acts and one in Galatians) describe the divine attention to Paul's particularity, and to the transcendent source and validation of the event; they all lay claim to the momentous need for transformation if one is to know Christ.

There can be no doubt that the transforming event must be felt as one's own. Saul was addressed and authorized in his own right by this moment; he was addressed in terms of the particular struggle in his own soul, which may well have been connected through his conscience with Stephen's martyrdom. If so, his own inclination and strict Pharasaical training made him vehement against Christianity; and at the same time he was inwardly in conflict over his vehemence. Whatever the exact nature of the inner conflict, Christ's brief word to Saul addresses him as one who is in a state of self-contradiction ("Why do you kick against the pricks?") while seeming to be singular in his purpose. The moment convinced him—ecstatically, if you will—that he was "seen," known, and understood, even in ways he had not been able to understand himself.

It is significant not merely that Saul the individual is here seen and known, but that he is *authorized*, first by this direct meeting, and later by confirming events, to be as authoritative as any of the other apostles in the communication of the Gospel. Particularity is a necessary part of authorization, but authorization is the claim of the historical on particularity. That is, Paul is not addressed by Christ merely to satisfy the subjective longing to be free from hidden conflict and to experience the ecstasy of being known by God, but he is addressed so as to be called into the making of history. Thus, the first observation is that ecstasy is supposed to make history, but one cannot make history without ecstasy; that is, without in some sense standing outside it and apart from its determinants.

A major consequence of this first observation, confirming what we said earlier in connection with the human sciences, is that no one can know or comprehend the central meaning of a convicting experience from a standpoint outside it. That is, no one making observations from an objective viewpoint, such as those who were with Saul on the Damascus Road, could know what was really happening to him. In all accounts, Saul is described as having an experience that is not of "flesh and blood," and so it is not subject to the sort of verification that flesh and blood might invent. However, God does not ignore the need for validation; Saul is not simply left to "take it from there." This leads us to our second observation.

The validation of a word from God is uniformly established by God's initiative, not by generally recognized human procedures. Ananias comes to baptize Saul and to restore his sight because he, too, has received a divine visit, and one no less remarkable than Saul's. Some might want to say that here we have a corporate validation, an acceptance by "the church," which in its own way is how any community (social, scientific, or artistic) determines what is or is not acceptable. However, it is exactly *not* corporate; it is not a communal agreement. There is a synchronicity between the Lord's word to Saul and his word to Ananias, but there is no causal or positive socialized connection between the two men; there was no basis in common experience for Ananias' bold venture to the house of his persecutor. Yet it validates Saul's experience and his own because he finds things just as "the Angel of the Lord" had said they would be.

The connection between them is, as it always is, between Christians: it is social in that it involves two or more people, but socialization and causalities have nothing fundamental to do with constructing the relationship. The second observation, then, is that God alone can finally validate the claim that God has spoken. However, we must go on to say that human judgments may examine and falsify a claim, either that God has spoken or that one has sufficiently understood how one is being addressed by God.

This leads us to our third observation, that whenever Saul's moment of transformation is described it is not the moment but the transformation that is stressed. This is to note that Saul's conversion stresses an intertwining of continuity and discontinuity according to a recognizable pattern. Much that follows is devoted to an explanation of this transformational pattern and how it pertains to knowing generally, as well as through such events as Saul's conversion.

At this point, it should be emphasized that Paul, as evidenced by his speeches recorded in Acts and by his letter to the Galatians, is seeking the same sort of transformation for his hearers as he has had himself. When he speaks to the angry mob of Jews in their own tongue, quieting their vehement tempers, he is clearly attempting to identify with them so that they might be willing to identify with his (and Israel's) mission to the Gentiles (Acts 22). When he speaks to Agrippa, it is clear from Agrippa's own comments and Paul's response that he is seeking to bring everyone present to the same sort of transformation he has experienced (Acts 26). Even when he is writing to the Galatians, he is recounting his experience, not only to establish his authority, but in a fundamental sense to reclaim for the Galatians the authority of the transformation through which they too had passed (Gal. 1:15-17; 3:2-3).

This third observation, which stresses more the weight and moment of transformation than the transforming moment, suggests that far from being an isolated episode—that is, a bizarre intrusion that should be explained away, like epilepsy, hysteria, or sunstroke—Saul's conversion exhibits a pattern of knowing that seems unique. It interweaves discontinuity and continuity in a logic of transformation that is open to all people as the way of coming into the knowledge of

Christ. Here I return to the view already stated that a claim to having heard God's word may be falsified by human means but not finally and ultimately validated except by God. Thus a presumed experience of Christ may be weighed against the pattern and implications of transformation, as the logic behind knowing Christ. Falsification is possible when the experience is not transformational, is opposed to transformation, and/or is not apt to become such. Transformation does not finally validate experiences of Christ, but one cannot know Christ apart from transformation. Transformational logic, then, provides a proximate norm for the ultimate claims of a convictional experience.

All three of these observations and any others that might be made hinge on the central decisive fact of Saul's vision. There is no personal calling, no history-making, no divine validation or transformation apart from Saul's imaginative leap into another reality, the reality of Christ's Presence. Any attempt to grasp the meaning of this experience by ignoring the vision is simply avoiding the issue. However, as with all vision, he sees a reality that is partially constructed by his own intelligence. That his intelligence does constructive work in the knowledge he has of Christ does not detract from the authenticity of his envisioning. That Christ takes the initiative to provoke the constructive act by which Saul envisions his Presence does not eliminate Saul's participation in what he sees, hears, and comes to know. It is Saul's imaginative leap to certainty that marks this remarkable event as an act of knowing. It is in this that we have the bridge between convictional knowing and ordinary knowing.

By imaginative, I do not mean imaginary. The imaginative thought, act, or word puts you into history; the imaginary takes you out. The imaginative links the private to the public world; the imaginary is hidden in privacy. God's action in history can vindicate the imaginative vision; his action shatters the imaginary. The imaginative drives toward a transformation of the given; the imaginary arrests transformation. It is Saul's imaginative leap to certainty that constitutes the key to events—convicting events, in particular—as a way of knowing truth.

It is by an imaginative leap that the depth of one's personal being reaches the level of consciousness. By this leap, Saul himself knew the reality of Christ that had first indwelt him, and he became increasingly conformed to it. Interpreting a convicting experience as mutual indwelling helps to overcome any assumptions about an absolute dichotomy between convictional and secular forms of knowing.

Knowing *anything* is to indwell it and to reconstruct it in one's own terms without losing the essence of what is being indwelt. Indwelling is preparatory; as we shall see, it winds the mainspring of the imaginative leap in which subjective involvement and objective provocation combine to constitute a spontaneous image, the crux of the knowing event. Subsequently, it is by indwelling the new imaginative reality that one becomes informed by it, and it, in turn, enters history.

Although this is fundamental to what happens in all knowing, I do not presume that it is *all* that happens, nor do I expect to ignore the differences that pertain between convictional knowing and knowing in general. If I fail to establish continuities based in ordinary experience, however, any foundation for explanation and interpretation of the extraordinary will be lost.

The continuity from convictional knowledge to everyday knowing is also familiar to the New Testament. The Greek word for "knowing" that is most commonly employed — whether one is speaking of human knowledge of a state of affairs, or human knowledge of God, or God's knowledge of us — is *gnosis*. Gnosis implies the same sort of imaginative leap I have been describing; it suggests a coming together of things in a convincing way, so that one who has gnosis has certainty. It is not confined to any particular organ of knowledge (such as the senses or the mind) nor to any innate capacity or competence (such as language or reason). Rather, gnosis occurs as an event in one's dealings with and experience of the world. Consistent with the way the imagination serves every aspect of personality from bodily action to the highest forms of abstract thought, gnosis assumes the power to exist in and act on the whole soul of the knower.

There is always a rational element involved in gnosis, but rationality does not stand apart, policing or censoring gnosis. Rather, gnosis contains a rational quality as one of its constitutive elements, and its inherent reasonableness comes into more expressed prominence as ethical and theological reflection on what is already known. Thus, gnosis is to be distinguished on the one hand from the demonic, the fantastic, madness, or self-absorption, and on the other from a purely rational, speculative, reflective, or empirical view of knowing. Gnosis emphasizes the participatory quality of knowing that is so dependent on the imaginative act. Just how rationality is contained as an element in gnosis, and especially in the imaginative leap to certainty, is something I will discuss at some length in the following chapter when we return to the transformational logic of the knowing event.

In the New Testament, the object of gnosis is *aletheia*, "the truth." The implications of this important word are that a matter or state of affairs that had been hidden (latent) has now been disclosed; its true being has become self-evident. The disclosure of this truth seemingly takes possession of the knowing mind and prompts, from the side of what is known, that eventful leap of certainty on the part of the knower. Taken together, the two words *gnosis* and *aletheia* imply a mutual indwelling of the knower and the known; of course, this is especially significant where the truth to be known is the reality of Christ's Presence.

Now this claim for continuity between knowing generally and knowing Christ might seem to rest too much on the idiosyncrasies of New Testament times, its ancient language, and literature. That is, the sort of vagary implied by an imaginative leap to certainty is not a part of the more highly differentiated modern mentality, which is well informed and daily instructed by the methods and findings of the "exact sciences"—or so it might be argued. Actually, of course, the opposite is the case; modern scientific thought is just as dependent on the imaginative leap as was the gnosis of the New Testament or as was that sudden event by which Saul knew the truth of Christ's Presence. However, that is the subject of the following section.

A NEW THEORY OF ERROR

It would be a new theory of error if I declared that nothing can be known without an imaginative leap and that the bolder the leap the more significant the new knowledge is apt to be. I emphasize "error" because imagination is usually thought to be the source of error, not a necessary organ of truth. It is usually assumed that where there is a mistake, there imagination has worked some foul play at a point where only reason—especially reason refined by the canons of scientific method—has the right to say what is true. A new theory of error would be: any assertion of truth that does not recognize and accept its primary dependency on some leap of the imagination, some insight, intuition, or vision, is guilty of intellectual dissimulation. Reason thinks it secures an objective, airtight case when in fact its processes are open-textured, its sources are rooted in "personal knowledge," and its conclusions are laced with human interests.[7] Knowing as event unequivocally depends on the image and its cognates to draw together

---

7. J. Habermas, *Knowledge and Human Interests* (Boston: Beacon Press, 1971). Habermas makes a strong case for the way in which "interest" has shaped the history of

an integrated picture, to put things in a new perspective, or to construct a new world view. I have yet to show that all knowing is eventful, but my claim is that a rationalistic eclipse of the image eventually cuts off reason from its substance — indeed, from the truth it seeks to order and communicate. For convenience, I will refer to this error as an "eikonic eclipse" and will attempt to show that it is not merely an error of omission but is an error of commission because eclipsing rationalists thereby lose their perspective on themselves and whatever they know.

Now a common rationalistic retort to this view of error might run as follows:

Your view of error is covert sacralization of imagery and an invitation to personal and religious chaos. We say a thing is "true" if it fits some determinant reality. Thus, the flight of a jet plane is "true" if it is *on course,* opinions are "true" if they square with the *known facts,* and one's character runs "true to form" if one acts in consistent conformity with *what one's public expects.* Indeed, all things are finally to be determined true or false depending on whether they conform to the *canons of reason.*

The canons of reason in the everyday exercise of a rational determination of truth, and the canons that are most appropriately applied to convictional experiences, are twofold. *First,* the process for establishing truth is a combination of induction (whatever happened in the past under certain conditions should continue to happen in the future under those same conditions) and deduction. (If a certain Reality R is normative for all cases and Episode E does not conform to R, then E is false. Conversely, if it does conform, it is true.) In short, the determination of truth is the end result of a rational process combining induction and deduction.

The *second* canon says that in the exercise of any rational process the thinking subject maximizes truth to the degree that he or she excludes his or her subjective involvement in the determination of that truth. Objectivity in the determination of truth is considered to be an unequivocal asset. Thus, the rational process objectively exercised with respect to a determinant reality (ultimately, reason itself) is what establishes truth.

In relation to convictional experiences, if the vision is allowed to speak and if reason is thereby dethroned, we are at the mercy of blind impulse. In the face of these overpowering experiences that

philosophical thought, which otherwise seemed based on the most solid rational footing. Also strongly implied in this assertion and the overall position here is M. Polanyi, *Personal Knowledge* (New York: Harper Torchbooks, 1974).

pivot precariously between revelation and private heresy, abundant health and devastating psychopathology, release of new energy and hysterical uncontrol, new knowledge and bewildering confusion, the holy and the demonic—surely here we need sound rational processes and an objective point of view. In fact, the more rational thing would probably be not to face them at all until the person involved can be rational about them. Error is a failure of reason, not a failure to include the image.

This general line of reasoning is a common one, so we must take a more careful look at these rational processes and especially at their highest refinement in "scientific method," where so much confidence in the rational process rests its case. This method of determining and establishing the truth must be reexamined lest one regain the "secure" ground of a strictly rational view of truth by eclipsing the image and losing the truth hidden in these remarkable experiences.

To begin with, let us briefly reexamine inductive thinking. A well-known critique of the inductive method is that no number of confirming cases can establish the truth of a hypothesis, because some new observation may come along to disconfirm it. Thus, one never knows the truth, one knows only hypotheses. A less well-known but more penetrating critique is that inductive thinking tends to work against, rather than in favor of, new knowledge. For example, consider the hypothesis, "Water boils at 100°C in open vessels." Note that if one comes against a disconfirming circumstance (for example, water does not boil at 100°C on a mountaintop) the inductive tendency is to modify the hypothesis so as to take account of the disconfirmation: "Water boils at 100°C in open vessels at sea-level atmospheric pressure." But that really begs the deeper issue. Suppose instead one were to ask, not "How can I restate this hypothesis so as to amass more confirming cases," but, rather, "Why does this contradiction occur?"[8] This sort of question drives directly into the contradiction, challenges axioms, and forces new thinking and bolder imaginative work. It is due to just such contradictions, boldly faced with imagination and insight, that the major turns in the history of Western thought have occurred.

In essence, inductive thinking is a psychological phenomenon, a mind set that moves toward wider generality, but at the same time tends to move away from new knowledge. It is precisely in this sense

---

8. B. Magee, *Popper* (Glasgow: Collins, 1979), especially p. 24. Magee has helpfully focused Popper's case as stated here.

that inductive thinking may be said to be in error. In fact, Karl Popper argues that there is no such thing as "a logic of induction"; the notion that theories are somehow logically constructed on the basis of observations is fundamentally wrong.[9] It is previous theory, more or less latent, that determines *what* we observe and *how* we observe, and it is from the imaginative leap of the mind rooted in previously established theories that our new theories come.

What Popper declares about induction in scientific theory is true of deductive thinking as well. Consider that tightly constructed logical sequence, the syllogism. Everyone follows the force of its movement when it unfolds the famous example: "Socrates is a man; all men are mortal; therefore, Socrates is mortal." However, following it is fundamentally different from constructing it in the first place. As Aristotle himself pointed out, the syllogism is constructed not by the most structured mind but by the "quick-witted" *(agchinoia)*.[10] The one most apt at syllogistic reasoning is one who readily makes new associations, because the syllogism is based on an imaginative insight called "the middle term": namely, *man* in the preceding example. The entire sequence depends on this link between the major and minor premise, and there is no structured way to arrive at this; one must simply "get it" by intuition or insight—in brief, by an act of imagination. Now if the key linkage within the syllogism depends on an imaginative leap, however small, how much more do those linkages that connect syllogisms to form theories and systems of theories depend on the vigilant work of the imagination. Even for deductive reason, the truth is first grasped by an imaginative leap, then demonstrated.

What is true for scientific method is surely true of knowing generally. It proceeds not inductively or deductively but imaginatively; knowledge moves forward by imaginative leaps and bounds. To be sure, such leaps are not totally blind to observation or reflection, but in the discovery of new knowledge, the facts do not determine the theory. Instead, the theory creates the facts, and it is contradiction that creates theory through an act of the imagination.[11]

---

9. Karl Popper, *The Logic of Scientific Discovery* (New York: Basic Books, 1961).

10. Aristotle, *Analytica Posterioria* II, 3, 90a, 35. For commentary on this passage and other implications of syllogistic reasoning for creative thinking see G. J. Seidel, *The Crisis of Creativity* (Notre Dame, Ind.: Notre Dame Press, 1966), pp. 11-20, especially p. 15.

11. Einstein agreed with Popper that theory was not able to be created from observable data. It has to be invented by what we have called a leap of the intellectual imagination (Popper, *Logic*, p. 458).

What about the second assumption, objectivity? The issue here is directly related to the nature of the imaginative leap. This phrase could mean that one took a wild, flying guess in the face of contradiction, and, of course, that would amount to a projection of subjective nonsense into (or out of) a problematic situation. In the case of convictional experience, it could amount to unmitigated sanction for subjective intoxication. To avoid this sort of error, scientific method has introduced an alternative that invites the opposite sort of error; the assumption that the subjectivity of the knower can be completely removed from what he or she knows to be true. Like most errors, it is only half wrong; to be sure, subjectiv*ism* is the way to solipsism, not the way to truth. But "objectivity" needs to be understood not as excluding the subject, but as growing out of the mutual indwelling of subject and object.

What we call "object" is an emergent synthesis of so-called subjective and objective factors. Thereby what is known becomes knowledge because the knower has been addressed, struck, confronted, attacked, or attracted by an "object," and in response he or she has sensed, felt, or incorporated it on the basis of previous analogous experience. Whatever has violated the serenity of his or her senses, sensibilities, or good sense enough to become an "object" has also been embodied by the knower on the basis of some bodily, sensate, propriate—in short, some subjective—basis.

In knowing anything, we respond more subliminally and thus more totally than is fully recognized. "We know more than we can tell," says Michael Polanyi.[12] That is, "objects" impinge on our knowing in ways that we scarcely recognize and figure into the results of our presumably rational process in ways that we do not readily acknowledge. Words interjected into movie films at a rate too rapid to be detected consciously have nevertheless been apprehended by viewers, significantly affecting behavior. For example, "unseen" popcorn commercials increased sales at intermission. "Undetected" words to the effect that "Mother and I are one" caused schizophrenics of a regressive type to score higher in mental health tests. These give evidence that we all probably ascertain a great deal more than we can say. Moreover, that "more" can make an immense difference in presumably rational judgment and conduct.

On a more complex level, we have already said that in scientific inquiry the theory creates the facts or the presumably indisputable aspects of knowledge—but where does the theory come from? It

---

12. M. Polanyi, *The Tacit Dimension* (New York: Doubleday, 1967), p. 4.

comes as contradiction forces the subjective mind of the theoretician to explore tacitly held theories, assumptions, and opinions, many of which are as vague or beyond the periphery of consciousness as the popcorn stimulus is beyond the consciousness of the movie audience. Theoreticians produce theory and new objects of knowledge /not/ because they excluded subjectivity but precisely because they included it and thereby drew on resources they did not know they had. The objects of our world or of our minds are "out there" because they were in some latent sense first "in here."

How they got "in here" even in a latent and potential state is a complex question that would take us too far afield at this point. But it can be said that what is true of scientific knowledge is true of the development of knowledge in general. Infants first indwell the objects of their world, turning them over and over, putting them in their mouths, in their ears, dropping them and so on until they have incorporated the objects or grasped a sense of their totality. What this exploration does physically, they eventually learn to do mentally, turning things over in their minds instead of in their hands. It is on the basis of previous bodily experience that has been internalized that the tacit basis for the more abstract mental operations of intelligence is constructed. A particularly striking and familiar example is that learning to crawl as an infant is fundamental to the coordination and organization of the mental operations involved in later learning to read. This is all to say that subjective involvement is not arbitrary, nor is it a matter of choice. It is inevitable in the knowledge of any and all objects.

"Objectivity" is not only an impossible goal in knowledge but striving for it may actually be destructive of knowledge. Thus, we come to some of the deep dangers of an eikonic eclipse. To bring all that is subjectively entertained or tacitly held out into the presumably lucid light of "objective knowledge" may dissipate or destroy what is known.

Try repeating a word several times, attending carefully to the movement of your throat, tongue, and lips, and to the sounds you are making. Soon the word will become hollow and lose its meaning. By concentrating attention on the action of their fingers, typists can temporarily paralyze their movements. We can make ourselves lose sight of a pattern or someone's physiognomy by examining its several parts under sufficient magnification.

It is one of Kierkegaard's observations that the more we rationally refine our proofs for God's existence the less convincing they become. Subjective or tacit participating in knowing, in academic subjects from theology or literature to science and mathematics, is as essential as it is to functioning in complex acts such as speech or typing. Because this is so, driving toward "objectivity" in these disciplines is potentially as distorting and productive of fallacy as it is in those complex actions.

It is not merely that imaginative subjectivity is inevitably involved and so must be acknowledged as such, but that any effort to eradicate it may well work against the creation and establishment of knowledge. The imaginative, indwelling aspect of knowing, always inevitable to some degree and more widely essential than recognized, keeps knowledge alive and open to change and makes it evident that the "world" is very much our composition of things. The ideal of objectivity drives toward shutting out the subject, shutting up the object in itself, closing off the future, and determining "true" knowledge in terms of inert entities. This shut-up-ness of knowing is the end of meaning, and the "world" ceases to be a living and livable reality. Hence any pretense to "complete objectivity" is at best a half-truth potentially threatening to knowledge and to the vitality of the "world."

The sum of what we have said about objectivity is this. In any absolute sense, objectivity is impossible, because "objects" are a synthetic, imaginative composition of so-called subjective and objective factors. Thus, subjectivity is necessarily involved in the most refined knowing act from start to finish. This leads us to reassert and restate that an eikonic eclipse is a fundamental error in the knowing act. Any rational view of knowing that fails to acknowledge an imaginative leap at its center and/or makes a pretense of perfecting objectivity as a goal is ipso facto in error. A rationalistic eclipse of the image not only invites the fallacies implicit in an uncritical reliance on reason, but it also forfeits the truth that may be disclosed, even thrust on us, by an imaginative construct, integration, or vision of things. Because some of the most recognizably powerful ideas of the modern world—including those of Friedrich A. von Kekulé, Albert Einstein, and Erwin Schrödinger in science; Karl Marx and Arnold Toynbee in history; and Sigmund Freud and Carl Jung in personality theory—have broken in on their authors in imagistic or visionary form, it is an obvious error to presume that truth must necessarily come on us otherwise when it bears a religious message. It would seem that to eclipse the image in relation to convictional experience in the name of rationality is not rational; it is an unexamined prejudgment.

Of course, this is not to eliminate rational elaboration and our ongoing concern to speak of "verification" (meaning "not-falsifiable"). It is simply to relegate rational processes to a subordinate role, having more to do with ordering, examining, and communicating truth than bringing it into being or discovering it in the first place. Rational processes can add no knowledge that is not first imagined. In the discovering and generation of knowledge, the rational can at best focus conflict that provokes an imaginative leap in the creation of a knowing event.

In summary, knowing—generally and convictionally—is first, foremost, and fundamentally an event. At the center of an event is a nonrational intrusion of a convincing insight. It is constructed by the imagination and constitutes a leap that may be found in any seemingly closed sequential movement from proposition to proposition, and a similar sort of leap is found at the crux of every convicting event. This is the central common feature that makes every convictional event an act of knowing and every act of knowing an event.

Even if "eikonic eclipse" is granted as a theory of error, I still am not in a position to answer those who are anxious about the destructive potential of convicting experiences, but I am in a better position to avoid the reductionistic tendencies and temptations that so easily take possession of judgment when these startling, convicting experiences appear. The answer to those who are concerned about the destructive potential of convicting experiences, for personal development as well as social and ethical life, depends, I claim, on an understanding of transformation. That is the key pattern that structures those events through which one must pass in the knowing of Christ and that potentially structures knowing at nearly all other levels. Indeed, I will eventually argue that all transformational knowing participates in the knowledge of Christ as its norm and paradigm. But first, what is transformation, and what is knowing as a transforming event? How does it operate at different levels of human experience? In particular, how does it operate in those events by which we come to know the truth of Christ?

Two

KNOWING AS
TRANSFORMING EVENT

TRANSFORMATIONAL LOGIC

➤ LET US BEGIN with the notion of "event," and if possible an experience as well as an understanding of its essential nature. If you are not already familiar with the following nine-dot puzzle and do not have an established frame of reference for solving such puzzles, you will be able to experience the key steps that constitute what I call an "event." If you have already solved it, you may recall the process you went through when you took on this sort of puzzle for the first time.

The puzzle requires that you draw four continuous straight lines through nine dots arranged in a square; you must not take your pencil off the paper.

.　　.　　.

.　　.　　.

.　　.　　.

If you are new to this, you will probably attempt to fit the four lines into the frame of reference set by the nine dots. You will soon discover that this procedure is impossible without adding a line or drawing curved lines. You may then begin to sense the conflict that constitutes the puzzle, and the very discomfort will usually make it more difficult for your mind to let go. Even if you dismiss it consciously, the common human drive toward closure or completion will send

your unconscious into an underground search, scanning inner resources for a solution. From time to time, the puzzle will resurface,
and possible solutions will be checked against its conditions. Thus,
after a sufficient period, perhaps in relation to an associative trigger
and probably when the puzzle seems farthest from your immediate
awareness, the insight will come imaginatively through a mental
reversal of figure and ground; that is, a reversal of the relationship
between the lines and the dots. Instead of assimilating the four lines
to the nine dots, you will break out of the set within which the puzzle
was framed, and assimilate the nine dots to the four lines as follows:

Those who arrive at this on their own usually do so with a sense of
"Aha!" The tension or extra energy invested in puzzling breaks into
relief because the stress of the conflict has continued under the surface
since first seeing the problem. Finally, you will make an explicit
public test of the insight, determining whether you have indeed
produced an imaginative insight fulfilling the conditions of the
puzzle. Thus, you will write out or explain the conception for the one
who gave you the problem and for some new public. If consensus
follows, you will have verified your transformation of the conflicting
elements in the original puzzle. Moreover, because this is a human
process, you will have made a gain (however slight) in self-esteem,
reinforcing mental agility or whatever personal meaning solving such
puzzles may hold for you.

What has here been spelled out as a process of solving a puzzle
constitutes a sequence that encompasses all the essential features of
"an event." Solving the puzzle is, of course, a minor event but
valuable as a relatively pure sample of the basic steps involved in more
complex and personally transforming events. How and why this is so
will become evident; but let us first examine what this specimen event
can teach us.

Notice first that the conflict appeared in a situational context, a
social and cultural "world" in which it could be understood and with
respect to which it was recognized as a puzzle. It might be possible to
imagine other worlds in which it would not seem problematic at all.
Suppose we thought automatically in terms of curved surfaces shaped

like a globe instead of flat surfaces like a map. Then, instead of curving the parallel pencil lines to cover the three rows of dots, you would automatically conceive of the nine dots on a globally curved surface. Of course, vertical, parallel lines would meet as they curved toward the poles, and then (instead of being one line short) the problem would be what to do with the extra line.

This is a puzzle because of the larger assumptive world in which it is placed, and because of the mental set it can presuppose on the part of the reader. Thus the first observation is that a knowing event always takes place in some context. Knowing events are situated; they depend initially on assumptions about and within their situations for the meaning of the knowing act.

The second observation concerns the inherent pattern or logic of a knowing event. The first step begins when there is an apparent rupture in the knowing context. *Conflict* initiates the knowing response, and the more one cares about the conflict the more powerful will be the knowing event. In fact, one cannot come to know what one does not care about. This is what makes the puzzle a *minor* event; there is little here to care about. Still, most of the time we respond to any rupture in the knowing context the way nature responds to a vacuum. No matter how trivial, we tend to want to set it right or know that it is all right that it not be settled (for example, "recognized paradoxes" and the accepted "ambiguities of life"). Also it is a knowing event of far greater personal significance if the initial conflict is not artificially generated from the outside (such as by the puzzle) but a conflict that the knower had had all along but not recognized (for example, inability to solve puzzles may raise a deeper and more enduring conflict over one's intellectual ability).

The second step we will call an *interlude for scanning*. To be temporarily baffled over a conflict in one's situation is to be drawn both consciously and unconsciously into the familiar psychological process of searching out the possible solutions, taking apart errors, keeping parts, and discarding others. This is indwelling the conflicted situation with empathy for the problem and its parts. In order for this to occur, one's attention must at least for a moment be diverted from the problem as such. This interlude may take place for only a second, as when one stares out the window briefly to recall a telephone number, or it may last years, as when one labors inwardly to resolve piece by piece some of the deep psychological hurts of childhood.

Scanning is not only a search for answers outside the problem; it is also scanning and differentiating the terms of the problem and playing possible solutions against various interpretations of the ruptured situation. Note that it takes an investment of caring energy to hold the problem, partial solutions, and the whole state of irresolution together. It is this step in the formation of the knowing event that leads into the fuller or more comprehensive implications of the conflict and accordingly searches out a solution in the most universal terms. This is the step of waiting, wondering, following hunches, and exhausting the possibilities.

The third step in the knowing event is the *constructive act of the imagination*; an insight, intuition, or vision appears on the border between the conscious and unconscious, usually with convincing force, and conveys in a form readily available to consciousness the essence of the resolution. Arthur Koestler's term "bisociation"[1] is a handy way to summarize the crux of such an imaginative construct: it is two habitually incompatible frames of reference converging, usually with surprising suddenness, to compose a meaningful unity. In the puzzle, the four straight lines and the nine dots, which at first appeared to be fundamentally incompatible frames of reference, are "bisociated" as the problem is restated and the nine dots are assimilated to the four lines, instead of the reverse. "Bisociation" is the smallest unit necessary to an imaginative resolution and reconstruction of the problematic situation, but, on the other hand, its inherent complexity may be almost infinite, as in Einstein's famous formula E = MC^2, where energy is bisociated with mass around a constant, the speed of light. This example demonstrates that a vast range of complexity may be mastered by a relatively simple formulation. Thus, bisociations may become infinitely complex as they are combined and compounded, but may also, as in E = MC^2, become statements of a higher order, i.e., bisociations of elegant simplicity.

The range and depth of possibilities here is controlled by the contextual situation, the shape of the original conflict, and its implications as ferreted out in the preliminary scanning interlude. That is, the resolution is imaginative, as opposed to imaginary, depending on its power to deal comprehensively and parsimoniously with the elements of the conflict in its context. It is this third step, the construction of insight sensed with convincing force, that constitutes the turning point of the knowing event. It is by this central act that the elements of the ruptured situation are *transformed*, and a new perception, perspective, or world view is bestowed on the knower.

The fourth step in the sequence is marked in two ways, first by a *release* of the energy bound up in sustaining the conflict and second

1. A. Koestler, *The Creative Act* (New York: Macmillan, 1967).

by an *opening* of the knower to him- or herself and the contextual situation. The release of energy is a response of the unconscious to the resolution and the evidence that one's personal investment in the event has reached a conclusion; the conflict is over. The opening of the knower to his or her context is the response of consciousness to being freed *from* an engrossing conflict and *for* a measure of self-transcendence. We might say consciousness is expanded by, and to the measure of, the resolution. Without the release of bound up energy and the liberation of the self-transcendence of consciousness, it must be assumed that the conflict has not been sufficiently resolved and the unconscious mind will continue to search for solutions. In the minor case of the puzzle, the release of tension that emerges with the "Aha!" is accompanied by an opening of one's mind; if the sense of self-transcendence is voiced, we say something like, "Now that is off my mind." We mean not only that now consciousness has expanded to include the puzzle, its solution, and us as its solver, but also that we are able to be more fully aware of new elements in our context now that that matter has been resolved. In fact, it is often the case that solutions will come in with a wave of related new associations, carrying the implications further than the original conflict suggested and thereby immersing the knower more richly and deeply than ever in his or her assumptional world. Solving the puzzle example will make one more ready to take up a book of puzzles and perhaps even more ready to engage puzzling situations on other levels of experience, such as the puzzling behavior of a colleague or a conundrum of feelings in oneself.

The fifth step is *interpretation* of the imaginative solution into the behavioral and/or symbolically constructed world of the original context. This interpretation works in two directions, both backward and forward, so to say. Working backward I will call *congruence;* this makes explicit, congruent connections from the essential structures of the imaginative construct back into the original conditions of the puzzle. Working forward I will call *correspondence:* this makes the apparent congruence public and a matter of consensus. Thus, the imaginative construct is examined for its correspondence to a consensual view of the world.

This fifth step is not a matter of conformity, because in the creation of new knowledge congruence cannot finally be sacrificed to correspondence, nor is the reverse satisfactory: both must agree before the event is completed. There are a variety of ways this can happen. The puzzle solution is most obvious, because one is "discovering" what is already known by some other quarter of the world or by the originating public. It is less obvious when one is discovering what must yet be proven to fit an established assumptional world. For instance, Kekulé, the noted nineteenth-century chemist, discovered the structure of the benzene molecule and for the first time showed that molecular structure could be circular. It is even less obvious when the discovery challenges the basic axioms of the assumptional world within which it takes place. When Einstein overturned the Newtonian world and by the sheer intellectual beauty (congruity) of this theory challenged and changed presumably established facts, he brought about correspondence by the inherent power of the congruities he constructed so imaginatively. Thus, the event originates and concludes in an assumed situation that includes the knower himself via his or her imaginative leap. However, as congruence and correspondence combine, the impact of the event on that world is a transformation of at least some of its elements and an essential gain over the original conditions.

In summary, then, the key steps in transformational logic, or the knowing event, are (1) conflict, (2) interlude for scanning, (3) constructive act of imagination, (4) release and openness, and (5) interpretation.

Now I must make some observations on the sequence as a whole. To begin with, this sequence is clearly a mixture of continuity and discontinuity. As to the first, the sequence is held together not by any formal logical necessity; in fact, I argued in the previous chapter that formal logic is held together by an implicit event. Rather, what establishes continuity is the knower's built-in intention to complete the knowing act. When I discuss human development in later chapters, it will become clear why this is a built-in tendency. The word *intention* here is helpfully interpreted etymologically as a condition, which one finds in oneself, of being in *tension* and stretching toward completion through the *tenses* of time, from the past through the present, toward the future. In contrast to phenomenological thought, which confines intentionality to consciousness, intention here cuts across the boundary between conscious and unconscious, driving toward a continuity of the event for the whole person.

Continuity may be conceived as a linear gestalt or an implied series held together by an inherent or immanent principle. When we expect to hear phrases such as "tick-tock" or "bow-wow," tension quickly appears if the first phoneme is followed by silence: "tick————" or "bow————." We have an urge to complete what we inherently sense requires a conclusion. This is what Frank Kermode calls the "sense of an ending" that most of us feel in relation to narrative.[2] Unfinished stories, like unfinished dreams, leave us in suspense, and we often invent endings just to satisfy the urge toward completion. The complete "tick-tock," Kermode says, is a kind of a miniplot that stretches from the genesis of "tick" to the apocalypse of "tock"; the tension built up at the center and resolved at the end classifies this as an example of intentional continuity. The knowing event is a much more complex example, but it is held together by the same sort of force: namely, the intention to resolve conflict through the creation of new knowledge.

This leads directly into the opposing force of discontinuity in this sequence: namely, the *mediating* image, insight, intuition, or vision. Note that there is no way to reproduce this sequence because its very heart and center depends on a mediating discontinuity, or more fundamentally, on a mystery. No matter how one searches with penetrating conscious analyses to make logically tight connections, the insightful resolution to conflict is always a gift that takes awareness by surprise. This is the first manifestation of the mystery that underlies this process. The second is that, when the resolution is given, self-transcendence (conscious of being conscious or freedom to choose) springs into being spontaneously like a still heart suddenly resuscitated.

This striking discontinuity at the critical juncture of the knowing event suggests intentionally cooperative intervention from a realm of reality beyond consciousness itself. From the creative unconscious on the one side comes a mediating image, insight, or vision that quickens self-transcendence on the other. The imaginative mediator liberates the "I," impels the knower toward new explorations of his or her world and toward those choices that promise to exercise transcendence and hold open the future. Discontinuity effected by an imaginative construct is the key and center of the knowing event; indeed, it is just this discontinuity that makes transformation possible. Mediation via an imaginative construct springs from an engagement and indwelling of a conflicted situation, its faults and dissonance; but then, from a point seemingly disengaged from the conflicted situation, emerges a transformed construction of those elements ready to be interpreted back into the situational context, liberating a sense of resolution and constituting a substantial gain in knowledge. Thus the first observation on the series as a whole is that it describes a coherent pattern of

2. F. Kermode, *The Sense of an Ending* (Oxford: Oxford University Press, 1967).

transformation whose inherent logic combines continuity and discontinuity through a persistence of intention.

As shown in the following section of this chapter, this transformational logic transposes from one context to another in the same way that grammar as the relatively stable underlying structure of language transposes from context to context and thereby gives coherence and meaning to a potentially infinite variety of semantic forms and expressions. Thus transformational logic may be called the grammar of the knowing event, and the knowing event may occur in contexts as seemingly alien as puzzle solving, scientific discovery, poetry writing, psychotherapy, and religious conversion. Such expressions of transformation vary at the surface, but the deep, underlying pattern remains the same. It is innate to want completion of transformational logic wherever it appears, just as we want completion of any recognizable sentence or any narrative form. The transpositions of transformation are manifold; I will cite certain major instances in the following section.

The second observation to be made has to do with conscious entrance into the knowing event. Owing to its transformational structure and the coherence of the sequence that this provides, one may enter consciously into the sequence at any one of the five points and still be drawn to work through the whole. I have already suggested with the puzzle how one enters at the point of initial conflict. However, there are also times when answers precede the questions. This was Einstein's entry into the formulation of the theory of relativity. Even before he ascertained the nature of the conflict, Einstein sensed error in the Newtonian world view and knew instinctively that he had the solution somewhere within himself.

As we will see, this is often, if not most commonly, the case with convictional experiences. Saul's Damascus vision was a powerful mediating Presence that brought with it both a negation of his previous circumstances and the conviction that the answers to life's deepest questions were packed into that moment even before he had formulated any questions beyond the first, "Who are you, Lord?" In sum, if one enters the process with the discontinuity of the middle step, transformational logic will preserve the continuity of the sequence and draw the knower backward into generative conflict and forward into the final stage of interpretation.

One may also enter on either side of the middle step of transformation. Sometimes one is working on a latent conflict, scanning for an orientation to a problem that has not yet been articulated, and expecting a solution that has not yet come forth. People who regularly enter the sequence at this stage are "seekers" or "wonderers" who sense an as-yet-undisclosed beginning and ending to an inherently meaningful process in which they find themselves already immersed.

One may also enter on the other side of the insight with a sense of new energy to reinvest. Awakening from a dream in which insight and resolution have occurred, one may forget the dream content while still enjoying a heightened sense of well-being. The inherent logic of the transformation would call for a working back through to the source of the resolution, recovery of the dream if possible, and a grasp of what latent conflict had been resolved. It also calls for working forward into an interpretation of the new imaginative construct.

Before going on, it will be helpful to make distinctions between three terms used in the subsequent discussion: *transformation*, *transposition*, and *transfiguration*. *Transformation* is the major term, designating a change in form from lower to higher orders of life along a continuous line of intention or development. A typical case of transformation is the change in form that occurs when a caterpillar turns into a butterfly. In the human personality transformation occurs between distinct registers of behavior and within them. When mature intelligence develops from sensory motor behavior, transformation crosses registers of behavior (organic to psychological); when intelligence develops from one distinct stage (concrete operations) to the next higher level of complexity (formal operations), transformation occurs within the same register of behavior. *Transposition* refers to the placing of a patterned unit of behavior; I will refer mostly to the transposition of transformation. When transformation appears as a pattern in a particular context, such as psychological behavior, social organization, or cultural phenomena, it is said to be transposed, because the pattern is presumed to be a movable unit that finds different positions in different contexts, but it remains recognizable as the same pattern. *Transfiguration* (see Chapter 5) refers to the illumination and divination of an otherwise unenlightened or mundane phenomenon. The implication is that the phenomenon as transfigured is the fundamental reality; the darkened version is its common appearance.

We must now turn to some examples where it will be possible to observe a transformational pattern unfolding and generating knowing events in widely different contexts. There will be different emphases in each case, but the force of the event—that is, its transformational logic—will be evident throughout. Each of the following contexts has some bearing on transformation in convictional experience — that is, it illuminates certain important aspects — but none of these instances, nor all of them collectively, will be sufficient to account for convictional transformation. This lack is what will lead us on to subsequent chapters.

SCIENTIFIC KNOWING

The logic of transformation transposes into scientific discovery with such outstanding examples as Poincaré, Kekulé, Einstein, and Schrödinger. The list could be considerably extended, but the point would be the same. In these and similar cases, the scientist has followed some deep sense of order other than that on which conventional science would insist. I am suggesting that the logic of transformation is governing the spontaneous disclosure of truth as these central figures experienced it.

Consider some comparisons and contrasts between conventional science or textbook knowing and those transformational knowing events that have so measurably influenced the history of science. Conventional science follows generally the five-step account of thinking set forth by John Dewey in his influential study *How We Think*.[3] This general model has governed for many years what we take to be textbook science, or indeed, straight thinking in any problematic situation.

1. The *sense of the problem* is when thinking begins. There must be an interesting sense of a crossroads, an unresolved problematic situation, to get thinking going.

2. There must be a *rational formulation* of the problem. Dewey said that eventually the sense of the problem has to be "intellectualized," and then one can know what has to be solved.

3. Once the problem has been rationally formulated the *exploration* of possible solutions or *hypotheses* begins. Here one gathers and observes the data, and formulates in propositional terms the possible solutions that are available, dependent on the relevant facts and theories.

4. As hypotheses present themselves, they are mentally examined for their potential adequacy in meeting the conditions of the problem as intellectually formulated until the *most likely hypothetical solution is selected.*

---

3. J. Dewey, *How We Think* (New York: Heath, 1933), pp. 106-118.

5. Finally, the most adequate *hypothesis is tested* to see whether or not it meets the conditions described in Step 2, the problem as "intellectualized." This verification may fail, in which case the whole sequence would be repeated, beginning with a reformulation of the problem, Step 2. Thus, the solution is always to the problem as "intellectualized" within some known reference frame; it is not a solution to the problem as "felt" or "intuited."

Most of us can recognize this sequence in our own efforts at problem solving. The familiarity of it is due partly to our schooling, in which problems in chemistry or American history were set up to train our thinking in this way. Moreover, it is partly due to the innate tendency of our thinking to strive for this kind of practical clarity and order.

Regarding innate developmental potential, we must also consider Jean Piaget, who is a more contemporary advocate of the essentially same procedure.[4] Generally uncritical of Dewey as an educator, Piaget affirms this procedure as embodying the major characteristics of what he considers the highest form of intellectual operation. Dewey's sequence embodies the procedure for "formal operations," Piaget's notion of mature intelligence. That is, one *propositionalizes* and formulates problems, moving them *from the concrete to the abstract;* the selection of hypotheses leads to inductive and deductive reflection, *thinking about thinking* and *anticipating* consequences. Finally, testing the hypothesis in the public sphere is an effort to establish evidence demonstrating a major Piagetian assumption: *mental structures bear an isomorphic relation to the reality of one's environment.* In effect, when one thinks properly one can prove time after time that the structure of the mind fits the structure of reality "out there." The demonstration of this assumption is thinking properly, according to Piaget. Although Piaget speaks differently from Dewey about the internal structure of intelligence, the actual practice of thinking for both is at its optimum when it follows Dewey's paradigm.

The sort of illustration Dewey used is that of a mechanic or physician. Examining a patient, the physician will not take what "pops" into his or her head but will intellectually formulate the problem in established medical terms, formulate the most likely hypothesis, and proceed to test it in practice. The process is similar for the skilled mechanic who will practice in terms of his or her established frames of reference. Surely this is the mode of thinking to be

---

4. J. Piaget, *The Growth of Logical Thinking from Childhood to Adolescence* (New York: Basic Books, 1958), especially pp. 255-271.

advocated for such situations in which the problem and the desired solution already presuppose an established theoretical frame of reference, and the only task at hand is adapting that frame pragmatically to the immediate situation.

The difficulty with this textbook procedure, whether it is in the pragmatic educational hands of Dewey or the structuralist developmental hands of Piaget, is surely not that it is unworkable in everyday life. Indeed, it is not only practical but transformational wherever the "sense of the problem" can be adequately "intellectualized." If it could be assumed that intellectualizing would always expand to encompass the richness of what is "sensed" and/or that we "sense" nothing of essential significance that cannot ultimately be intellectualized, then this might be an adequate description of transformational knowing. In actuality, one's sense of a problem tends to be cut down or trained to fit what can be intellectualized. Thus, what can be known as true cannot be greater or exceed the boundaries of formal operational intelligence as applied with established frames of reference.

This is the eikonic eclipse in its most familiar form; it is a well-known everyday version of inductive reasoning (see Chapter 1), easily adapted to a wide variety of practical purposes where efficiency in adaptation is the main point. It is not merely the creeping-conformist tendency toward technique that is problematic here. It is also Piaget's unfortunate assumption (I think partly due to his early negative relationship with psychoanalysis) that imaginative understandings are all inferior or subordinate versions of formal operational intelligence. This constricts and dehumanizes knowing in favor of rationalistic structures, reinstating the dangers of rationalistic reduction described in Chapter 1.

Einstein, whose own thinking procedure was inveterately transformational and who was not reluctant to get "solutions" from the "felt" or "intuited" level of knowing, should be quoted here: "If you want to find out anything from theoretical physicists about the methods they use, I advise you to stick closely to one principle: don't listen to their words, fix your attention on their deeds."[5] What is true of theoretical physicists is true of theoretical thinkers in psychology and education as well. Dewey and Piaget have both created knowledge with immense intuitive genius; they themselves have taken bold imaginative leaps

5. Einstein, as quoted by W. Percy, *The Note in the Bottle* (New York: Farrar, Straus & Giroux, 1975), p. 233.

that characterize the knowing event. However, what is advocated in this paradigm of thinking is a distillation that eclipses the imaginative aspect of thinking in order to eliminate as much discontinuity as possible. The consequence is that the transformational aspect of knowing is sacrificed to the technical need for consistency in performance and conformity to known frames of reference. Had Dewey followed this procedure, he would have remained a philosophical idealist; Piaget would have stayed with Simon in Paris constructing standardized tests, and neither one would have made the contributions for which they are so widely noted. The transformational thinking that characterized their "deeds" should inform us better than their "words."

This is not merely a matter of looking behind the teaching to the teacher, but what is taught here about thinking is actually capable of seriously distorting a given situation. Again, Einstein is a case in point. His discovery of relativity was written up in textbooks as having followed this procedure, particularly in having its basis in the Michelson-Morley experiment on the speed of light. However, in a personal correspondence with Dr. N. Balazs, Einstein said the Michelson-Morley experiment had no influence on his thinking.[6] Moreover, in the textbook account the Michelson-Morley experiment gave the wrong result to serve as a foundation for relativity theory. Historically, the experiment had to be reworked in light of Einstein's theory, and only then did it give support to Einstein's claims. In effect, theory based on intuition and insight bypassed experimental findings to generate new facts—just the opposite of what the paradigm of conventional science would advocate.

Let me draw out the full implications from this contrast before I return to an appreciation of the Dewey paradigm. Knowing as event discloses that ultimately there may be no hard and fast boundaries to the production of insightful coincidences between hitherto unformulated or unconnected frames of reference: factors seemingly remote even in space and time may generate coherent insight and new understanding.

In the accident recorded in Chapter 1, prayers were said for me from nearly a thousand miles away and, coincidentally, I experienced a substantial healing. More remarkably and more specifically, Ananias, far removed from his persecutor Saul, went to meet him as a brother,

---

6. M. Polanyi, *Personal Knowledge* (New York: Harper Torchbook, 1962), p. 10, fn. 2.

because, without having seen him, he knew what had happened on the Damascus Road. When C. G. Jung wrote that "for the unconscious psyche space and time seem to be relative," he was saying that, at the deep level of awareness from which our most imaginative insights are drawn, knowledge finds itself in a space-time continuum where "space is no longer space and time is no longer time." In science, knowledge generated at this level may have a visionary quality, as if the visionary were able to "see" beyond space-time boundaries and read new knowledge directly out of the essence of things. It was a visionary capacity that enabled Michael Faraday to discard the ether theory and postulate that light was electromagnetic radiation. The remarkable thing about this is not only its accuracy but that Faraday lacked any mathematical education or special gift. He simply "saw it" that way without the help of a single mathematical formula.

Such a visionary grasp of the order of the universe is what guided Erwin Schrödinger, one of the founders of quantum mechanics. As Paul Dirac, with whom Schrödinger shared the Nobel Prize in 1933, said, "Schrödinger got his equation by pure thought, looking for some beautiful generalization . . . not by keeping close to the experimental developments of the subject."[7] Seeing, sensing, or knowing something *through* rather than strictly *bound by* the familiar space-time frame of reference has had a more powerful effect on the history of science than we are conventionally willing to acknowledge.

Having said all this to stress the importance of transformational knowing, I may now add that, once the results of transformational thinking are given and one enters the last step of "correspondence," Dewey's paradigm becomes useful. Here, relevance to known frames of reference is necessary because now the problem is entirely one of cognitive and technical inquiry. Designing ways to demonstrate, let us say, Kekulé's unique theory of molecular structure in the benzene molecule or Einstein's theory of relativity drew, of course, on known frames of reference, observable data, and a consensus from the appropriate scientific community. Yet it is notable that in neither of these two cases did the theorist himself make the test—that was left to the experts in experimental technique.

In sum, conventional science emphasizes demonstration and so tends to reduce all knowing to the shape of what can be demonstrated in terms of current facts and theory. However, the most significant knowing in the history of the sciences takes place in a way that draws

---

7. Koestler, *Creative Act*, p. 245. See also p. 170 on Faraday.

deeply on personal intuition and the creative unconscious. It is as if the history of science (where rational demonstration is so important) testifies that what is known in and through personal being, imaginatively and transformingly conceived, is the deepest and most comprehensive truth. Yet it does not exclude but contains as an element that which is rationally demonstrable.

ESTHETIC KNOWING

Esthetic knowing waits on and celebrates the imaginative turning point in the transformational knowing event. It is not information or idea, but the intuition or image and its symbolic expression, that the artist (of whatever sort) cares for and wants to make known.

In contrast to scientific knowing, when the chemist Kekulé, baffled by the molecular structure of the benzene molecule, arrived at its unique, circular structure by seeing a dancing circle of snakes in a hypnagogic image, he was not interested in the intuitive roots, contours, substance, or power of the image. It was the internal structure of the image that he cared about; it was the essential abstraction that he wanted to extract from the image and communicate to the scientific world. If Kekulé had been as great a poet or painter as he was a chemist, the meaning of and response to the same image would have been quite different.

The most evident difference between esthetic and scientific knowing is that the esthetic appears to be intrinsically more gratuitous. That is, it does not apparently originate as a solution to a particular problem. Moreover, esthetic knowing has not had to submit to empirical tests and standards for verification at the hands of a normative community usually more interested in rigor of proof than vigor of insight (although Kekulé did admonish the Chemical Society of London in 1929, "Learn to dream, gentlemen"). Thus esthetic knowing has rested more easily with the conviction and release that characterize Steps 3 and 4 of transformational logic, than with pressing through to interpretation so as to move on.

What follows is not a general theory of esthetics, but an interpretation of esthetic creation as a knowing event that exhibits transformational logic with emphases distinctly unique to the arts. To be specific, I will limit illustrations primarily to the work of imagery in poetry. Of all the arts, poetry can best be contained on the printed page and will probably reach farthest into what we will eventually say

about convictional experience in the context of the Eucharist.[8] However, by implication and with minor modification, the following
analysis of transformation in esthetic knowing could be applied to all
the arts.

Although I am not advocating any particular school of poetic
creation or criticism, it is fruitful at the beginning to look at Ezra
Pound's approach to poetry called "Imagism." Here the force of the
image itself carries the full weight of artistic meaning:

> In writing poems, the author must use his *image* because he sees it or
> feels it, *not* because he can use it to back up some creed. . . .
>
> All poetic language is the language of exploration. Since the beginning
> of bad writing, writers have used images as ornaments. The point of
> Imagism is that it does not use images as ornamets. The image is itself
> the speech. The image is the word beyond formulated language.
>
> The image is not an idea. It is a radiant node or cluster, it is what I
> can, and must perforce, call a vortex, from which and through which,
> and into which ideas are constantly rushing.[9]

What Pound describes regarding "image" in poetry may be seen
analytically as combining three layers of imaginative awareness into
one. The first is the *intuitive*. Cryptically, this means that one knows
that one knows, but one does not yet know the content of that
knowledge. This layer binds bodily sense, pathos, and desire to an
expectation of new awareness. This is stronger than a hunch because
it seems both decisive and conclusive, and it is less explicit or clear
than a passing notion or fancy because as intuition it does not yet have
any conceptualization or objectifiable content. As the word "vortex"
suggests, this is the power aspect of the general image; it is intuitive
force. Like a magnetic force under a thin paper covered with iron
filings, intuitive force compels a wide range of surface factors (that is,
symbols and ideas) into its field of influence and at the same time
anchors the final poetic creation deeply in the personality of the
artist.

---

8. I am using the term *Eucharist* for conceptual, not liturgical or denominational,
reasons. The Greek word *Charis*, which stands at the center of the term, implies both
"grace" and "gratitude." *Eu-charist*, than, is a heightened form of these terms: the
Presence of Christ in the Eucharist is both his grace toward us and a cause for our
gratitude. Transforming experiences approximate the Eucharist so they are to be seen
as gifts of grace that give rise to worshipful gratitude. *How* they approximate the
Eucharist is in large part what this and following chapters discuss.

9. E. Pound, *Gaudier Brezeska, A Memoir* (New York: Lane, 1916), pp. 99, 102, 106.

The second layer is the *compositional* aspect in which intuitive certainty is united with perceptual images and memories. As the magnet approaches the random arrangement of filings from beneath the sheet of paper, reaching a certain degree of closeness, the filings begin to quiver in anticipation. When the critical point is reached, the whole mass of filings is suddenly and beautifully ordered into a symmetrical bipolar scheme. In the formation of the artistic composition, perceptions and memories dance in and out of the intuitive vortex, finally shaped by it into an internally coherent "radiant cluster," composed of manifest content and felt with intuitive force. This unifying layer of imaginative awareness may combine the most distinctly opposed extremes, such as light and darkness, life and death, or male and female, because the manifest content is held together not by the objective perceptions or structure but by the intuitive order of the poetic artist. The constellation takes on a life of its own, hovering between being thrust into objective consciousness, on the one hand, and being submerged again beyond the reach of the intuitive force, on the other. Its brief, brilliant life is so tenuous that many such mental images of potentially powerful significance are lost before they are caught in any public form; others, rushed into objectification at the expense of their intuitive roots, are stillborn.

The third layer is the poem, "the formulated language." This is the *symbolic expression* by which the poet attempts to bring the full force of the creative act into public view. The fundamental instrument of poetic expression is the metaphor whereby, as Aristotle defined it, one can gain an intuitive perception of the similarity in the dissimilar. To take an unambiguous example, in the familiar dead metaphor "table leg," dissimilar things — that is, animals and tables — are united in the similarity of "standing things." By this example, it is evident that when a metaphor establishes a connection between hitherto unconnected things, it is also implying the existence of a higher class of objects. In more lively and complex metaphors, the range and multiplicity of implied higher classes can be almost inexhaustible. This is to say that in the final analysis metaphorically constructed unity is potentially an infinite, open-ended connection. Thus particulars are made to imply an almost infinite series of more universal meanings.

The immense power of the metaphor to connect the intuitive life of the poet with his or her public lies first in this: in combined metaphors, particularities are made to carry the full range of meanings embedded in the poet's original intuition. As a result, the reader or audience, if the poem is read aloud, is able to replicate the poet's creative act. The audience moves through the same sequence as the poetic artist, but in reverse, from the outside in rather than from the inside out.

The poet, in what we have called "scanning," builds up the intuitive potential, following hunches, sensing directions, and moving toward that gratuitous internal coalescence that eventually takes on a life of its own. Coalescence occurs when explicit content is fused with and infused by the force of the intuition. Thus every inward composition, whether in the poet or the audience, begins in expectant waiting, and, through indwelling a series of leads, searches and scans until the inner composition is born. The audience, starting from the "outside," must indwell the poet's symbolic expression, the work of art, with sufficient intensity to break the tyranny of surface meaning. it must come under the spell of the underlying "word beyond formulated language," to sense the pull and contours of the underlying connection between pathos and idea, universal implication and particular percepts and memories, that inspired and governed the poet's creation and choice of metaphors. As this primary poetic "word" takes hold, the audience can be taken up by the generative intuitive awareness of the artist to such an extent that it "knows" why the poem *had* to be the way it is. Thus it might be said that by performing the creative act in reverse, the audience approaches an intuitive transparency between itself and the poet. Of course, the audience is not merely getting into the poet's narcissistic psyche. It is indwelling what the poet intuited at the same level of preobjective awareness.

On the other hand, of course, this is not to say that the poetry, or any work of art, is created to suit its public; that would apply only to the cheapest sort of creation. Rather, the poet's art implicitly puts forth the entire, creative movement, from the empowered intuition to the expressive symbol, directed preeminently toward the *congruence* of the process. Thus congruence is the most common controlling norm in esthetic knowing, not *correspondence* with public expectations as in scientific knowing. The public is important to the artist, but, as was said of P. Renoir's work, it establishes its own norms for evaluation;[10] the integrity of the creative act, from intuition to expression, is what makes it reversible and hence powerful for the appreciative audience. The expressive symbol, the complex of poetic metaphors, does the unique thing of holding the creative act open at both ends, open to the public and open to the reality intuited by the

---

10. M. Merleau-Ponty, *Signs* (Northwestern University Press, 1964), p. 63.

poetic artist. Thus, congruence creates correspondence, or original creative integrity produces audience reversibility.

Wallace Stevens' poetry is perhaps the most efficient and vivid way to illustrate esthetic knowing. It is "efficient" because so many of the overarching concerns of transformational knowing are caught up in his poetry and its fundamental intention to draw the reader, via the imagination, into "moments of enlargement." It is "vivid" because his imagery is not only striking in itself but designed to catch "the instant of change" in flight. As with the Impressionists, or, better, Paul Cézanne, in painting, Stevens' poetry is designed to catch a reality that is simultaneously subjective and objective; hence at blurring speed he lays hold of the impact of transforming change.

From his earliest published poetry, in 1923 when he was age forty-four, Stevens' poem "The Curtains in the House of the Metaphysician" is a representative example of his poetry as a whole. It is both a symbolic expression of the process of esthetic knowing we have been discussing, and in itself as a poem it is a symbolic paradigm of transformation as I will be discussing it later in relation to the Eucharist (Chapter 4).

> It comes about that the drifting of these curtains
> Is full of long motions; as the ponderous
> Deflations of distance; or as clouds
> Inseparable from their afternoons;
> Or the changing of light, the dropping
> Of the silence, wide sleep and solitude
> Of night, in which all motion
> Is beyond us, as the firmament,
> Up-rising and down-falling, bares
> The last largeness, bold to see.[11]

The slowly drifting motion, as it appears first in a description of the curtains, is then reflected metaphorically into the vistas, cloud, sunlight, night, until finally it embraces the entire cosmos, including the reader. Hence in the title, the word "house" is metaphorically linked with the universe, and the metaphysician is one who finds a home in the universe. As the scope of our attention changes from "*these* curtains" to "the last largeness," our mode of consciousness is taken from descriptive awareness to metaphorical, and thence to

---

11. I am heavily indebted to A. McGill, *Celebration of the Flesh* (New York: Association Press, 1964) for this selection and commentary on Wallace Stevens' poetry.

intuitive metaphysical. A metamorphosis is suggested as we move from seeing the "objective" reality of the curtains, open to any naked eye, into the final "see," which has a visionary quality that has clearly broken with "the tyranny of the naked eye," as Stevens called it. Actually the transformation effected is one in which the reader has moved from being an observer, through a metaphorical reflection of what is observed, to being overtaken by and taken up in the reality that at first resided outside. This sweep of movement remarkably contained in a single sentence catches the breathtaking "moment of enlargement," as Stevens so persistently sought to do. Arthur McGill, commenting on this movement, says that as "imagination is led from the curtained room into the open spaces of earth and sky and finally to a point where 'all motion is beyond us,' and we stand in the presence of an ultimate immensity, there develops a growing sense of release and exultant invigoration."[12] The rhythm of this poetic sentence changes to bring forth the cosmic release, expressed in the final words, "bold to see." This cosmic conclusion is implicit in the curtains from the beginning, but as this movement unfolds there is a grand-scale figure-ground reversal that puts the observer within the reality observed. Thus, the scope and self-involving power of the reality implicit in the author's original intuition is finally disclosed as embodied in the particulars and at the same time embodying us who regard them.

The further richness in the transformational effect of this poem is twofold. First, if we turn the movement of the poem back on the process of its creation, then clearly the poem is an outward symbolic expression of the inner creative act that gave rise to it. The reader is led through the very process, from particular to universal, that will enable intuition of the author's original vision. Unlike poetry that talks *about* objects (such as mountains, roses, wind, or fog) as entities to be enhanced by poetry, this poem does not leave the dynamics of appreciation up to the reader. Either the reader is caught up into the same vortex of many-faceted apperceptions of movement, both visible and invisible, that first entertained the author, or else the poem is not appreciated at all.

Second, this poem's mirroring the key turning points in its own creation does not beget a narcissistic result. This is partly because the intuition of a primal sweeping motion is a reality beyond the poet's creative process. It is also because that motion is drawn out of a series

---

12. McGill, *Celebration of the Flesh*, p. 154.

of metaphors such that the particulars of the world are vivified and enlarged. Thus, the poetry produces in the appreciative reader a kind of "mundane ecstasy" with respect to ordinary things. That is to say, the ordinarily inward appreciation of external objects and action is now turned inside out: one is met and taken outward into a heightened sense of the world; it is not merely that a heightened sense of the world is thrust inward.

The ultimate power of the poem is limited by the fact that the reality envisioned in particulars is no more than a slow, undulating motion, however cosmic it may be. If a more powerful reality were envisioned in the particular and subjected to the same symbolic process, the effect would be immensely more significant. Such is the aim of the symbolic aspect of the Eucharist, which we will eventually see is normative for convicting experiences. I will have much more to say about this in Chapter 5, but for the moment note these parallels. As with curtains, so with bread and wine as common objects of experience. Then, if we move via metaphorical expansion from the elements' inherent life-giving and quickening power into their representation of the body and blood of Christ and from there into all creation, the vast reality hidden in the elements from the beginning becomes increasingly more apparent. Finally reaching an intuitive transparency with the inner life of Christ, one is overcome by the Author and Authority behind the sacrament and over all. Thus the outside observer of common objects moves to become active participant and from active participant to become a passive recipient of the reality hidden in those common objects from the beginning. I do not want to suggest that the Eucharist is nothing more than a symbolic transformation, but rather that the power of any poetry successfully conveying transformation lies in its capacity to represent symbolically what Christ actually does in the Eucharist. Thus from a faith perspective poetic transformation does not reduce the Eucharist, but the Eucharist includes and expands the poetic.

Now, if esthetic knowing is gratuitous — that is, if the intuitive force spontaneously generates its own imagery — how does it conform to the conflictual aspect of transformational logic? We said at the beginning of the chapter that the logic of transformation necessarily includes a rupture in the knowing context; yet esthetic knowing appears without an apparent problem to solve. Does this mean that the logic does not apply, or is there always a conflict implicit in the act of esthetic knowing? I suggest that the logic does apply and that it does in fact focus our attention on one of the most important aspects of esthetic knowing: namely, its power to break the numbing spell of "everydayness," to renew and restore both the human spirit and the particulars of the world. Dynamically, the human spirit, whether it be the artist's or the audience's, is characterized by its power to break with the tyranny of the obvious and compose some aspect of the world, in its (the spirit's) own terms.[13] The integrity of the human spirit, and the protection against random creativity of its transcendent relationship to the world, is preserved by the coherence of transformational logic.

Transformation in esthetic knowing cannot occur in the artist if his or her spirit has been violated, stifled, or perverted. Similarly, the replication of the artist's creative act is lost if the audience has been so subjected to the stereotypes, techniques, and calculations of everyday life that it cannot make even a beginning move toward indwelling a work of art. When the creative act does occur, then the human spirit is immediately in conflict with the reductionistic, habituating tendencies of the human organism to find its most satisfying equilibrium and stay there. But the truly imaginative vision and its symbolic expression will, for a while at least, break the spell of everydayness and restore the spirit to the particulars of its world.

Here we must return to the earlier distinction betwen imaginative and imaginary. Poetry—indeed, any work of art—becomes increasingly imaginary and less transformational to the extent that it gets caught up in reflections of reality, never returning to particulars and never rekindling the spirit (except as escape may be refreshing). The tendency of poetic artists to become charmed by their compositional powers, to enclose themselves in their metaphors, and to confuse the reality of their images with the reality of their own souls haunts esthetic knowing the way textbook knowing haunts transformational knowing in the sciences. Just as scientific knowing, which depends on proofs (even if they are only proof of falsity), can begin to define its knowing as proving, so esthetic knowing, which depends on metaphor, can begin to define itself as nothing more than reflecting this in that or establishing similarities between dissimilar things. Transformation, the implicit logic in any complete knowing event, will, however, continue to press toward the release of new life and the truth gain that comes from resolving those conflicts, which (latent or manifest) permeate every knowing situation.

---

13. *Spirit* in western philosophical thought has been associated with reason, love, freedom, universality, personality, and creativity. A working assumption in this book is that creativity is the generative source of the other manifestations of spirit, and it is the patterned process of transformation that most aptly defines creativity.

It is important to note that in neither of these transpositions (scientific or esthetic knowing) has the person or the self been the central matter of concern. In therapeutic knowing, transformational logic is transposed into a context in which the self itself undergoes transformation. Because this is such an important aspect of transformation in convictional experience, we must examine how therapeutic transformation works.

THERAPEUTIC KNOWING

Transformational logic is also transposed into the therapeutic context as a patterned process of healing. That is, when clients in psychotherapy, following in the psychoanalytic tradition, reach a point of substantial "improvement," they will have gone through a process of transformational knowing such as we have described.[14] The therapeutic process is complicated by the wide variety of defenses that enable the client to avoid being known; but most of these maneuvers simultaneously expose the secret desire to be known. Thus, the healing process is essentially a knowing event working transformationally on defenses and the conflicts buried beneath them.

In psychotherapy, both therapist and client are mutually involved in a process of coming to new knowledge—or a rediscovery of old knowledge—about the client's personality. The client must come to it from the inside out; the therapist must come to it from the outside in. The therapist utilizes deeply felt experience as well as rationally constructed theories of personality and its disorders in empathically indwelling the particular case. Before anything like therapeutic knowing can take place, the therapist and the client must establish a shared "world," a context of *rapport.* Rapport here means that the client is willing to let the rational capacities and judgments of the therapist guide his or her self-understanding, and the therapist is willing to let the personal knowledge of the client guide his or her use of those rational capacities. There is, in other words, a dyadic relationship established between them so that they can enter into a shared "world" and eventually replicate in a joint effort what takes place in individuals as a knowing event.

As rapport permits, the therapist makes analytical and appropriately timed interpretations to focus key conflicts. These are more or less latent ruptures in the client's situation that through their

14. See J. E. Loder, *Religious Pathology and Christian Faith* (Philadelphia: Westminster Press, 1966). The technical argument for this viewpoint is developed in this study of Kierkegaard and Freud.

rapport the therapist has indwelt and come to understand but not identified with. Thus, the *first step* in therapeutic knowing may be described as focusing *conflict in the context of rapport*. Notice that the therapist, however informed he or she may be by theory, intuition, and experience, must follow the lead of the "personal knowledge" of the client, both as to timing and as to content. If it is ever otherwise, interpretations fall on deaf ears or become coercive, and the aim of the process — that is, knowledge of the client — will have been set back by confusion and/or repression. As with transformational knowing generally, so with therapy; tacit factors give the lead to rational processes that then work elaboratively to delineate conflict.

In the second step the therapist assumes that the client, confronted by conflict and supported in the face of it, will work toward its resolution. If the rapport is not broken, the client and therapist will together indwell the conflict and the resources for resolution. They *scan* the client's psychic terrain, making new connections in a genuinely creative way. Thus, as in transformational knowing, an *interlude* in which *deep scanning* takes place follows the focusing of and bearing with any given conflict. Most of the reflective or interpretative aspects of scanning will be done by the therapist; most of the affective and unconscious scanning will be done by the client. Together they will persist in the search awaiting the third step, insight.

Insight is preeminently — both in its significance and in its power to effect change — the imaginative work of the client. His or her personality must finally reintegrate those fragments that comprised the conflict — both as felt and as rationally focused. In approaching this step, the therapist must simply trust the transformational potential of the client to create a fresh constellation that will integrate the conflicted aspects of the personality. However, the psychic abhorrence of conflict is so great that the client will repeatedly produce false solutions, escapist configurations of the conflict's features, or only proximate resolutions, such as transference. All imaginary configurations must be met again and again with rational judgments that refocus the essential aspects of the conflict for the client. This is to ensure that transformation, not fantastic escape or clever defense, is the outcome of the process.

Sometimes it is the therapist's construction of the latent conflict that is imaginary. Recognition of such an error may be called *negative insight*. Then the conflict must be restated to take account of new data or deeper intuitions. This works, in principle, like scientific transformational knowing when the scientist realizes the wrong problem is being studied. Although the therapist may have negative insight, any constructive, healing insight must in the final analysis be the property of the client.

When insight comes to the client, extraordinary connections are made; or ordinary connections are given new or extraordinary significance. It is as if scales fall from the eyes, and distorted perceptions of people, especially of oneself, are corrected. Defenses become optional rather than compulsive; acceptance of self and world become possible. But this gets us ahead of the sequence.

The fourth step is also primarily the property of the client and may be described as *release of tension;* this is a felt decathexis of the conflict that makes new energy available for reorganization of the personality and its "world" relative to the insight gained. New energy is available because the mind has found an easier way to assemble all the aspects of the conflict. Instead of holding them in unresolved tension, the imaginative leap of the client contructs an original, meaningful whole out of puzzling fragments that had seemed inherently incompatible. Thus, meaningful insight becomes the mediating integrator in the transforming act of coming to know oneself.

The "aha!" and release are the surest sign that genuine insight has been attained. Of course, there is no way such a release can be effected in the client from the analyst's side of the rapport; but it can be recognized and affirmed together with the client, thus solidifying the gain. In some cases, the therapeutic sequence terminates here without any further interpretation; in fact, when dreams prove to be healing, they do their work often without the full benefit of a final stage of interpretation. The client simply knows that the world has changed, and whatever was conflictual has disappeared.

However, in such instances the knowing process is not finished, and the therapist does a more complete job if there is a feeding back of the insight into the initial conflict, and the continuity between the insight and the conflict is established for the client. In other words, the completion of the jointly conducted knowing process brings the new knowledge into a shared, public arena where client and therapist test presumed interpretations to see whether they correspond to the client's subjective sense of congruence between insight and conflict. Ultimately, the client and the therapist must be mutually satisfied that congruence corresponds to reality.

It is only at this final point that the goal of therapy is reached and established. As Freud once put it, the client is "given the freedom to choose for or against the neurosis."[15] The freedom of the "I" to

---

15. S. Freud, *The Ego and the Id,* trans. J. Strachy (New York: Norton, 1960), p. 69 n.

choose to reconstruct its world is first liberated with the insight, but it must be secured by completing the transformation sequence. That is, it must work through to congruence and correspondence to ensure the continuity of intentionality with respect to the original conflict. Before reaching this conclusion, the "I" is immersed in the underlying conflict, not being free to choose because the conflict exercises unconscious control. When the self-transcendence of the "I" is secured by completing the transformational process, an unwitting reinstatement of the conflict is far less likely to occur.

Of course, various types of psychotherapy will emphasize one or the other aspects of this process. A more thoroughly "client-centered" approach will tend to eliminate the interpretative step all together, but the interpretation is nevertheless operative implicitly, because the nondirective method is also governed by an elaborate theory of personality. A more "reality-oriented" therapy will actually teach the patient how to think on the premise that the cognitive and interpretative aspects create the cultural world and sense of meaning to which the client will conform. There are other variations in which the client is actually "created" by the therapist; in these the last step of interpretation is used not so much for verifying insights gained as for convincing the client that the process gives life and new vision. The "I" is set free for recomposition of the world, and the "test" is the reproduction of the process.

As I have discussed at length elsewhere (see p. 57, n. 14), the essential process of transformation described here is a core process in any therapeutic sequence following in the psychoanalytic tradition. My emphasis at this point is to describe the steps involved in coming to know the client and the client's coming to know self in a transformational way; it is not to exposit variations imposed on the process by different techniques.

The following case serves as a summary illustration. Christina was an attractive young university student of twenty-one. Threatened by strong lesbian feelings, she sought counseling at the university clinic. Christina did not like her desires. She wished to relate to men, one in particular, and yet she was not able to respond emotionally to any of his overtures.

Christina assumed that the source of the difficulty lay mostly with her relation to her mother, because she saw herself as very much like her mother and because there seemed to be a subliminal seduction from her mother toward her. She worked with this for a period of time, but it became increasingly evident that the problem was more closely related to her father, and her notions about her mother were more like extrapolations from a textbook; that is, what she had read and presumed must be the case.

As she worked with her counselor to refocus the conflict (helped by the negative insight that they had been working on the wrong one), a more deeply felt connection for Christina emerged when she saw her father as both seductive and mothering. The mother, it turned out, had actually been hostile and competitive toward her daugher. The result for Christina was that from her father she derived unusual anxiety over the heterosexual experience, and from her mother unusual uncertainty about being a woman. The apparent result was a narcissism in which her intense self-love worked as a compensation for the lack of any clear expression of love from either parent. Her young women companions were strikingly attractive persons with strong personalities, but they, like Christina, had little or no capacity for intimate, empathic feeling. Apparently, each partner gratified herself in support of a neurotic, narcissistic obsession. Ironically, in that seemingly intimate setting each was in the act of reinforcing the other's denial and distrust of intimacy.

The irony in this description of the conflict rang true to Christina, and she seemed to absorb it with a deeply embarrassed silence. She then left the university for a vacation and soon found herself in bed with one of her female companions, but this time it was different. As her companion approached her, she was seized with an overwhelming need to vomit. She jumped from the bed and ran to the bathroom where she heaved herself dry. When she returned, she felt absolutely no attraction for her companion, and in fact no further troublesome lesbian feelings appeared in the course of her therapy. Amazingly, as she had earnestly hoped, the catharsis and transformation seemed complete, and happily, she left school at the end of the spring term engaged to be married. Unfortunately, follow-up information is not available, but this vignette will serve to illustrate the process I am describing.

The sequence in this case illustrates therapeutic knowing in which a client is freed, finally, to choose the self whom she had come to know and whom she and her counselor considered to be authentic for her. Christina wrestled long with a problem that rankled under the surface, but the dynamics remained hidden. By working together, they scanned the situation—the therapist, working more at a rational level, and Christina, scanning her own field of feeling and images. The first major insight was negative, so a reformulation of the conflict had to be both sensed and stated. When this point was reached, a resolution of apparently remarkable power took place. In a catharsis of vomiting, her psyche created a remarkable body-image reversal of the sexual act that had become so repulsive to her. Instead of taking in and moving toward climactic orgasm, she heaved out in an orgasmic expulsion of what she perceived as vile contents under the surface.

The body metaphor reversing aggression and surfacing self-disgust is striking in itself and in the mystery of psychic resources on which it seems to draw; but more than that, it was central to a transforming act of her personality, radically reconstructing the world from the inside out. It was clear that the elements of the conflict had been dramatically rearranged from a sudden turning away from the narcissism to a commitment to a man for whom she had real heterosexual feelings. Her position with respect to her parents had basically changed, but there was much more that needed work. However, the therapeutic relation terminated at the end of her semester with the understanding that the central process of coming to some new knowledge of herself had been accomplished. Further work on parental relationships was not pursued, although Christina was left with an interpretation of what she had been through and was in a position to do some of the work on those relationships by herself.

Therapeutic knowing is clearly relevant to the thinking we want to do about convictional experience. The transformation of conflictual factors that lie at the base of one's person is often involved in coming to conviction. I will speak much more about contaminating factors in convictional experience in the last chapter. For now, note that this form of knowing is distinguished from the others in its cooperative or dyadic aspect. Transformational knowing is carried on conjointly, but imagination and personal intuitions interact with reflective or theoretical knowledge in essentially the same pattern as in any other transformational knowing event. As a consequence, what is known imaginatively and therapeutically is a gift from both a personal creative unconscious (the client) and the intelligence of the caring other (therapist). The gift is the knowledge of oneself, including as the essential ingredient the freedom to choose for the self one has come to know.

Therapeutic knowing, like the scientific and the esthetic, is subject to characteristic perversities, most commonly the reduction of personal uniqueness to "the theory." This is certainly not to say that theory will not help in the discovery and recovery of one's uniqueness, but it is a violation of the knowing event so central to the human spirit to assert that no matter what may appear "you must believe the theory," as one analyst with whom I studied told me in no uncertain terms. This is one facet of a general perversity: instead of therapy's being a knowing event, it becomes like conventional science, a matter of incorporation and socialization into the therapist's view of what is theoretically "normal." I will say more in Chapter 6 about what is abnormal about "normal," but now we must briefly focus the main contribution this transposition of transformation has made to our overall discussion.

First, therapy understood in this way confirms the assumption that the logic of transformational knowing may be carried on conjointly by two (or more) people. What has appeared here in a professional relationship is carried on with the same sort of result in other face-to-face relationships where two people mutually create each other. This general observation is especially important for working with people who report having had a convictional experience.

Second, as with none of the other types of knowing discussed here, therapeutic knowing makes it evident that what is known in the event may indeed be oneself. Such self-knowledge often comes through an eikonic awareness; that is, a spontaneous coalescence of many personal, often repressed developmental, fragments. I will discuss this further in Chapters 5 and 6. What should be mentioned here is that the surest sign that healing has occurred in therapeutic knowing is the freedom of the "I" to choose for the self and against patterns of self-destruction. As we will see, this same self-disclosure appears as the appropriate human response to convictional experience.

Finally, the essential health of the transformational knowing event has been articulated and illustrated. One may say that the inducement of this process with respect to a felt conflict may be assumed to be a movement toward health. It is important to emphasize this because the threat of a contaminating pathology in convictional experience is very real. However, the threat is met by the coherent logic of transformation. Indeed, the coherence of this logic may be taken as the very sort of reasonableness that is built into and fostered by convicting experience.

OTHER TRANSPOSITIONS

Other contexts could be cited where the logic of transformation might be spelled out as the underlying guiding order in an otherwise disparate or random situation. There is neither space nor sufficient relevance for all of these in this book, but certain ones should be mentioned.

A major figure whose work is explicitly on the transformation of the human ego is Carl Jung. His view is not far removed from what I have cited as therapeutic knowing except that he bases all transformations of the personality on archetypal forms buried in the human psyche.[16] Although his view of the personality is more complex than anything I have discussed, his notion of transformation follows the same logic. I will refer more explicitly to his work in Chapter 5. Interpersonal knowing has been explicated by Charles Hampden-Turner in a transformational pattern whereby one's identity, in intense one-to-one interaction, becomes more fully itself.[17] Social transformation in the limited context of revitalization movements has been set forth in some detail by Anthony Wallace.[18] Social transformation on a broad political scale has been set forth by Manfred Halpern.[19] Cultural transformation has been provocatively developed by Claude Levi-Strauss' extensive studies of myth.[20] My point in making this list, which could of course be much longer, is that no realm of human life is without its versions of transformational logic. It is not merely the property of the "creative few," nor is it merely an incidental aspect of the human psyche, nor is it strictly the concern of "religious types." The logic of transformation, by a variety of other names (conscientization, dialectical process, and so on), has been the subject of study and the guiding principle in nearly every area of human experience.

The position I will be taking and one that I contend is central to the Christian faith is that human transformations must themselves be transformed. From the standpoint of Christian conviction, all of the preceding transformations, transposed from context to context, are forms of knowing that reflect, in respect to the character of each context, that decisive transformation by which we come to know Christ. As "the Logos" (John 1:1), he is the ultimate ground for all order and so also the order of transformation. Yet we participate fully in that order only through a redeemed knowledge of him, only as we

16. C. G. Jung, *Symbols of Transformation*, trans. R. F. C. Hull, Bollingen Series, vol. 2 (Princeton, N.J.: Princeton University Press, 1967).
17. C. Hampden-Turner, *Radical Man* (Cambridge, Mass: Schenkman, 1970).
18. A. Wallace, "Revitalization Movements," in W. A. Lessa and E. Z. Vogt, eds., *A Reader in Comparative Religion* (New York: Harper & Row, 1965), pp. 503-512.
19. M. Halpern, "Transformation and the Source of the Fundamentally New," paper presented to American Political Science Association, Chicago, September 1, 1974.
20. C. Levi-Strauss, *Structural Anthropology* (New York: Doubleday, 1967), chap. 11.

are reconciled to God through Christ's mediation. Other proximate forms of transformation participate "sacramentally" insofar as they are visible forms of that infinite and invisible truth, or propaedeutically, in that they "prepare the way of the Lord" (Isa. 40:3).

As preparation these proximate forms of transformation alert us to the ultimate mystery of Christ's redemption of the world, and they open our awareness to the forms of everyday life that do or do not point toward or participate in Christ's transformation of all things. As "sacramental," they repeatedly represent to us the redemption in which we already live and suggest the full significance of the Eucharist, in which that reconciliation is celebrated directly. However, before making the connections between created and uncreated knowing more explicit and before attempting to say what is meant by transformation transformed, we must explore and interpret the ultimate dimensions of the knowing event as I have already described it. This means that what I have discussed as instances of transformation need to be seen in terms of their full implications for all being. Putting it more sharply, Is transformational logic a convenient fiction imposed on life or perhaps an incidental part of reality that is noticeable but not essential? Or is it anchored in the very marrow of existence as convictional experiences tell the convicted soul?

Three

THE
FOURFOLD
KNOWING EVENT

INTRODUCTION TO BEING

➤ THE CONVICTED PERSON believes that the very nature of one's being is changed by the Convictor through the transforming event. Now, if conviction is not merely subjective intoxication, an altered state of consciousness, wish-fulfilling eruption from infancy, or some other transient, accidental aspect of our nature, how is the whole matter of transformation connected to the essence of being human, and indeed, to being itself?

To begin with we must say a preliminary word about "being." C. S. Lewis once described two parents who, trying to avoid anthropomorphism, taught their son to think of God as "pure substance." After growing up, the son confessed that he had always thought of God as a huge tapioca pudding. The same opaque and impenetrable murkiness sometimes takes possession of our thoughts when we start to think of "being." By "being," I do not mean a vague substance that oozes into everything. "Being" as it is used here is simply that which is logically and phenomenologically presumed by all knowing, transformational knowing included. We cannot think, know, doubt, or deny without presuming that our thinking, knowing, doubting, or denying *is*. Thus, "being" is the implicit assumption behind everything that is and occurs. To say, as some philosophers do, that "being is nothing" is quite clear when you realize that being is "no-thing" in particular but that which is necessarily presumed by all particulars. Thus, what is meant by being is that which is so universal that it cannot be classified, and so close to each one of us that it cannot enter into explicit awareness, yet "the understanding of which is included in all things whatsoever a man apprehends" (St. Thomas Aquinas).[1]

Before continuing, I should pause to take note that ordinary language is not well suited to the discussion of "being," because we cannot talk about it without shrinking it to the units and structures of our grammar, thus making it a being among others. Thus we must agree that talk of "being" is stretching grammar beyond its proper limits.[2] Using what was said above, I will be asking you to read "being" metaphorically. As we saw in the discussion of esthetic knowing, it is precisely in the stretching of language by metaphor and symbolic expression that it is able to be more inclusive. Thus "stretching" is not distorting language; it is drawing it closer to the universal source of being itself. Thus, I will assume that talk about "being" or "being-itself" is a hidden metaphor that moves from the beings we know, primarily human beings, toward the universal, which stands behind and beyond them.

Far from the static implications of "pure substance" or a tapioca pudding, the notion of being is inherently dynamic. The Sanskrit roots are significantly vital. The verb "to be" derives from the Sanskrit *bhu*, "to grow or make grow," and the English forms "am" and "is" derive from the same Sanskrit root *asm*, which means "to breathe."[3] At its roots, being is vital and constantly increasing itself in life. John Macquarrie wants to make being the condition on which all beings exist; hence being is that which "lets be." "Letting be" should not be understood laconically, as the mildly depressed motto "Live and let live" suggests; it is, rather, "Let flourish!" It is not difficult to see how this translates into the creative and loving activity of God, once "faith" has recognized that what phenomenological reason calls *being* has revealed itself as God in Christ. However, we must pause here and say more about explicitly theological matters later.

Any direct investigation of being-itself will also be set aside at this

1. J. Macquarrie, *Principles of Christian Theology* (New York: Scribner's, 1977), p. 110. As any reader familiar with Macquarrie's work will notice, this chapter is indebted to Macquarrie at many key points.
2. Ibid., pp. 106-107.
3. This etymology is taken from J. Jaynes, *The Origin of Consciousness in the Breakdown of the Bicameral Mind* (Boston: Houghton Mifflin, 1976), p. 51.

point while I pursue the issue of human being. Of course, the two are not separate investigations, because the most immediate, and I would argue the most necessary, avenue to the essence of being-itself is through human being. This is the case first because of what we have already said about imagination and its inevitable mediation of personal existence into any rational process. If our earlier discussion holds true, any presumably direct, rational investigation of being-itself would already presuppose the full scope of human being as tacitly shaping reason through its underlying intuitions and images. Furthermore, only in human being, so far as anyone knows, is being self-aware. In fact, being human entails the awareness that one is a being and to some extent what sort of being he or she is; to be human is inevitably to open being to itself. Thus, simply because it is existentially unavoidable, I will be implicitly discussing being-itself as I pursue more directly the matter of being human.

Being human entails environment, selfhood, the possibility of not being, and the possibility of new being. All four dimensions are essential, and none of them can be ignored without decisive loss to our understanding of what is essentially human. First, I will discuss environment under the rubric "the lived world" to stress the constructive, compositional character of the environment. However, this is in no way to disembody human being as if to enclose it in subjectivity; it is to stress the claim that reality is created, not fixed and normative. Authentic human being must always view itself from inside a composed situation; it cannot rise above it either in gnostic fantasies or in metaphysical speculations. Embodiment in a composed environment is the first essential dimension of being human. In the following pages, "world" (in quotation marks) refers to a particular, lived composition; the general term *world* refers to all possible composed "worlds" taken collectively; and *World* means God's recomposition of the world.

The second dimension is "the self" that transcends the embodiment of being human in order repeatedly to recompose its "world." From the standpoint of the transformational knowing event, this is "the knower"; the self is embodied in the lived "world" and at the same time stands outside it. By virtue of this duality of the self, it is evident that human being both *is* its environment and *has* an environment. Some will want to stress the transcendence of the self, in which case environment is taken in the weak sense; others emphasize the reverse, in which the environment is the stronger dimension. My view is that both self and lived world may be taken in a strong sense. Ontogenetically the lived world is engrossing and very largely determinative of the ontic, or particular shape of the self; in this sense, the environment composes the self. Ontologically the self is primary in that (1) self-transcendence or openness to one's own being is universal and independent of the environment and (2) the lived world must finally be the self's own composition of the environment as given with birth. Otherwise the self, as self, collapses into prefabricated "worlds" (business, fashion, academia, and so on), the uniqueness of self as composer is lost, and human being becomes *nothing but* a reflection of its culture.

Later on (Chapters 5 and 6), I will have to speak of "ego," to keep faith with the language of human development. Ego includes the "I" and the "self" as described, but it is seen by psychologists as the hypothetical psychic agency that seeks to equilibrate intrapsychic reality with external reality and so establish a reliable, realistic pattern of defenses and interrelated coping capacities (the part processes such as thinking, imagining, and speaking). Thereby it ensures survival and long-term satisfactions in life. The "I" or "self" refers to the *sine qua non* of the ego: namely, the capacity to make choices freely — even choices that may break out of established patterns of defense and coping.

However, both these dimensions of human being are weak with respect to the third: the possibility of annihilation, the potential and eventually inevitable absence of one's being. I will discuss this dimension under the rubric the "void," because this is the end result of each human being, implicit in existence from birth and explicit in death. The "void" is understood as the ultimate telos toward which all experiences of nothingness point; "nothingness" refers to the "faces of the void" taken collectively.

When being is present not only implicitly in beings but explicitly *manifest* as being-itself, then we experience "the Holy." The *mysterium tremendum fascinans*" that Rudolph Otto described so vividly is not a privileged awareness. Rather, it is essential to being human that one worship what is holy. A sense of "the Holy" may be projected onto the profane, in which case "worship" (and being human along with it) collapses into the embodied environment as idolatry and thence into nothingness. However, at the center of transformational knowing in science, esthetics, or therapy the imaginative, constructive insight or vision is an undoing of nothingness; it is a proximate form of the ultimate manifestation of "the Holy" in revelation. That which is unique, set apart, and manifest as new being, reversing and overcoming annihilation, expresses the graciousness of being-itself. Faith sees that being-itself may be interpreted as "God" and that the ultimate manifestation of being-itself is Jesus Christ. (Exposition of this aspect must await a subsequent chapter.)

With this preliminary overview in mind, I must now attempt to be more explicit about the ways in which these dimensions or aspects of human being intrude on experience. The assumption always is that if convictional experience is more than superficial change, it must engage and be articulated in terms of four dimensions. Under authentic conviction, all four dimensions become mutually supportive of human being; that is, they become consciously and intentionally dimensions of being human.

THE LIVED WORLD

In the beginning is the body, the only entity we know from the inside and outside simultaneously and spontaneously. Early in life we "take in" all we can and we "get into" all we can; we have an innate restless desire to know things both inside out and outside in. Especially if the "objects" we encounter are people, we "take in" and indwell them as if it were a matter of life and death—because it is. With sucking mouth and clutching hand, through gazing eyes and hearkening ears, and through myriad tactile perceptions of the skin, we take in and indwell, holding and molding everything to suit the structure, activity, sensitivity, and corporate model of the body. Even in rest and sleep the body is at work constructing matrices for the lived "world" of waking life. While the infant does all this in an obvious way, the nurturing mother also does it with her child and "world," in a more subtle but no less pervasive fashion.

The body is magnificently transposed and extended into personal, social, and cultural "worlds" by the common genius of the imagination and the symbolic process. It proposes from its store of latent potentials, it organizes "worlds" around and like unto itself as our master model of unity, totality, and diversity. Nothing is in our "worlds" that is not somehow rooted and grounded in the body.

A point to be stressed here is that as concretely anchored in the action of the body as our "worlds" are, they are nevertheless spontaneously composed. This is to say they are prevolitional; ordinarily consciousness does not have to *try* to construct its situation. One's "world" is spontaneously projected, and sustained by the primordial need to live in a unified, comprehensive, and meaningful context.

In a psychological depression this "world" shrinks or collapses and ordinary reality becomes empty, pointless, even dreamlike. In elation, as when one is falling in love, the "world" expands, and the lover senses that ordinary reality has become almost infinite in time and space. Reality "out there," as we ordinarily speak of it, is an elaboration on, but not the foundation of, the lived "world"; it is a reflective objectification of whatever lived "world" one may spontaneously compose. The lived "world" underlies and sustains what we ordinarily call "reality"; objective reality cannot sustain the lived "world."

Thus, we see that the "worlds" which live in and through us and on which we build our notions of reality are not in themselves fixed entities or established places with immovable boundaries. In fact, the everyday assumption that we are "in here" and the world is a fixed reality "out there" is another instance of the eikonic eclipse, implicitly severing the personality from itself and its environment. Actually we do not know any reality separate from our composition of it; nor could we live in a world that was merely fixed outside us and for which we had no internal, embodied analogue. We compose "worlds" and reflectively set them "out there"; they in turn feed back and "compose" us; but, whether moving out or moving in, what we ordinarily call reality is included in and sustained by our spontaneous competence to compose a "world."

Some "worlds" to which we attribute reality are more distinctly private (one's own style of life), others more public (business, fashion, athletics, academia), yet others more natural (earth, sea, sky). The unconscious supports consciousness in composing these, but by itself it cannot create more than a dream "world." It is when the capacity to compose conscious "worlds" ceases that reality collapses around us. It is this that occurs in insanity; indeed, it occurs after one loses no more than seventy-two hours of sleep or after undergoing prolonged sensory deprivation. Reality, which we are fond of assuming is so stable, is in fact as fragile as it is flexible. Of course, this is part of the excitement and miracle of being human, because if reality were not as resilient, flexible, and fragile as it is, adaptation and creation would be infinitely more difficult. If we could not compose and recompose "worlds" symbolically and culturally, we would be far more stable but far less human.

Consider, in passing, the fact that mice removed at birth from all other mice and from every vestige of mouse culture continue in their mouselike ways; but on being removed from human culture, a person must return to the most primitive sort of behavior, living what we would call an uncivilized existence. Our dependence on culture makes us less stable but far richer in meaning and values.[4]

In sum, we live an increasingly fragile, fascinating, and creative life precisely as we take up and exert that with which we are already endowed at birth, the capacity to compose the "world." Being human means not only being destined to compose, but also choosing for one's destiny; the human being either risks "world" composition or loses the sense of what it means "to be."

To experience an instance of this primordial dynamic, shut your left eye, put your finger at the beginning of this line of type, and, with your right eye fixed on the beginning letter of the line, follow in your peripheral vision the tip of your finger as it traces the line from left to right. If your eye is about normal reading distance from the page, then approximately three-fourths of the way across the page, the tip of your finger will disappear and then reappear as it moves on. This blind spot in the visual field is where the optic nerve connects with the eyeball. The point is that you and I regularly compose the world so as to eliminate the blind spot. We live not in a strictly physical environment but in a "world" our minds compose out of physical input.

What is true of vision is true of the total comportment of the body. There is a well-known psychological experiment in which specially prepared glasses reverse the image on the retina of the eye so that through these glasses the whole "world" looks upside down. In the course of about a week, however, the mind adjusts the organism to the upside-down "world" so that things seem normal again. The inherent compositional capacity is always at work to create, integrate, equilibrate a "world" that will be livable in terms of the body we have been given.

Our social, cultural, and natural "worlds," of course, have considerable power to reflect back and compose us. Yet they cannot captivate us altogether. A classical illustration of this was reported by anthropologist Colin Turnbull, who was investigating the life of the Ba Mbuti pygmies in a tropical forest so dense that one could hardly see more than a few yards in any direction. When he took one of the pygmies named Kenge to a clearing and showed him a herd of about a hundred buffalo grazing some miles away, Kenge asked what kind of *insect* they were. He insisted that they were insects even as Turnbull

---

4. A. Hardy, *The Spiritual Nature of Man* (Oxford, England: Oxford University Press, 1969), p. 12.

took him in the car down to the grazing herd. As they were approached, the animals seemed larger, and Kenge became frightened. Even after recognizing the buffalo, Kenge wondered if they had suddenly grown larger or if some kind of witchcraft was being worked on him.[5]

This episode is striking because it concisely dramatizes what occurs in culture shock as one's lived "world" collides with that of another. Even then, in the face of such collision, we make adjustment and work to recompose the unknown into the familiar. Although it varies in flexibility from person to person, our compositional capacity to maintain meaningful "worlds" is dauntless, even if it entails interpreting buffalo as insects under a spell.

Certain structures, latent in the body and differentiated out of global human experience by personal and social development, are constantly employed to make composing the "world" more efficient and negotiable. The structures of intelligence, grammar, and moral judgment are examples on a personal scale; the oedipal pattern, the avunculate, and other kinship structures are examples on a social scale; the "composito oppositorum" and mythic structures are succinct examples on a cultural scale. However, all these only structure a lived "world"; where the connections within a structure (as between a major and minor premise) or the connections between structures (as between moral judgment and kinship patterns) are lacking, it is the compositional power of the imagination that produces a way across and beyond the dichotomy.

More than that, when the given structures of personal, social, or cultural "worlds" prove adequate for adaptation but remain unsatisfactory to the inner spirit of person, the imagination may create a transformation of structure. This was exemplified in both scientific and esthetic knowing as discussed in the foregoing chapter. Although in much of day-to-day life the imagination serves established structures, in a transformational knowing event the very opposite priority appears. The structural egg is cracked, and a new, living "structure" inherent to the vitality and coherence of the imagination emerges. Thus, the imagination, either within or beyond given structures but never without them, becomes the *formative* power behind the lived "world."

In relation to transformational logic, the "world" is the situational context within which transformation begins. Thus, it is the "world"

---

5. Episode cited in P. G. Zimbardo and F. L. Ruch, *Psychology and Life* (Glenview, Ill.: Scott, Foresman, 1977), p. 235.

that suffers the rupture that initiates the knowing event, and finally it is the "world" that is recomposed to include the gain that is accomplished by transformation. For example, in the nine-dot puzzle, the "world" allowed you to receive the puzzle coherently as information, and to sense the implict incoherence, or to see the puzzle as puzzling; finally, the lived "world" was recomposed to include the puzzle as solved and you as solver.

Because the "world" is the context of transformation before and after the event, it is evident that the unfolding of transformational logic is not able to depart from the "world." Nor can it disavow the body even when the ecstasy of insight seems overpowering. In this sense, transformational logic is a bodily and worldly matter, although body and "world" are themselves always subject to transformation.

Because the "world" is recomposed by this patterned process, then, by implication the process must be in some respect transcendent. Because the "world" is recomposed in the transformational knowing act, there must be a knower or composer in and through whom recomposition occurs, but who, in him- or herself, is not recomposed. This leads us to the second distinct aspect of human being inherent in transformational knowing: the self.

THE SELF

In *The Mystery of the Mind*, famous Montreal neurologist Wilder Penfield makes the following striking observation. When he probed the brain with an electrical stimulus, the subject (who remained conscious during the open-brain exploration) told him what awareness the probe had provoked. However, when Penfield touched a part of the brain that made the subject move a limb or recall a particular childhood experience (the so-called memory tapes that transactional analysis has used so extensively), the subject would respond, "You did that, *I* didn't!" What was striking to Penfield was not only the memory tapes but the "I."

Try as he would, Penfield could not find that "I" with his electrical probe. He concluded that this aspect of the mind dwells in a "separate essence," distinct from all other aspects of the brain. It is, he claimed, the independent essence of the mind that enables it to be the programmer for the brain. Although Penfield was criticized by colleagues for promulgating this sort of hypothesis (he was challenging an axiom of neurological research by positing a double-essence theory), this remarkable observation has far-reaching consequences.

Although mind and brain function as a unit in Penfield's view, the mind has the specific function of focusing and sustaining awareness, reasoning, deciding, and understanding. With these functions, the mind uses the information stored in the brain and composes it for the meaningful conduct of everyday life. Mind, then, is the maker of meaning, the creator of objects, concepts, and myths.

Left to itself, without the intervention of mindful activity, the brain will carry out programs established by the mind from some previous time. Penfield notes that he was so habituated to getting up and driving to the Montreal Neurological Institute that if some morning he wanted to go to the airport, he had to make a conscious effort to program his brain that way. Otherwise, what he calls the "automatic mechanism" would deliver him to the institute. Without mindful monitoring, the brain will repetitively take the person through familiar patterned activity.

Mindful activity, then, by focused, conscious attention blazes a new trail, so to say, through the seemingly infinite maze of neuronal connections, marks it, and thereby lays it down for retracing. This kind of activity requires an energy or power of its own, above and beyond anything that could be touched by Penfield's probing electrical stimulus. It is with this quality of energy that one says "I," that one transcends any structural pattern, previous experience, or accumulation of data and creates new meaning.

Penfield's observations in this regard are quite unique, but not entirely so. Probing with a different instrument—his dialectical genius—Søren Kierkegaard formulated a similar picture of the mind and how it works. The point in turning to his view is that he pushed beyond the mind-brain relation to the notion of the *self* implicit in Penfield's findings but never explicated by Penfield.

What follows depends heavily on Kierkegaard's thought,[6] but you will not have to be a Kierkegaard scholar to follow this discussion. I have not used his language except at key points, and I have used other existentialist views to fill out what he described in all too succinct a manner.

For Kierkegaard, the self is not an entity but a relationship entirely unique in relation to its "worlds." Were it not for the self, it might be correct to say that given the bodily anchorage of the "lived world," we know nothing that we have not somehow first experienced through the

---

6. See especially S. Kierkegaard, *Fear and Trembling* and *Sickness unto Death* (bd. together), trans. W. Lowrie (New York: Doubleday, 1954), *Sickness*, pt. 1.

body. However, the self is one aspect of human being that, although it becomes embodied, is not created through any extension of the body.

The first aspect and key to the self itself is the phenomenon of *self-reflection*. This is not merely the person looking at his or her body, it is looking at looking; it is not the person thinking about what to do next, it is thinking about thinking; it is not merely knowing *that* one is a human being, it is knowing *what* is human and what is *not* human (abstract use of negation is implicit in all self-reflection). It is impossible to "learn" this self-relatedness through bodily experience or, indeed, intentionally to compose anything without presupposing it.

Such self-relatedness is not, so far as we know, a property of rocks, plants, or animals; it is uniquely human and in some respects it is the antithesis of the body. As Penfield suggests, the "I" is using a quality of energy uniquely its own when it blazes new trails down the neuronal pathways and thereby embodies meaning and purpose. Of course, it is not completely antithetical. For instance, when Penfield's patients said "I," they did not say "Ich" or "je," or some other cultural embodiment. What Penfield observed here, although he did not spell it out, was the dual nature of self-relatedness as packed into a single symbol, "I." The self both *is* a body and it *has* a body; to the extent that it says "I," it is embodied, but to the extent that it creates new or unprogrammed meaning or when it declares "You did that; I didn't," it *has* a body and uses it to express transcendent purposes.

Being and having a body, occurring at the same time, constitutes a unique relationship between mind and brain; it represents what Douglas R. Hofstadter reductionistically calls a "strange loop in the *brain*" (italics mine).[7] It is an interaction between the two levels, mind and brain, in which the top level (mind) reaches back down toward the bottom level (brain) and influences it while at the same time mind itself is being determined by the bottom level. That is, the culturally embodied "I" (lower to higher) gives new shape and "program" to the neural connections of the brain (higher to lower), which stores the culture in which the self is embodied (lower to higher).

However, for Kierkegaard the self was not merely this relationship between "brain and mind." This sort of self-relatedness was for him a "negative" or empty relationship because the relationship *as relationship* was hidden or buried in the unified utterance, "I." In the Penfield example, the buried relationship had already sped past the patient's

---

7. D. R. Hofstadter, *Gödel, Escher, Bach: An Eternal Golden Braid* (New York: Basic Books, 1979), p. 709.

attention, and I think Penfield's as well, when he said "I." The key to
the self lies in unpacking the "I." For Kierkegaard, the culturally
embodied "I," the loop of self-reflection, is not the self, although it
may masquerade as such. Self-reflection must be broken open; the
hidden relationship must be exposed and become something in and
for itself.

This takes us into the second aspect: the self in *self-relatedness*.
You can begin to get a feel for this if you consider how two people
often relate to each other at first, more or less unconsciously, accepting the interpersonal programming of appropriate role structures;
but then they fall in love. In the love relationship, the relationship as
relationship begins to take on a life of its own; and eventually, if the
love continues to grow and deepen, it will relativize roles and come in
large measure to define the two people. In this example, the love has
become a "positive relationship." It is not a subliminal connective
taken for granted, slipping by unnoticed; it is that which gives locus,
direction, and true significance to the people being related—a thing
in itself. The relationship has become a positive third term.

Now put brain and mind in place of the lovers, and recognize that
the self is not the fact that they relate. The self is not the fact that the
mind and brain mutually reflect each other; the self as the relationship *is* something, and it needs to gain a life of its own.

Breaking open the mind-brain connection, or unpacking Penfield's
"I," is essential to being human, and I would argue that it is inevitable
in the course of human development in a social context. That is, when
you are encountered by another self-reflecting person whose presence
gives evidence that he or she has taken your sense of "I" and put it into
a reflective process of his or her own, then the potentiality for
unpacking your own "I" is awakened. I suggest this has nothing
fundamentally to do with *how* one is encountered—that is, whether
one is treated as a "Thou" or an "it"—but only with the notice given
to the self that *as a relationship* it may relate to itself even in the
absence of another.

I said it makes no difference whether or not one is met as "Thou,"
because in the state of just being awakened to the positive potential of
the self, every self-engaging encounter with another is potentially
threatening. In such encounters, one is "seen" in a way that one has
not seen oneself; in a sense, one is violated, and, until such times as
the self has been authentically grounded beyond itself, it cannot
respond as a "thou." It can at best compose a "world" in which "thous"
are possible and even desirable, but it cannot become one to another

person. This is the inherent problem of the ego, which will be discussed in Chapters 5 and 6.

The self as a positive relationship—"a relation that relates itself to itself" as Kierkegaard put it—is "conscience" in the generic sense. It is knowing within and together with oneself *(scientia and con-)*. This is the self that has chosen itself and in that choice determined to be itself, in, but not of, its "worlds"; in, but not of, its embodiment; "having" but not "being had." This represents a choice against the endless mirrors of self-reflection, against socially constructed selves and the superego, against world-denying mysticism and against absorption in a world of kindly "thous." The self as conscience is generated by the power to choose. One must choose to choose the self, otherwise all choices will be consumed in self-reflection and "world" composition.

Although the freedom of the self to be itself is salutary as relief from a variety of self-destructive alternatives, it is not a closed unit. Integrity of conscience does not imply an isolated unit, but openness and illumination. Now more open than ever because of the richness of its self-relatedness and the complexity of its many connections within and beyond the person, the self seeks a ground for its being. As open to its world, to its embodiment, to new meaning and purpose, the self is extremely vulnerable; it experiences what Kierkegaard called "the dizziness of freedom" and out of this dreadful condition it will fall into false grounds for securing itself, paradoxically attempting to establish its integrity of openness by locking it into universal systems of value or doctrine, enclosing it in a presumably "open community," or by exercising a compulsive openness emulating Protean behavior.

In effect, the self as conscience seeks to ground itself as such, but it cannot find its ground the way it found itself: namely, by unpacking its own nature. This leads to the third stage of the self: the *self as spirit*.

The one place where openness belongs and where the self can remain itself is in its Source. If the self is to remain authentic, it must be, as Kierkegaard says, "transparently grounded in the Power that posits it." The self is itself when it expresses the nature of being-itself as that which "lets be" or "lets flourish." The self is grounded in the power that posits it when it lets the being of others flourish. In less abstract terminology, the self is truly itself in the ongoing act of giving love. Once grounded, the self composes the "world" in a new way. "Thou" is transformed from threat to privilege or gift, and the self becomes a "thou" even where there is no "I" responding. More-over, it finds the Presence of being-itself illuminated in every particular of its "world." Thus, the self free to be itself loves the World and so lets it flourish with the same integrity, freedom, and love with which "I" (the self as spirit) came into being (see "The Way of Love" in Chapter 6). Thus being-itself is disclosed in the third stage of the self. You might say this stage represents a transformation of the self-reflected self into a self that reflects its groundedness in being-itself.

It should be emphasized that the self as spirit does not exclude or eliminate the self as conscience nor the self as reflector. The self as spirit includes other forms of the self and makes them relative to its center and ground in being-itself. The self as spirit may function reflectively or function as conscience, but its identity is with being-itself. I will say considerably more about this "transformed ego" in Chapters 5 and 6.

Of course, this whole discussion from being-itself through human being and back again would be just a self-vindicating circle if it were not that being-itself is revealed as "Holy." As "Holy," being-itself is present with manifest power to break self-reflection out of its vortex and to establish in itself (the Holy) the ground for the self as spirit. The dynamics of this supreme transforming event are discussed in the next chapter. Here suffice it to say that this is a work of love that the Holiness of being performs on behalf of the self, and the self remains itself by replicating this act of love in its own works of love.

Transformation of that unique phenomenon "I" into that yet more remarkable phenomenon, the self that gives love, is in many respects the essential theme of this entire study. If, in the case of convictional experience, such transformation does not occur, then it is doubtful whether one experienced the "Holy," the ground of one's human being; it may just as well be that some new "world" has intruded—mystical, cultic, or otherwise—and promised power, health, freedom, or some other virtue or reward. However, Kierkegaard's claim for the transformed self, and the position described here, is that the self cannot be itself unless it is grounded in the Source, that which "lets it be," in such a way that it spontaneously replicates and expresses that Source by "letting be" in all its "worlds."

THE VOID

Any talk of "void" is of course a semantic anomaly; it seems to be speaking of nothing as if it were presence; nonbeing as if it were being. Thus many modern theologians would rather speak of "limit," or the "boundary" where one has come to the ultimate edge of finite experience. I prefer to speak of void with the implication that nothingness, or negation of being, is not beyond experience; indeed, it is part of the uniqueness of human being that negation is meaningfully included in the composition of our "lived worlds" and in our sense of "self." Many people live not only on the near side of the limit, but in a real sense beyond it as they choose to enact self-destructive patterns of behavior. We will be concerned to describe not only extreme behavior but also the pervasive nature of nothingness in ordinary experience. Void is the ultimate aim of all proximate forms of nothingness; the implicit aim of conflict, absence, loneliness, and death is void.

Void is implicit the moment the lived "world" is ruptured and the process of transformational knowing begins. If the lived "world" is the context of transformational knowing, and the self is "the knower," the face of the void intruding into the two-dimensional existence of the self-world is the "conflict" that moves transformational knowing into action. However, the void has many faces as it intrudes into two-dimensional life, and all represent a need on the part of the un-grounded self to recompose the lived "world" in some imaginative way so as to remove the intrusive threat of nothingness.

In this connection, Jean-Paul Sartre suggests how to speak about "absence": the slow, depressing awareness that comes over Sartre (*Being and Nothingness*) as he waits in the cafe for Pierre, who doesn't come. The "world" composed by Sartre with the expectancy of the meeting is violated by a third dimension: the absence, silence, void. The response of Sartre, or any of us, is to attempt immediately to recompose the "world," so that the absence does not take its toll. At first, we say, "He is merely late, delayed in traffic." Then, "He is not coming; I hope nothing has happened to him." Finally, "Perhaps he has just forgotten; I must ask him what happened." Without fail, we rush to fill the absence with a recomposition of the world just as we compose out of awareness that blind spot where the eye connects with the brain.

However, we always have difficulty composing out or covering over the nothingness because it is not merely "out there," it is embedded in the very heart of the untransformed self. The deepest sense of absence we have is the separateness of the self from its Source. As "self-reflection," the self reflects nothingness everywhere by making everything depend on the "I" and the lived "world." There is no positive self in this posture; it is only negatively or implicitly present as the person makes an ongoing series of culturally absorbed choices. Absence of the positive self will often seek to diffuse the painful inner sense that being human is empty and meaningless by proliferating meaningless activity to the cheers of an equally self-alienated society.

An example of this is the irony of achievement-oriented behavior in a modern, highly mobile, industrialized society. In the Western world, the addicted achiever has set out on the profoundly misguided assumption that personal worth is capable of being gained and established by what can be achieved. Modern society perpetuates and lavishly rewards this illusion. The irony is that the achievers cannot thereafter accept any sense of worth that they have not earned; they cannot allow themselves to receive any more love than they feel they deserve. This is ironic because, of course, love establishes worth quite apart from what the beloved deserves. Accordingly, it must be accepted as a gift if it is to be received at all; "earned love" is not love but reward, making "love" depend on the world rather than the other way around. Hence the achievement addiction is a fundamental violation of human being at its Source and in its self-transcendence.

Tragically, the empty self, in its separateness from its Source (which would graciously "let flourish"), constantly drives achievers to higher achievement with every new sense of absence, loss, or void. The lived "world" they try so desperately to recompose and inflate with trophies cannot be made to fill the vacuum that intrudes between the self and its Source. Yet it is precisely this that addicted achievers seek to accomplish, and ironically the addiction only deepens. As we know from contemporary studies, achievers are more planful and purposeful, but also more tense, domineering, and cruel. The number of heart attack victims among people living alone is significantly higher than elsewhere, but achievers, accepting no undeserved love, live always with loneliness inside, whether in a family or not—hence the "Type A syndrome" that directly links heart ailment to achievement as an addiction.[8] Achievers desperately try to compose the world so that the inner emptiness is not noticeable, but there is no hiding; as one remarked to me, "I just hope I die before I ruin my reputation." The inner nothingness expands as years advance; one noted writer and professor said that the only way he could get back to

---

8. Several works could be cited to make this point. Consider two: M. Friedman and R. H. Rosenman, *Type A Behavior and Your Heart* (Greenwich: Fawcett, 1974) and J. J. Lynch, *The Broken Heart: The Medical Consequences of Loneliness* (New York: Basic Books, 1977).

sleep at night was to think of his next promotion. But suppose the reputation is ruined or the promotion is denied—then what? Then we have the conditions of trauma in which the outer nothingness matches the inner, and the world collapses into the nothingness at the center of the self.

Harry Stack Sullivan, noted psychoanalyst, said he could bring patients to relive almost any experience from anxiety to violent trauma, but he could not bring them to relive loneliness. The horror of being caught between outer and inner emptiness is the worst shock of all. This, I suspect, is because loneliness, when it is both inner and outer, is the closest we can come to experiencing our own death.

Loneliness is proximate death, yet even death is not ultimate. It too is a metaphor supplied by the end of life to suggest dissolution of existence into absolute empty silence. Void is the ultimate end of all creation and as such it is, ironically speaking, the "goal" of evil. Not every absence is evil, as for instance the absence of pain; but every absence that reflects the inherent brokenness in the self, aggravating the disability of the self to be spirit, evokes evil. All evil presses toward the reversal of God's creative action; God created everything out of nothing, but evil seeks to return everything to nothing.

In order to help you feel this a bit, let me take you into a hypothetical scenario. Let's suppose I'm working late in my Princeton home one fall evening, and even though it's 2 A.M. I decide to take a walk to clear my head. Let's also suppose I slip into some heavy boots because of a recent rain and put on a coat still carrying some tools from a recent camping trip. I don't plan a long walk but go down the hill to Carnegie Lake. At 2 A.M., Princeton is very still. There is music from a few dorm parties in the distance, but houses are dark and there are no street lights. Now let's suppose I trip on a root as I walk along a steep embankment, fall forward, strike my head on a limb, and plunge into the lake. Unconscious, I sink to the bottom; my coat snags on a branch buried in the mud, and I drown.

No one sees me fall or hears the splash. The circles soon disappear into the smooth surface of the water, and all is quiet again. Dark stillness pervades, and time passes. About 3 A.M. my wife wakes up, realizing I've not come to bed. She gets up, goes downstairs, turns out the study light, and calls softly so as not to wake the children, but getting no answer, she goes back to bed. The alarm awakens her at 7 A.M. but still no husband. She jumps up, wakes up the children, and gets them into the routine of the morning. "Where's Daddy?" "Oh, I'm not sure—hurry up, you'll miss the bus!" They set off and the search begins, but no one has seen me and certainly dragging the lake is the farthest thing from anyone's mind, because I never walk down there. Time passes, and the search dissolves into futility and is abandoned. My family lives three more months in the seminary housing. There are a few tears, the seminary holds a brief service, and a memorial minute is spread on the faculty record. Classes are rescheduled, and the institution returns to normal. The family moves west to live with grandparents, and gradually the children ask less and less, "Whatever happened to Daddy?" They give up the hope—it is too painful to sustain without reward—that he will turn up somewhere unexpectedly. Ten years later the fellow my daughter is dating asks, "Whatever happened to your dad?" And she answers, "Oh, we don't know; I wonder if we'll ever know. But don't let that spoil our evening."

After fifty years almost no one wonders. This book and others gather dust in the library, and silence settles over all the activity I now so vigorously sustain and intensely value. The irony is deep and powerful. All this comes to absolutely nothing. Now that is probably not *how* it will happen. But it *will happen* to me—and you. There is not the slightest doubt that the two-dimensional world you and I now so intently sustain will come to nothing at all. This is the perfect statistic, one death per person every time in a material universe that is ultimately destined to silence. That, of course, makes our obsession with meaning, and the meanings by which we live, absurd. It seems as if we dare not live with too large a perspective (one that includes the void), or we will not want to live at all. It is small wonder that we screen this inevitable fact out of our minds and out of the "worlds" we create. We don't include the third dimension in our world compositions because it makes the first two meaningless and composition becomes a waste of effort. Yet there it is, unalterable, universal, and the absolute truth. Thus void pervades the self and the world, absence in each dimension reinforcing itself in the other.

The void, then, is the third dimension of being human, but it has many faces, such as absence, loss, shame, guilt, hatred, loneliness, and the demonic. The void is more vast than death, but death is the definitive metaphor; "nothing" in itself is ultimately unthinkable, but death, shrouding all our lived "worlds," gives us our clearest picture of nothing. Although its origin for experience is in the self's inability to be itself, the sense of void goes far beyond this in society, culture, time, and the universe, so that consciously we dread to include it in our "worlds." We tend to compose it out as if it were a great blind spot; but after birth, death is the one absolutely unavoidable experience, the one we finally cannot ignore.

THE HOLY

So why do we continue to live? Why does the self continue to create its "world" and compose new meanings and enact its story when the whole theater of its existence is dark and the building has been condemned? First it must be noted that we *do* go on living; the fact is that people who have had some of the most horrendous encounters with the void surrounded by all its faces are most prepared to create new meaning and remold the world. We make a mistake if we look for answers to why in some place extrinsic to our existence; the answer, like the question, is intrinsic to our selfhood. We continue to live precisely because in the center of the self, for all of its potential perversity, we experience again and again the reversal of those influences that invite despair and drive toward void. Kierkegaard repeatedly insisted with bewildering brilliance that the faces of the void become the faces of God.

This I would say is precisely where we must begin to discuss the "Holy." The reason we do not cease to live is the deep sense that we are not merely three-dimensional creatures. No one who has taken the void seriously would propound the credo that we are in effect only three-dimensional, or that life ends in void and all is merely chance. Such a one would not declare anything at all; authentic encounters with the void are paralyzing or deadening. French existentialists, such as Sartre and the early Camus, have furthered a philosophical movement of atheistic absurdity; but the books they wrote and the vehemence with which their followers press their points witness to *another reality*. To take the void seriously, to let the magnitude of its implications wash over and soak in, is not to write books, organize protests, or make pronouncements; it is to fall into deep despair and to identify with the overpowering aggressor. They do not believe what they say; the void or nothingness fascinates and awes them. Sartre declares that, like an unholy ghost, "nothingness haunts being." His nothingness is little less than a negative surrogate for the Holy.

Even those who are the enemies of the beneficence of being live by it and diligently create their position by the countless transformations indigenous to human being and its ways of knowing. The power of the Holy is not pious wishing, but solid truth, as illustrated by the case of Julia de Beausobre, author of *The Woman Who Could Not Die* and *Creative Suffering.* She was taken into a Russian prison and subjected to severe and systematic torture. Her sadistic training officer was a master at breaking down every defense; yet she continued to search for ways to find meaning in her absurd situation. When she tried to shrink into a negative posture, he came on stronger; if she tried to fight back, she whetted his sadistic appetite. Finally she prayed and found herself asking the right question: "What are you [God] doing in this situation?"

Praying in this way, she found herself "permeating the situation with consciousness." By such permeation, she began to look at the training officer with a new awareness of the dynamics of his selfhood. Yet if she became even subtly sentimental toward him, or overly indulgent of his perversity, he brutalized her all the more. Furthermore, if she became self-pitiful, or overindulgent of her own plight, he did the same.

The upshot was that she gradually found a balance between indulgence on either side, a fine edge of serenity which she said was founded on a divine "Rock." This place was the Presence *in* her, on which the core of her personality was founded and of which she was a part. This shining center of herself, she learned, was strengthened and brightened with every new act of brutality. She found herself so grounded on and so much a part of the Rock that she grew perfectly quiet despite the pain. Realizing he could not disrupt her serenity, the training officer lost interest. This was not only merciful but redemptive, because the Presence of the Holy in her freed the sadist from his obsession and freed her for centeredness in God.

The root significance of the Hebrew word *Qadosh* ("holy") is "separate." There is no compromise of that separateness in saying that in the midst of the deepest extremity a sense of the Holy *in* us cries out for a manifestation of the Holy *beyond* us. This describes the quality of the Presence of the Holy as that which is indeed separate but not unknowable; rather, it is separate and remaking us in its image.

From earliest Hebraic notions of the Holy as "banned" or essentially negative, through the more personal expressions of the Holy in the Old Testament prophets, to the Holy revealed and present first in Jesus as the Holy One and then in the Holy Spirit, we have essentially a transformation of the concept. By the time of Paul's New Testament letters, the Holy has gone from being negative and strictly contained materialistically and cultically to a new plane in which all material and cultic life is contained in and given its significance by the Holy

Spirit. De Beausobre experienced the Presence of the Holy as that which grounded her selfhood beyond her context of nothingness. Thus, she experienced the fourth dimension of human being that is always intuitively present; in her case, it was manifest directly, or "revealed" in the face of nothingness, with the result that the situation, including the nothingness, was transformed and the whole matter became redemptive.

Even those who would not agree that being is gracious implicitly live by that premise with every affirmation of scientific discovery, esthetic intuition, or therapeutic success. The central turning point in the transformational knowing event, the imaginative vision, is an eruption of new being in the presence of imminent void; it is a manifestation of the abundance with which being-itself supplies the deepest needs of human being. What appears to scientific, esthetic, or therapeutic knowing is only a superficial expression of the depth and power of being-itself to bring forth new being. The graciousness of being-itself serves a priestly function after the order of Melchizedek who, having no evident origins, comes out of nowhere and mediates between God and humanity.[9]

I will illustrate the emergence of the Holy within the context of the void by one further case—this one my own, and not unrelated to the accident story with which this book began. Having been a philosophy major in college, I was in my first quarter of seminary, where I had come more to think than to pray. I was called home unexpectedly when my father was diagnosed as having brain cancer. It was a long siege; we watched for nine months while he slowly died. Profoundly depressed afterwards, I was in bed with a glandular infection. The sense of void was all-pervasive. The things he had worn were now still and useless, and so was the "world" in which I tried to compose meaning. Everything had turned to cardboard, flat and empty; every day was the same dull experience regardless of whom I saw or what occurred.

In a desultory mood at first, but gradually more adamant, I began to pray. Since there was seemingly nothing to pray to, it helped me to write out the prayers. Finally one morning I got so angry I threw down my pencil, smashed my fist into the pillow, and shouted at God, "If you're there, *do* something!"

He did something, but it was not what the philosophy major wanted. It was instead a warm life, like gentle electricity, that started

---

9. Gen. 14:18-20; Psalm 110:4; Heb. 6:20-7:22.

at the bottom of my feet and rushed through my entire body, filling me with such strength and vitality that it almost threw me out of bed. I leaped up singing what no good philosophy major should sing, "Blessed assurance, Jesus Is Mine!" In my excitement, I picked up Emil Brunner's little book, *The Scandal of Christianity*, and I think I must have read it in ten minutes. It was as if I had suddenly entered into the central intuition out of which the book had been written. So I recognized, more than I read, everything that was being said.

Finding at first that others understood little of my experience, I was delighted nevertheless in the magnificent Presence of the One who enabled me once again to compose a meaningful "world." Moreover, it was recomposed with a richness, depth, and excitement I had never known before.

This was the first time I had experienced the presence of God's Spirit in any palpable sense. This manifestation was very similar to that of the accident episode described in Chapter 1. Indeed, the seminary experience may well have been the basis for the recognition of God's spirit in that accident which occurred exactly sixteen years to the day after my father's death. In both crises, the Holy brought to me a sense of self anchored on the Rock de Beausobre spoke of: separate, beyond the reach of the void, yet thoroughly redemptive, the immanent sense of the Holy constituted the fourth dimension of my being.

In the case of my father's death, what I went through in a remarkably short time was the sequence by which Alfred North Whitehead (who may have been speaking out of his own experience) characterized all religion: "It is the transition from God the void to God the enemy and from God the enemy to God the companion."[10]

This concise sequential summary, I think, combines two movements, one psychological and the other transformational. The *psychological* movement is the undoing of the depression. Based on aggression against oneself, depression may be relieved by externalization in anger. My anger released pent-up aggressive energy, which could then be reinvested in another object—the very One against whom the anger was initially directed; but the Enemy had now been radically reconceived as Companion.

The *transformational* movement includes the psychological dynamic but, employing a wider frame of reference, it turns the depression into an occasion for finding the ultimate ground of the self. Once the stage of Companion is reached, the initial depression in

10. A. N. Whitehead, *Religion in the Making* (New York: Macmillan, 1927), pp. 16-17.

retrospect will appear gracious, a development necessary for the transforming moment. Psychology is interested primarily in adaptation, while transformation of the self works to redeem the significance of the whole sequence, including the depression, as a passageway to centeredness in the Holy.

Other cases could be cited, but the pattern should be clear. When serenity comes up out of anxiety, joy out of depression, hope out of hopelessness; when good is returned for evil, forgiveness replaces retaliation, and courage triumphs over fear; then we recognize the movement of something beyond the personality and mental health. Such profound manifestations of the human spirit are the faces of the fourth dimension, which I have called the Holy.

The Divine Companion or the Presence of the Holy remains Other, even though its faces appear in human experience. Under its influence, the self becomes truly itself for the first time, and its "worlds" are recomposed in new ways. Subsequent experience is drawn into forms of awareness and behavior that include but go beyond two-dimensional humanity and scandalize the pessimism of three-dimensional existentialism by positive recognition of void as essential to human transformation. The three-dimensional view will say, "It is too good to be true," implying the tautology that three-dimensional pessimism is the truth, so it could not be overcome by two-dimensional good. But tautology can be played both ways: suppose we shift the tautology and say the Holy is the truth. Then such behavior is so true, so filled with the Holy, that it is beyond good and evil as defined in two- or three-dimensional terms. Genuine forgiveness, inner courage, and sacrificial love all are too true to be "good" in any ordinary or pessimistic existentialist sense. Such scandalous claims point beyond everyday humanity to a quality implicit in being itself that is both awesome and magnetic. The *"mysterium tremendum fascinans"* as manifest in the earthiness of human existence via the faces of new being retains Otherness and inflicts profound ambivalence. The experiential mark of the Presence of the Holy is just this ambivalence that both draws and repels us, excites and overcomes us, intrigues and threatens us.

A student once asked me to pray for him so that he might receive the power of the Holy Spirit in his life. I complied; laying my hands on his head, I began to pray. Suddenly in the midst of the prayer he erupted, "Stop, I'm not ready for this yet!" Even though I was doing as *he* had asked, the ambivalence toward the Holy entering one's life is too powerful to be taken lightly. He was right; he wasn't ready.

Nobody is. That is why it comes with such disturbing joy and confounding clarity, leaving us so unable to think about it in ordinary terms. The idea of intimacy with the Holy is a paradox too great for us to entertain, but it is just such intimacy that establishes the authority of the Holy for the self.

In marriage counseling I often find, even among ministers and their wives, a readiness to work for rapport at every level, including sexual relations, but a deep reluctance and distrust when it comes to the intimacy of prayer. Inviting the Holy Spirit to enter the relationship is often something they do not even want to try. Each partner may pray well enough on his or her own, but to pray *together* at that level is the last thing either would consider. That quality of intimacy has decisive authority and power at the weakest and most vulnerable part of the self—namely, the point of transcendence—where the potentially dizzy self relates itself to itself and the internal dialogue of the self seeks a ground in its ultimate Source. No alien presence can be allowed in there, or the last stronghold would be lost. Of course, it is not readily shared, nor should it be; yet it cannot be forever held tightly and not shared at all without stifling its life. Moreover, it can be the life blood of renewed relationship once the self discovers that its very ground can be shared with another. The absolutely unique claim of Jesus that one could be on "Abba" terms with the Holy, and the same claim made by St. Paul, is based on simple trust; yet it is highly complicated by its offensiveness to two-dimensional existence and the demoralized outlook of three-dimensional atheism.

If the Holy has such an impact on us, it is not surprising in Scripture that even St. John is stunned by the revelation of the Son of Man and his glory. The appearance of the Holy One in Scripture is repeatedly accompanied by words of assurance, "Be not afraid," "stand on your feet," and so on, because the Holy cannot be made manifest without seeming to destroy two-dimensional existence and to fill the void with itself. The Holy by nature means the obliteration of "worlds" designed to screen out the void or "worlds" designed to revel in a perverse fascination with nothingness. The Holy intends the renewal and restoration of two-dimensional life as a gift in the presence of the void, like "a table prepared in the presence of one's enemies."

Thus, manifestations of the Holy extend, as Pascal suggested, from the little infinity to the big infinity and from irrepressible and scandalous ambiguity to an overwhelming flood of light, power, beauty, and glory. A vision of the Holy is a vision of a reality so magnificent that the human self longs for the Holy to be all in all, totally transforming existence in the fullness of its light and being.

In sum, the Holy is the manifest Presence of being-itself transforming and restoring human being in a way that is approximated by the imaginative image as it recomposes the "world" in the course of transformational knowing. As the Presence of being-itself, the Holy is both within and beyond people, but always it retains its essential character as *mysterium tremendum fascinans*. What I have described above are some of the contexts and forms in which the Holy may appear to a human being. Clearly convictional experiences that do not entertain a profound sense of the Holy have lost their significance as convictional because they have lost any sense of the Convictor. Notice that it is just for the reason of their *Holiness* that convictional experiences should not be burlesqued or treated reductionistically. However, it is because such manifestations are *only faces* of the Holy — that is, *manifestations* of being-itself in and through a particular context — that the manifestations themselves are not to be worshipped. Finally, any authentic manifestation of the Holy will convict human being of its four-dimensionality and call it toward its ground in being-itself.

Having described the four dimensions of human being as they relate to human transformation, we are left with a problem: how shall the universal claims and language of being-itself be brought into relationship with the particularity of human existence where convictional experiences always occur? This relationship is established by the language and claims of Christianity, whose center is Jesus Christ, in whom universality and particularity are perfectly united for the eyes of faith. How transformation in four dimensions is to be understood as Christocentric is the subject of the next chapter.

Four

CONVICTIONAL
KNOWING

➤ CONVICTIONAL KNOWING IS the patterned process by which the Holy Spirit transforms all transformations of the human spirit. This is a four-dimensional knowing event initiated, mediated, and concluded by Christ. In these next three chapters, I will discuss the nature, dynamics, and implications of convictional knowing to provide a Christian context of explanation for convictional experiences.

ANALOGY OF THE SPIRIT

To say, as I suggested in the last chapter, that the Presence of the Holy One creates the self as spirit is to imply that the self's transformational activity takes on the creative, "letting-flourish" nature of being. Thus, it is possible to look at the new spiritual life of the self and see not only an expression but a disclosure of the inner life of being-itself. That is, by making the self spirit, the Holy One manifests its inner life to the eyes of faith as *Holy Spirit*. In fact, we know the Holy Spirit as such only through the self as spirit; we know the Spirit only in his own medium, so to say.

This suggests not a fusion or absorption but an analogy. Paul wrote, "For what person knows a man's thoughts except the spirit of the man that is in him? So also no one comprehends the thoughts of God except the Spirit of God" (1 Cor. 2:11). His assumption here and elsewhere (see Rom. 8:16; Phil. 2:12-13) of an analogical relationship between the human spirit and the Holy Spirit is the key to convictional knowing, yet it is not a relationship that has often been spelled out.

Between two things considered to be analogous, there is both a likeness and a difference. I am suggesting that between the human spirit and Holy Spirit, the *likeness* is established by the logic of transformation. The same pattern applies to both, but it is transposed from one level to the other, making the human spirit conformable to the Holy Spirit and the Holy Spirit intelligible to the human. The *difference* is that on the human level, the ungrounded self is seen as the origin and destiny of the human spirit, but on the divine level human transformations are transformed and the origin and destiny of the Holy Spirit is the Holy One.

The process of transformation characterizes spirit generally (cf. Chapter 2), but this *analogy* becomes actual and historical only through Christ. However, Christianity is not alone in its concern for a four-dimensional transformational process, although as we will see it has important distinctions.

EASTERN TRANSFORMATION

One matter to be clarified at the outset is the nature of the distinction between four-dimensional knowing in Christian perspective as opposed to certain other religious viewpoints, also concerned for transformation and four-dimensionality. This distinction clarifies the Christian perspective at key points, especially in contrast to the traditions of the East.

The Eastern religions have in fact made much more of the four dimensions of human existence than the religions of the West. Consider this poem, ascribed to Lao-Tzu, sixth century B.C.:

> Void the mind:
> Abide in stillness.
> Life arises and passes,
> Birth, Growth and return,
> A Rhythmic arc from Source to Source.
> In the rhythm is quietude,

A tranquil submission . . .
And so, the Great Light![1]

This appears to be a four-dimensional poem describing at least a partial transformation. It describes focusing the concentrated attention of the mind on the finitude and fragility of the self and its "world," which move in pointless circles until there is the breakthrough of a fourth dimension, "the Great Light." This envisions the Great Light as the redemptive power in relation to the other three dimensions and the place in which the self must abide if it is to sustain ultimate meaning.

The process implicit in this poem is one that, elaborated variously as a spiritual practice, appears in most of the Eastern religions. It appears in Taoism, Buddhism, and Hinduism and may be characterized as the "way of release." The great religions of the East, particularly as practiced in Zen, the historical heir of Taoist practices, have found their way into a four-dimensional process that generates release and union with the "Great Meaning."

The process appears to follow the logic of transformation. Attention is concentrated on a conflict of existential proportions to the self, exposing the futility of any form of "transcendent" that merely reflects the passing world. Then the conflict is embraced and borne with expectancy as scanning the substance and limits of existence ensues. The intuition that breaks through is one of overpowering force, such that the intuition itself becomes *the* transcendent reality with respect to which self, world, and void all become relative. There follows the ecstatic sense of arrival at complete meaning or "Great Doctrine." Out of such personal coherence with transcendent meaning, specific practices have emerged with striking significance.

Contrary to the familiar Western assumption that Eastern religions leave the person in another world, the fact is that Zen practices, to take one example, have had a powerful effect on practical arts and crafts of everyday life. In premodern Japan, the entire range of Japanese culture was affected by a disciplined practice of this process. Ceremonies governing family life, such as the tea ceremony and the design of houses and gardens, were some concrete results. This

---

1. The translation quoted here is found in H. Rugg's *Imagination* (New York: Harper & Row, 1963), p. 158. The reader may also find a widely recognized translation of the same four-dimensional philosophical statement in Lao-Tzu, *Tao Te Ching*, trans. D. C. Lau (Baltimore: Penguin, 1963), p. 72. It should be stated that Rugg's work is the source for much that is included in this section of the text.

process has governed the educational program of the samurai (the warrior class) and the practical arts of archery and swordsmanship. It created ritual and techniques in ink painting and other graphic arts, and provided a basic philosophy of the No theater, the dance, and the movement arts.

A decisive difference that does pertain between four-dimensional transformation in Eastern and Western Christian contexts has to do with the role of God in history. In the Eastern scene, even if the practitioner does initiate spiritual activity in a historical context as a result of having seen "the Great Light," the ultimate conclusion remains that the historical world is unreal. This is because the continuity of intention in the transformational process has been broken off from the initiative of "the Light" and taken back into the hands of the practitioner. Of course, the practitioner's world becomes unreal because it has been separated from the direct action of the "Light," or "God," on history. The result is that the material world is to be dealt with "spiritually," and the movement of history, although markedly affected by followers of "the way of release," is itself irrelevant; that is, it plays no essential part in the transformation effected by the Great Light. The logic of transformation in the Eastern context, therefore, is truncuated at the point of "release," and people are "saved" by moving *out* of the historical reality, not by God's action in and through it.

An erroneous Western Christian view of transformation contrasts with this to a striking degree, emphasizing the historical, almost to the exclusion of the spiritual. If the Eastern view tends toward "the imaginary," the erroneous Western view tends toward conventional science and technology. If the West commits the error of eikonic eclipse, the East commits the error of eikonic inflation. Either way, the continuity, although not necessarily the power, of transformation is lost.

Both the continuity *and* the power of transformation are retained in an authentic Christian conviction. A contrast of saints leaves a clear picture. The Buddhist saint sits cross-legged in a lotus position, eyes closed, "looking" inward. The Christian saint, straining forward, holds his or her eyes open and follows what God is doing in the world for its redemption. Thus, Christianity, true to the complete logic of transformation, returns every insight, vision, or image to its historical context as the locus of God's redemptive action.

The key factor behind this and other differences that might be cited is the identity or nature of the Divine Presence. (See the second case illustrating psychological guideline 1, Chapter 7.) For instance, it is said that Zen enables one to do everything "spiritually" from sword fighting to serving tea, but what or who is behind that spirituality as the Source of its power to effect transformation? The Source without the process does nothing; the process without the Source makes the practitioner into god. Is the Source Buddha? Then one acquires the character of Buddha as one practices the spirituality of Zen. By the process of convictional knowing operating in "the way of release," one becomes more and more the Buddha that one already is (a typical paradox). The practice of transformation, even in broken or incompleted forms, leaves the marks characteristic of the presumed Source of transformation on the practitioner. Thus, the critical question is: to what or to whom am I becoming conformed when convictional knowing acquires the power to redefine my personal being?

We turn now to the dynamics of transformation when the Source and destiny of the transformation is Christ. When Jesus Christ reveals and identifies the nature of the Holy One, the logic of transformation still pertains, but personal transformation is seen in a broader perspective that includes the overall movement of history.

THE EMMAUS EVENT

It would be intriguing and helpful to pursue transformational logic as a key to biblical narrative, but that would be a separate book in itself. Here I will simply use a biblical narrative to illustrate transformational logic transposed into four dimensions under the authorship and mediation of Jesus as the Christ. By this device, I will spell out the analogy that pertains between human and Holy Spirit in convictional knowing and, finally, say what the analogy implies for convictional experiences. The particular narrative will be Luke 24:13-35, the story of Cleopas and Simon on the road to Emmaus.

This text has been selected because, rather surprisingly, it embodies in one pericope all of the central turning points in the process of convictional knowing. Also, it appears historically that this text not only describes a particular episode but also the life of the early church as it sought to interpret its existence and nature in light of the transformation of Israel as mediated by and consummated in Christ. Moreover, it provides us with the opportunity to develop a position using a fairly pure specimen.

If for any reason this seems too removed from the complexities of daily experience, note that the process of convictional knowing will be integrated into the fabric of human development in the following chapters. Thus, this text is a way of getting the whole sequence of Christian transformation before us in a form that is concise, properly emphasized, and fully four-dimensional. Finally, by way of introduction to this narrative paradigm, I am making the assumption that what the risen Christ does in the narrative articulates what his Spirit does in the contemporary transformation of human being.

That very day two of them were going to a village named Emmaus, about seven miles from Jerusalem, and talking with each other about all these things that had happened. While they were talking and discussing together, Jesus himself drew near and went with them. But their eyes were kept from recognizing him. And he said to them, "What is this conversation which you are holding with each other as you walk?" And they stood still, looking sad. Then one of them, named Cleopas, answered him, "Are you the only visitor to Jerusalem who does not know the things that have happened there in these days?" And he said to them, "What things?" And they said to him, "Concerning Jesus of Nazareth, who was a prophet mighty in deed and word before God and all the people, and how our chief priests and rulers delivered him up to be condemned to death, and crucified him. But we had hoped that he was the one to redeem Israel. Yes, and besides all this, it is now the third day since this happened. Moreover, some women of our company amazed us. They were at the tomb early in the morning and did not find his body; and they came back saying that they had even seen a vision of angels, who said that he was alive. Some of those who were with us went to the tomb, and found it just as the women had said; but him they did not see." And he said to them, "O foolish men, and slow of heart to believe all that the prophets have spoken! Was it not necessary that the Christ should suffer these things and enter into his glory?" And beginning with Moses and all the prophets, he interpreted to them in all the scriptures the things concerning himself.

So they drew near to the village to which they were going. He appeared to be going further, but they constrained him, saying, "Stay with us, for it is toward evening and the day is now far spent." So he went in to stay with them. When he was at table with them, he took the bread and blessed, and broke it, and gave it to them. And their eyes were opened and they recognized him; and he vanished out of their sight. They said to each other, "Did not our hearts burn within us while he talked to us on the road, while he opened to us the scriptures?" And they rose that same hour and returned to Jerusalem; and they found the eleven gathered together and those who were with them, who said, "The Lord has risen indeed, and has appeared to Simon!" Then they told what had happened on the road, and how he was known to them in the breaking of the bread.

Conflict in Four Dimensions

In the opening situation, two men—possibly representing the early church—are engrossed in a deeply felt conflict. It may be assumed that Israel is the lived "world" for Simon and Cleopas; its history, culture, and destiny have constituted the horizon of all life for them. "Israel" is not strictly an empirical entity, but a "world" composed and sustained by the vision of her people, often in defiance of the deep contradictions that lie at the base of her existence. Restoration seems to mean a reconstitution of political and economic reality in conformity with the vision of her religious destiny. All this is now threatened from without by the Roman occupation, but more important to the two men, it is threatened from within by "chief priests and rulers." A deep-running complex of oppositions is embedded in this struggle of nation against nation, but deeper and more intense is the apparent sense that the current leadership of Israel is in fundamental contradiction with the hope and destiny of Israel.

The void has opened up before these men because in the crucifixion of Jesus the redemption of Israel has collapsed. His tragic death and their consequent disillusionment in the early part of the narrative are the face of a deeper void, the total annihilation of their lived "world" and the expectation that not only their hopes but also the hopes of their fathers will come to nothing. The void is the gathering darkness into which they are walking because their transcendent basis for recomposing the "world" is dead. They have nearly lost all faith.

It is important to recognize that their disillusionment is commingled with hope because, as Luke describes it, they have received from "the women" the report that the tomb was empty and angels had appeared. The report is unverified, but they are a bit intrigued with this improbable glimmer of hope in the midst of their disillusionment. Because they have no capacity to transcend the conflict situation, they are not capable of meaningful, purposeful action in regard to Israel. Thus they are immersed in a four-dimensional conflict at the hands of the Holy One, who presumably came to redeem Israel but has died. Only the glimmer of hope remains.

Notice that they are, at best, only partially aware of the extent of the divine initiative involved in creating the conflict with which they are confronted. For instance, they do not recognize that the conflict they feel is not fundamentally derived from their broken hopes for Israel, but from the fact that they had inadequate hopes for Israel to begin with. Jesus' death only *begins* to expose the conflict in which they were already unconsciously involved; their hopes for Israel had always been too small because their inherited separation from the greatness of the Holy One of Israel made them too dependent on their cultural heritage in spite of their criticisms of their leaders. Thus the divine initiative whereby Jesus submits to crucifixion is not *creating* a conflict but is exposing, focusing, and intensifying a conflict they unconsciously brought into their original acquaintance with him. So it is with the Spiritual Presence of Christ in contemporary experience as well.

In more *general terms*, it can be seen from the narrative that the first step of transformational knowing is transposed into a convictional context as follows. "Conflict embraced and borne with expectancy" is now a consciously four-dimensional affair marked by the human condition that the "I" cannot transcend the situation and recompose it, nor can the "I" escape the situation and move, as it were, into another "world." In essence, the conflict *has* the "I" or the alienated self; the self does not *have* the conflict. The conflict resonates through the self into the lived "world" and back again, threatening ultimate void; and yet it is truly conflictual — that is, not yet overwhelming — because the possibility of new being, however marginal, stubbornly persists, offering the hope of transformation in the midst of an otherwise hopeless situation.

Scanning and the Inner Teacher

The interlude for scanning is the next step in transformational logic. In the narrative, Christ's disguised presence is the key to the scanning process. Note that this represents four-dimensional scanning as personal; his disguised presence introduces a dialogue. Under the guidance of "a stranger" and beneath the surface of the conflict, Cleopas and Simon (and by implication, the whole of the early church) are led into the implications of their own scriptural tradition. This is apparently a deeper indwelling of their own past than they have ever experienced before, especially as the past is connected for them, via the dialogue, with present events. It is "heart warming" (see Ps. 39:3, "my heart became hot within me," and Jer. 20:9, "There is in my heart as it were a burning fire shut up in my bones") not in the sense of a warm bath, but in the sense that something in them of vital concern to their relationship with God is about to break forth. They are "getting hot"; they are approaching the breakthrough.

Now note what both Augustine and Calvin called "the inner teacher."[2] The Teacher is not to be separated from the scriptures and the historical community being illumined; yet this Teacher transcends that community as these two men know it, because he is relating them to it in a new way. This is a relationship they themselves could never have invented, nor were they raised by their own community to interpret their tradition in the way this "Teacher" instructs. It is this link with the historical community, and at the same time transcendence of it, that builds up in these two men the anticipation of transformation.

The shape of the transformation is established in part by the condition of "the Teacher." Before Christ is recognized, his condition is exactly the reverse of his condition following the recognition. At this point, he is the unrecognized visible Presence; then, after they know who he is, he becomes the recognized invisible Presence. This is important because the reversal supplies us with a sense of the transformation as both continuous with the past and and yet involving a radical change of those past conditions. The story builds, as convictional knowing always does, toward consummation and completion of the transformational sequence. The result will be a definite gain over the original situation; but it is not a gain made by denying continuity, the original context, or its inherent conflicts.

Thus Christ joins them as they walk. By cultivating and directing the process in which they are already immersed, he fosters through historical prototypes and interpretation their discovery of what, in their own time, has been revealed in the crucifixion and resurrection. The dialogue between the Presence of Christ and the self-in-conflict is the means by which he seeks to reopen the self to the transcendent, in order that it may become "spirit." Thereby the self gains the capacity to represent the Divine in the World. This, however, gets us a bit ahead of the story.

In more *general terms*, scanning in four dimensions is a process in which one's immersion in the conflict is seemingly undertaken by another initiative. Scanning is usually, although not totally, based on

---

2. J. Calvin, *Institutes of the Christian Religion*, trans. John Allen (Philadelphia: Westminster Press, 1936), vol. 1, book 3, chap. 1; A. Augustine, *Concerning the Teacher and On the Immortality of the Soul*, trans. George G. Leckie (New York: Appleton-Century-Crofts, 1938), pp. 48-51.

"leads" or hunches. An analogy to therapeutic knowing may be helpful. Here another initiative working at first as a "stranger" facilitates an inner integration that does not contradict but complements the integrative potential of the subject, refocusing the conflict so as to maximize potential for a resolution that deals squarely with all four dimensions. In simplest terms, scanning is an internal dialogue that finds and grows the hope that is already there by establishing a context of rapport and tracing down the roots of that hope in the realities of personal, social, and cultural history. There one finds, in solutions of the past, prototypes for the "new" solution that will open the future. In the therapeutic situation, this is the work of the therapist in cooperation with the personal history and creative potential of the client; but the Other can as well be a "sense of spiritual direction" or "governance," as Kierkegaard called it. Under any such form of guidance, prototypical patterns of the past come together to give new meaning and purpose to the present situation.

Many people experience a synchronistic conjunction of events, which directs the scanning process or sets it on its way.[3] As is well known, coincidence is frequently a catalyst to scientific discovery and religious illumination. Consider the coincidences mentioned in the opening narrative of this book, in Paul's Damascus experience, and in several other New Testament accounts. Synchronicity, then, may be thought of as the four-dimensional equivalent of two-dimensional bisociations in the psychological process of discovery. Things coming together like this in four-dimensional terms suggests to the subject that inside meaning is being correlated to outside event in a way that transcends the inside-outside distinction. Thus, in religious terms

---

3. Carl Jung has named a casual, meaningful coincidence *synchronicity*. He writes: "The wife of one of my patients, a man in his fifties, once told me in conversation that, at the death of her mother and her grandmother, a number of birds gathered outside the windows of the death chamber. I had heard similar stories from other people. When her husband's treatment was nearing its end, his neurosis having been removed, he developed some apparently quite innocuous symptoms which seemed to me, however, to be those of heart disease. I sent him along to a specialist who after examining him told me in writing that he could find no cause for alarm. On the way back . . . my patient collapsed in the street. As he was brought home dying, his wife was already in a great state of anxiety because, soon after her husband had gone to the doctor, a whole flock of birds had alighted on their house. She naturally . . . feared the worst." (C. G. Jung and W. Pauli, *The Interpretation of the Psyche*, trans. R. F. C. Hull [London: Routledge and Kegan Paul, 1955], pp. 31-32.) This account illustrates how synchronicity, when understood outside the Lordship of Christ and our cooperation with it, may become a face of the void, not of the Holy.

the immanent potential for being turned inside out[4] via transformation is often brought to awareness by such a causal phenomena (for example, see John 4:16-30).

Scanning in the context of convictional knowing is following the promptings of the fourth dimension as it prepares the latent sense of the Holy within to turn outward toward the Holy beyond. Recall that in four dimensional perspective it is not one's own initiative but the initiative of the Holy, working deeper than consciousness and well beyond it, that brings forth the inside-outside reversal in the transformed person.

Transforming Intuition of Christ

In the narrative, as the two men draw near to where they are going, they constrain the Teacher to stay with them (v. 29). The resolution — often threatening — ultimately must be *chosen*. Because "arrival" takes the form of a decisive intuition by which the full range of elements in the conflict are transformed through negation and integration, the moment that brings the elements of the conflict together is potentially threatening. Thus, some people prefer a familiar conflict to a new and unfamiliar resolution. Receptivity to convictional insight depends on a willingness to embrace the unexpected. Because of this and the inherent ambivalence toward the Holy, people may dismiss the resolutions to which they have been led. These two men invite transformation.

"When he took the bread, blessed and broke it, and gave it to them their eyes were opened and they recognized him; and he vanished out of their sight" (Luke 24:30-31). In these two verses are summarized the transformation of the four dimensions of the conflict. The broken bread is a spiritually charged symbol. It is, first, *Jesus'* body, broken on the cross. Jesus' own symbol for his crucifixion, now held by his resurrected Presence, is given to them. It is, second, *their* brokenness in four dimensions as taken into *his* body. Thus in the broken bread, his brokenness is united with theirs, and theirs is united with his as they are invited to take it into themselves.[5] This, however, is not merely a union of brokenness, because the bread is embraced by his resurrected Presence. It is a union of brokenness embraced and

---

4. The psychological significance of this inside-out imagery is given in Chapter 6 in reference to the "face."

5. This is the key to the personal effectiveness of the cross, a unity of contemporary brokenness with his crucifixion. This connection constitutes "the double negation" essential to transformation in convictional knowing.

upheld by his resurrected Presence, which is now theirs to incorporate. The crucifixion and resurrection are here drawn into the most
powerful tension possible; in this tension its polarities interpret each
other and so constitute in their tensive unity the new reality by which
void and Holy are to be combined without denial or absorption. Their
combination makes them both dimensions of human being, mutually
revealing of each other. The void is revealed by the Holy to be its
shadow; the Holy is revealed by the void to be the Source and ground
of its (the void's) transformation. As the two men "take this in," they
are not only exposed in the brokenness they brought consciously to
that room, but they are also exposed in the false hopes they brought
into their relationship to Jesus in the first place. Israel is not to be
merely restored, it is to be totally transformed, and out of meager
broken hopes like theirs will come its transformation. Indeed, breaking down all false hopes for its restoration is a necessary condition of
its transformation; such was the "cross" these two men had been
bearing without realizing that it was a dark foreshadowing of the
resurrected "Israel."

Thus the *broken body* received from the *risen Lord* presents a whole
new reality, a startling way of looking at things. In effect, and in fact,
"their eyes were opened." But he vanished! How is it that when their
eyes were opened, they could see less? This is of course a marvelous
thing because the new Israel will not be external to them, bound to
one place and time, one space and person; it will be the new reality in
which all persons can live. They have become able to compose the
"world" as his World; that is, as it is promised to be composed for
them—ahead of them, and from beyond them. They had been bound
to an historically ingrown transcendence, no bigger than historic,
Israelite enculturation; but the "new Israel" is to be a total transformation of all "worlds," of the void, and of all selves. The Holy is also
transformed (for them), from one who would establish his rulership
preeminently in the lived "world" of the cultic and political order of
Israel, to the Holy who establishes his World in and through all the
dimensions of human existence. Thus, as long as he remains an *object*
of their perception, he is a factor *in their* lived "world"; to that extent
he conceals his nature as the Christ, the revelation of all being,
including theirs. His vanishing as their eyes were opened means that
his true nature is revealed; they now "see" the universal range, depth,
and power of his Lordship, which also includes their particular
existence. Of course, they can no longer see him "out there" after he
has become the lenses through which they view all beings and even

being-itself. Faith as "seeing" always implies that his perceived physical presence — an object in the lived "world" — is to be transcended by the recognition that he is Lord of all that *is*.

Notice that neither the crucifixion nor the loss of "restored Israel" is nullified, nor is their longing to be with him in the flesh. It is merely that his absence and their loss turns out to be more powerful than his physical presence in accomplishing far more for them than they could have hoped. This is a foretaste of his final disappearance in order to become Lord over all, in and through the Holy Spirit. Once the self has become spirit, it can "see" to walk by the light of the Spirit.

In *general terms*, the structure of the transforming intuition works as follows. Human intention, self-defeating in its negation of divine initiative, is negated by divine intention. Cancellation is the result of this double negation such that human intention is now left free to choose for the Author of the cancellation. Thus the nature of the divine bestows itself through the freedom of human choice made in the context of grace. Three key movements are interlocked in this summation: (1) double negation, (2) liberation of the self's capacity to choose for itself as spirit, and (3) a four-dimensional integration composed by the Author of the double negation. Movements 1 and 3 constitute the context of grace within which this movement of faith (2) can occur.

At this point, it may be useful to recall the discussion of esthetic knowing and the two-dimensional transformation described there as background for understanding how the imagination connects four-dimensional transformation to the depths of the personality. The image that comes with intuitive power to reorganize the elements of the original conflict may be attached to a dream, a cluster of memories, a vision of the future, or even to a person or circumstance in the lived "world." Whatever the manifest content and medium through which that content is conveyed, the intuitive impact of the experience will accomplish each of the three key movements in the above formulation. That is, it will accomplish in four dimensions something like what Wallace Stevens' poetry accomplished for the reader in two dimensions. It is impossible to experience transformation in four dimensions without all three interlocking movements, but one need not experience all three *completely* or *all at once* to initiate and empower the transformation process.

The centrality of double negation as that which makes the image efficacious for transformation in this decisive phase of convictional

knowing cannot be overemphasized. Luther's commentary on Galatians dramatizes the double-negation theme very effectively for the
image of Christ and the whole sweep of world redemption. The
following selections will suffice to illustrate the point:

> Therefore when I feel the remorse and sting of conscience for sin, I
> behold that brazen Christ hanging upon the Cross. There I find another
> sin against my sin which accuseth and devoureth me. Now, this other sin
> (namely in the flesh of Christ) which taketh away the sin of the whole
> world, is almighty, it condemneth and swalloweth up my sin. So my sin,
> that it should not accuse and condemn me, is condemned by sin, that is,
> by Christ crucified: "Who is made sin for us, that, we might be made
> the rightousness of God through him" (2 Cor. 5:21).
> In like manner I find death in my flesh, which afflicteth and killeth me:
> but I have in me a contrary death, which is the death of my death; and
> this death crucifieth and swalloweth up my death.[6]

Note that any parallels between this process of spiritual formation
and that found in other religions such as Zen are decisively broken at
this point. The presence of Christ as the Holy identifies the process as
belonging to him. As Mediator, he implicitly identifies himself as the
Source of the transformational process by which the Emmaus trav-
elers (representing the early church and potentially all people) come
under conviction. The effect his identity has on the people who
undergo transformation by this process distinguishes Christian convictional knowing from other forms of convictional knowing.

In Zen, the "Light" or the "Great Doctrine" are the apparent
content of the mediating center of the process, but eventually the
subject and Buddha, the Enlightened One, become one in the ultimate
state of satori. Then the individual may say, "I *am* Buddha." The self
and its "world" become absorbed into the Buddha, and in that state
nothing becomes all.

The Christian experience is decisively different in coming to say, "I,
yet not I, but Christ." Here the distinction (see Chapter 3) between
the "I" in its integrity as the spiritual *self* and Christ as the *Holy One*
is all important. Christ is still the one to whom the process belongs,
but the consequence for the subject is not absorption; rather, it is a
personal interrelatedness with Christ. The self relates to Christ in

---

6. J. Dillenberger, ed., *Martin Luther* (New York: Doubleday Anchor Books, 1961),
includes several passages from Luther that focus this issue. See pp. 121-126.

such a way that the "world" it composes is recognizably created in response to his having "gone before." It is Christ's World that the self creates out of the freedom that Christ's grace has made possible. Thus while the self, world, void, and the Holy are reconstellated by his nature, the self is freed within that very context—the context of his nature—to choose for or against him. That one can actually choose to manifest in his or her own particularity Christ's own nature—a nature that preserves all the dimensions of human being in their interdependence—this is the impossible Christian possibility. Yet, absorption in Christ is a contradiction in terms, because "in Christ" one is never absorbed but is heightened in personal particularity and uniqueness.

The issue here is not this-worldliness versus other-worldliness but simply the nature of the relationship betwen the self and the Holy into which transformation leads. In Jesus Christ, the two sides of the self's relationship to the Holy are revealed. In Jesus' intimate relationship to the Father, whom he called *Abba* ("Papa"), he epitomized the transcendent movement of the self; through this relationship, he did only what he saw the Father doing. In effect, he composed the "world" after the Father and in accordance with the Father's composition of the World. In this, Jesus revealed what it means to be truly human.

On the other hand, by doing what the Father was doing he revealed the nature of God as one who loves the World sacrificially. Thus for the self the consequence of transformation at the hands of the Mediating Christ is to be led into conflict with all other "worlds" and into a sacrificial love for the World which the Father composes and sustains. The self, therefore, while being thoroughly grounded in Christ's nature, must remain both free and distinct from Christ so that love can be truly *self*-giving. If love is not given consciously and freely and as an expression of one's own being, then either the sacrifice is puppetlike and means nothing, or it aggravates self-alienation and heightens the dizziness of freedom.

Release and Mundane Ecstasy

Following Jesus' disappearance, the two men experience a coalescence within and correlatively a power of new being. Verse 10 reads, "'Did not our hearts burn within us while he talked to us on the road, while he opened to us the scriptures?' And they rose that same hour and returned to Jerusalem."

A creative integration and consummation has occurred in the course of their being "known" by the "Teacher." Being with them and remolding their lives in the molds of their anguish, he has indwelt and reconstructed their nature the way they ordinarily would indwell and compose the objects of the "world." In their being recomposed, they have become part of his World, and in self-transcendence can "see" it that way. As things fall into place around the central, integrative intuition of Christ as the revelation of being-itself, they feel less need to hold the "world' together against their anguish and conflict. The revelation of Christ has laid a judgment on them; they had missed the point from the beginning, and they had been living out a despair of their own making. However, they are judged in such a way that they are not condemned, but informed by a new and accurate picture of themselves as in and part of his World. With the release of their mistaken "world" comes a new vitality, a sense of assurance and enthusiasm.

The day is already "far spent," so they must travel four to seven miles back to Jerusalem at night. Walking the open roads in the dark is dangerous, but the intuition of Christ has redefined them and their place in the World. Threats from the dark, the known, and the unknown are deflated where death—that definitive face of the void— has been exposed as the shadow of the resurrected life. Thus, they are released for an enthusiastic (en-theos) return to Jerusalem under a four-dimensional conviction. Their courage is an expression of deeper self-understanding and an overpowering assurance that their "world" accurately reflects his World. "Seeing" things as they really are is a remarkable antidote to fear of the dark, particularly where one is convinced that the power that overcomes death is the ground of one's being.

In more general terms, when we spoke of the release of tension in two dimensions, it was in reference to the decathexis of energy from aspects of the conflict, a condition made possible by the fact that the image or intuition was now holding the conflictual pieces in place. Similarly, the vitality released in the Emmaus couple is a result of their recognition that the broken parts of their lived world had suddenly been reorganized into a new configuration. To this extent, their joy is an "aha!" experience. In four dimensions, however, the initiative of the personality is subordinate to the initiative of the Holy; so, in effect, the "Inner Teacher" has been as involved in the process as has the initiative of the learner. Thus the release that is a consequence of instruction in the Spirit is not merely the psychological catharsis of tension reduction for a return to equilibrium and known patterns of adaptation. It is a suffusion of the personality with the joy of the "Teacher" at his having "made the point," so to say. In biblical terms, he works "in us" for his "good pleasure" (Phil. 2:12-13) and "his Spirit testifies with our spirits" (Rom. 8:16).

The experiential content of such a release is what I would call a "mundane ecstasy." If that sounds like a contradiction, it is because we usually think of the *ec*-static as taking us out of our senses and therefore out of the world known and shared with others. Being beside oneself, as the word suggests, and so "out of the body" in some sense, is, of course, a possibility; but it is not a *distinctively* Christian form of ecstasy, although such ecstasy does occur in Christian experience (2 Cor. 12:1-4). In Christian ecstasy, one is beside oneself in depth as well as height, so to say. In the ecstasy of Christian experience, one perceives the world of common experience in a new way; one becomes absorbent of almost more "mundaneness" than can be contained. One is beside oneself in the perception of particularity and the essential goodness of being itself. This is a direct reflection of one's awakening to one's own particularity and goodness as given by grace. This is to say, one comes into Christ's World—his intended creation—out of those "worlds" that induce self-alienation.

Brief mention of a friend of mine may suffice to illustrate this phenomenon. She had been awake all night praying for her little girl, who had been burning up with fever. Toward morning, the fever broke. My friend went out into the kitchen and looked out of the window. "It was," she said, "as if I had never really seen the trees before."

The key here is my friend's paying attention to the Holy. "Paying" is used advisedly, for such attending usually involves a deliberate sacrifice of lesser interests and distractions. Yet the sacrifice is far outweighed by the gift of God's beauty within the attender, a gift that may be described as a quality of completeness, or a sense of no lack. Such a sense within allows renewed perception of every proximate form of beauty without. Then, too, the proximate forms of beauty without are often enabled to initiate the inner attending to the Holy. (This latter movement is illustrated in the conversion of Sergius Bulgakov in Chapter 7.) This beauty and the Holy are inextricably related.

When one's very being is graciously recreated by the Holy One, one is free to indwell and compose his World in all of its particularity, fascination, and beauty. One's eyes are opened to the particularity of goodness and the goodness of being-itself when one's own particular being has been embraced and affirmed by Christ Jesus, in whom being-itself became particular. In this the "transparency" of faith, as Kierkegaard spoke of it, is exhibited not only by the self toward its ground in Christ but also toward the World as the creation of Christ's intention.

Such an intramundane ecstasy has serious, long-range consequences about which I will say more later. At this point it should be noted that such an ecstasy is an affront to those personal, social, and cultural systems that are built on a systematic repression of the void and of the Holy. Confrontation of "worlds" is inevitable; hence the power of new being endowed by the indwelling presence of the Holy must reengage the void concealed in those "worlds" designed to deny it. Christian ecstasy necessarily makes history precisely because it is given to faith for the sake of the World *God* intends to compose, a World to be manifested through the anguish, tears, and joy of sacrificial love (see Chapter 6).

There is a second important distinction to be made here between the Christian spiritual process and the way of Zen. As I noted, the contemplative Zen practitioner makes an effort to attain release at the beginning in order that the "world" he or she creates may be engaged and molded "spiritually"; whether it be through a tea ceremony, sword fighting, or archery, the practitioner is seeking freedom and power to gain mastery over the "world" by submission to the Supreme Doctrine. This is, of course, distinctly different from the Christian's Worldly ecstasy in which one sees in bold outine the particularity and goodness of the World *God* intends. Consequently, in the mundane ecstasy of Christian conviction, the ecstatic does not do what he or she, the ecstatic, chooses or sees as good, but what Christ's Spirit intends through his action in the clash of "worlds."

To be sure, the Christian ecstatic is liberated by a new awareness; the "I," as in therapeutic knowing, is set in the position of being free to choose for or against the new World Christ intends. Yet this sort of freedom and power to create depends entirely on discerning the intentionality of Christ. The point is not to discover how to do things "spiritually," but to discover what the Spirit of Christ is doing so as to choose for *his* World.

Thus the Christian response is less likely to be marked by manifestations of spiritual power than by sacrificial love. But even here, one does not decide ahead of time what is loving and then seek spiritual power for doing that; rather, one seeks the Presence of Christ and receives discernment regarding *his* intention so that freedom, power, or whatever may be called for will have contours that fit what

God is already doing. In Christian terms, one seeks to compose only the World that God is composing.

One may say this is absurd, but then absurdity is inevitable as soon as one's awareness moves beyond two dimensions; or, I should say, beyond two dimensions one is aware that absurdity has always been inevitable. The absurdity for which the Christian chooses is not the absurd imposed by the void on two-dimensional existence. It is a *positive absurd*—that is, the negation of the void, or the way of sacrificial love as revealed in Christ. Mundane ecstasy is an exposure to the World "God so loved," in which faith already participates and for which it is willing to sacrifice, even perish. Anything less is a collapse into the negative absurd and the void; anything "more," in the sense of coercive achievement, is a collapse into two-dimensionality.

Verification: New People

When the two men from Emmaus arrive at Jerusalem, they are confronted with the very proclamation they themselves had planned to bring to the Jerusalem disciples. "The Lord is risen indeed, and has appeared to Simon [Peter]! Then they told what happened on the road, and how he was known to them in the breaking of the bread" (verses 34-35). This surprising coincidence points to the unique character of confirmation and congruence in the four-dimensional patterning of transformation. In two-dimensional transformation, the final step is one of investing released energy in a test of the insight or intuition, both for its congruence with the conflict and for its correspondence with some "public" in the new situation.

What appears in the final phase of this narrative is confirmation by a synchronistic reversal of expectations. The two men thought they would *tell* of Christ's resurrection, but instead they are *told*. Thus, they are put into a "public" in a way that could only occur by Christ's action independently of any verification process by an established body of experts. The creation of a "new people" is the confirmation of a shared intuition of Jesus as the Christ.

Of course, the disciples at Jerusalem had shared the same broken expectations and tenuous hopes for Israel as the two men of Emmaus. However, that they have also shared the same vision of Christ's resurrection and the same resulting conviction, without intervening contact with them, is a powerfully verifying experience. It is, in fact, the only way in which something genuinely new can be verified. That is, it must create its own public and its own criteria for verification.

The church's unsocialized, unlearned, unpracticed unity as a new people, who were constituted in a way that made the resurrected Christ the only necessary and sufficient condition of their existence, is the verification of their separate experiences. This is a basic argument the text presents for the validity of the Emmaus experience.

This dialectic between the historical and the acausal, the diachronic and the synchronic, is at the heart of the church and its koinonia. Paul Lehmann calls koinonia the "fellowship creating reality of Jesus Christ." By this he wants to insist that the result of Christ's action is a very definite social reality but that the origins, sustaining vitality, and ultimate destiny of that social reality are not bound up in socialization and the larger society. Koinonia is the consequence of grace; relative to temporal and causal terms, it is characterized by synchronicity; it is a unique meeting of people whose preeminent commonality, in but apart from all distinctions due to socialization, is the continuing Spiritual Presence of Jesus as the Christ. Hence community and communication all depend in the final analysis on people being communicants at his table.

Of course, the point here is not to tie down the church to those who have had "a sudden experience"; four-dimensional transformation is essential to knowing Christ, but it may be stretched out over years. Convictional experiences and their verification focus in fast motion, so to say, the unique way in which individuals are united over extended time in a particular fellowship that, in turn, enters into the broad historical, transforming work of Jesus Christ and explains itself in terms of his nature.

Verification: New Culture

To speak of the church's "explaining itself" brings us to the threshold of theology in the formal and systematic sense. Theology attempts to develop symbols and ways of relating them interpretatively so as to "thematize" the life of the church. Thereby the church accounts for itself to itself and to the secular order in relation to the scriptural sources of its existence. I cannot here venture into any extensive theological expositions, but I must account for the particular symbol system we call *theology* in relation to convictional knowing. I will take just a few examples of the unique character of theology as a culture designed to thematize the transformational, four-dimensional quality of being in Christ.

A synchronistically constructed community like the koinonia calls for a unique culture. Although appearing in two-dimensional contexts, synchronicity as a mode of relationship negates any sort of two-dimensional connectedness and implicitly points toward the transcendent reality of the fourth dimension. This four-dimensional synchronistic pattern is enshrined in nearly every major theological symbol. That is, synchronistic events (such as the Emmaus story and its climax in Jerusalem) do in experience what theological symbols embody at the level of culture. Such events begin in a two-dimensional context, but they negate every form of two-dimensional connectedness and point toward a fourth dimension. Similarly, key theological symbols are based in two-dimensional experience (e.g., father); then, in a third dimension, they are negated (e.g., not any ordinary human father); finally, they are heightened or magnified so as to point toward a fourth dimension (e.g., heavenly father). The same four-dimensionality is implicit in agape love, Kingdom of God, God's grace, etc. Thus theological symbols may be said to capture and preserve in a cognitive pattern the unique mode of four-dimensional relatedness that characterizes the koinonia.

However, theological symbols are not best understood analytically — that is, in terms of the modes of activity and relationship that give rise to them. Rather, they are best understood as evoking an awareness of the four-dimensional reality that called them into being. That is, theological symbols are not to be seen as human projections (i.e., projections of the human father) but as responses to the projection of the fourth dimension into the other three (human fatherhood to be seen as derivative from and defined by God's self-revelation as "Abba"). It is only when theological symbols are understood in terms of the higher reality which calls them forth that the synchronistic life behind the symbol is preserved. It is only then that the symbol has revelatory power for the full four dimensions of existence, and especially power to reveal the fashion in which the fourth dimension transforms the other three. Of course, a supreme example of this is the Eucharistic moment in which Simon and Cleopas recognize Jesus in the breaking of the bread, and are therein transformed.

Theology, however, is more than its symbols. Its overarching themes establish the larger context within which a text of Scripture or a knowing event may be interpreted. Ordinarily, if we were to pursue this text theologically we would probably put it in the context of a resurrection theme under the heading of Christology. The aim here, though, is not to pursue the usual procedures that would take us away from our concern for convictional experiences. Rather, we will return to the theological basis for selecting this text—that is, as an illustration of how the Holy Spirit works convictionally in the lives of individuals. If the analogy of the Spirit pertains as was said at the outset of this chapter, then the transformational pattern that was exemplified here should reflect the transforming activity of the Holy Spirit as understood theologically. Moreover, it should be made clear that the transformational work of the Holy Spirit converges with the Eucharist in a myriad of different ways, all of which draw us into the fundamental theological assertion that the subjective and objective sides of the revelation belong together; or more explicitly, the Holy Spirit testifies to the Word of God in Christ. It is to these themes that we now turn.

First, the text we have just been interpreting via the logic of transformation participates in a much larger theme running throughout scripture, which theme is also characterized by the same logic. It is a theme the church has classically called "Spiritus Creator" or the Creator Spirit. Lutheran scholarship, Regin Prenter in particular, suggests that Spiritus Creator is the best way to characterize Luther's entire theology of the Spirit.[7] Here the process of convictional knowing is taken up into classical theological categories as the "grammar" of the Holy Spirit; here the analogy of the Spirit becomes theologically explicit.

Luther himself wrote that the Spirit has its own "grammar" by which the Word of God is articulated.[8] "Grammar" may be translated into what I have designated as transformational logic, the unique sense of order that characterizes both the human spirit and the Holy Spirit. The Lutheran emphasis is that we cannot experience authentic transformation anywhere except in the work of the Holy Spirit. What I have called transformation in two or three dimensions is still alien to the Holy Spirit, so that all such transformations must be themselves thoroughly transformed. In the context of the analogy of the Spirit, this emphasis stresses not the similarity but the radical difference between human and Holy Spirit. The similarity is implicit in the way grammar is implicit in language. Luther's use of "grammar" and Prenter's development of the implicit order in Luther's interpretation of Spiritus Creator suggest that although the explicit relationship between the two spirits is as radically disjunctive as "glorification" and "damnation," the Holy Spirit's pattern of action does become

---

7. R. Prenter, *Spiritus Creator* (Philadelphia: Muhlenberg Press, 1953).
8. *Werke*, vol. 39:2 (Weimar: H. Böhlau, 1883-), pp. 104-105.

intelligible—that is, continuity and discontinuity are interwoven in a pattern that follows the logic of transformation. Transformation of all two-dimensional transformations is decisive for salvation because Christ the mediator must also become the origin and destiny of the process. Yet intelligibility implies that a transposition of transformational logic pertains between the two spirits. Thus, Luther's position implies a similarity at the structural level, even though it stresses, in agreement with our analogy of the Spirit, that the origin and destiny of transformation in the Holy Spirit is radically different from that in the human spirit.

Having taken this position on Luther's view of Spirit, we may look at his spiritual "grammar" and how it employed transformational logic. That "grammar" begins as the Spirit of Christ makes the Gospel meaningful for us; that is to say, it begins in "inner conflict." To have the Gospel come to us with meaning is to be thrown into a conflict of immense proportions. The Spirit of Holiness makes us sinners, the enlightenment makes us blind, dimensions of the Holy call into play the threats of evil, annihilation, and damnation. The self and all its "worlds" are exposed as alienated from each other and within themselves. This is the intention of the Spirit in Luther: to convict through conflict and then to overcome that conflict through the Word of the Gospel. Thus Luther himself came to a radical new consummation within himself. By the Holy Spirit, he was moved from fear of the just God who exposes guilt, toward the just God who justifies by faith. Between the mortification and vivification, the death and the new life, there is anguish and longing, a struggle of immense proportions, far beyond the dimensions scanned by the creative scientist or artist in the throes of productivity. In this, "eros is crucified," the human spirit is exposed in its brokenness and restored only as a gift of that same sovereign Spirit. The destiny of this regenerative work is a sanctifying unity with Christ in worship and in his ongoing redemption of the world.

In this highly condensed account, it is possible to see how transformation must be transformed. The logic of transformation remains constant, but *Spiritus Creator* radically transforms the origin and destiny of transformation in the human personality. As I have said, in ordinary experience transformation begins and ends with the development of the personality's creative and adaptational capacities, or, in simple terms, begins and ends with the human ego. But in theological context it is a pattern that begins with Christ's initiative borne in on the personality by his Spirit and brought through conflict into faith and worship, of which theology is the integral interpretative part. A similar kind of argument could be made for social and cultural transformations undergoing transformation by the Spirit of Christ. Thus does transformation transformed bring expression to Christ's Word in and through the history of his people.

As in the initial paradigm (see Chapter 2), the aspect of *continuity* in theological transformation is all important. (See theological guideline 3 and psychological guideline 5, Chapter 7.) The intention of Christ's Spirit toward us cannot be broken without our falling into some distortion—an existentialist's masochistic love of struggle, an enthusiast's repressive denial of it, or a rationalistic obsession with interpretation, to suggest just three possible distortions. From the origin to the destiny of the Spirit's work, from the inner to the outer aspects of human participation in that Spirit, continuity is to be maintained for the sake of the integrity of the Spirit's act of creation.

When transformational logic is operative in the creation of new being, the crucial feature of *discontinuity* is the new creation, the jolt into awareness whereby one awakens, as Karl Barth put it, to the ongoing transformational activity of Christ's Spirit. Thus Luther himself awakened to the just God who justifies. This awakening Karl Barth describes with dramatic bisociative language:

> The jolt by which man is wakened and at which he wakens . . . is not the work of one of the creaturely factors, co-efficients and agencies which are there at work and can be seen, but of the will and act of God who uses these factors and Himself makes the co-efficients and agencies for this purpose, setting them in motion as such in the meaning and direction which He has appointed. We are thus forced to say that this awakening is both wholly creaturely and wholly divine. Yet the initial shock comes from God.[9]

What is "wholly creaturely and wholly divine" represents the extreme in "habitually incompatible frames of reference" coming together to form a meaningful unity (Koestler's view of bisociation), especially when one considers the impassable gulf of sin that would otherwise eternally separate all that is creaturely from the Divine Creator.

Thus, the intertwining of ultimate continuity with ultimate discontinuity according to the pattern of transformation makes this

---

9. K. Barth, *Church Dogmatics*, vol. 4, part 2 (Edinburgh: Clark, 1958), p. 557.

which we call "conversion," or the "awakening into sanctification," or "being shocked into metanoia," a personal instance of the Word of God under the agency and initiative of God.

Let it be clear that the transformational activity of Christ's Spirit in the church and in history reflects the same logic expressed personally in conversion, but it is transposed and extended to the redemption of all creation. Conversion is not conversion out of but *into* the transformation of *all* things. Thus, as Arthur Darby Nock has pointed out in his classic study of conversion, the threat that Christianity posed to Rome was vastly greater than, say, Mithraism or any other sort of cultic conversion, since one could, so to say, be a Mithraist on the side.[10] Christ's Spirit transforms all transformations; so, one cannot be a Christian on the side.

Such is the analogy of the Spirit, but in relation to convictional experiences the sacramental work of the Spirit is especially significant. We must turn here to the Eucharist as the repeated, normative instance of a convictional experience in the larger context of convictional knowing.

A second decisive theological theme at the center of the Emmaus account and the transformation of the human spirit is the Eucharist, as image and as eschatology. This is decisive because without the mystery of the Eucharist at its center, transformation itself could be falsified and become an ideology or program systematically imposed on people and situations. When the Eucharist stands at the center of transformation, it means that here the human spirit itself, not merely this or that in one's life, but the creative dynamic of human life that generates science, art, and all culture, is about to be turned inside out. To explain this, I will turn first to the Eucharist as image; note that what follows is not a theology of the Eucharist but a description of how people participate transformationally in the Eucharist.[11]

In thinking of Eucharist as image, recall Ezra Pound's statement that an image is a "radiant node or cluster, it is what I can, and must perforce, call a vortex, from which and through which, and into which ideas are constantly rushing." The Eucharistic meal, surrounded by the celebration of its meanings, is a highly charged symbol expressing imagery that draws all four dimensions of human being into Christocentric focus. Macquarrie aptly summarizes the density and richness of the Eucharist:

---

10. A. D. Nock, *Conversion* (Oxford University Press, 1952), pp. 14-16.
11. *Eucharist* is being used in preference to *Lord's Supper* or *Communion* not for any denominational or traditional purposes but for conceptual reasons (see p. 50, n. 8).

It seems to include everything. It combines Word and Sacrament; its appeal is to spirit and to sense; it brings together the sacrifice of Calvary and the presence of the risen Christ; it is communion with God and communion with man; it covers the whole gamut of religious moods and emotions. Again, it teaches the doctrine of creation, as the bread, the wine and ourselves are brought to God; the doctrine of atonement, for these gifts have to be broken in order that they be perfected; the doctrine of salvation, for the Eucharist has to do with incorporation into Christ and the sanctification of human life; above all, the doctrine of incarnation, for it is no distant God whom Christians worship but one who has made himself accessible in the world. The Eucharist also gathers up in itself the meaning of the Church; its whole action implies and sets forth our mutual interdependence in the body of Christ, it unites us with the Church of the past and even, through its paschal overtones, with the first people of God, Israel; and it points to the eschatological consummation of the kingdom of God, as an anticipation of the heavenly banquet.[12]

The ideas and meanings that are united in this master image of the Christian faith require a four-dimensional, transformational perspective if they are not to be merely a list of teachings *about* the Eucharist. That is, unless the Eucharist becomes transformational for the participant its celebration will be a bearer of distortion and confusion. One has only to recall the dismay of those who heard Jesus say they would have to eat his body and drink his blood (John 6:10) to recognize possible misconceptions, from dull ritualism to cannibalism and Dionysian revelry. Thus, without the Eucharistic center transformation may become an ideology, but without transformation the Eucharist may become idolatry or sheer folly.

The intersection between four-dimensional transformation and the Eucharist as image, symbol, and celebration becomes the turning point at which a massive figure-ground shift can take place for the participant like that which occurred for the two men at Emmaus.

In this figure-ground shift the complex of meanings focused on Christ no longer resides outside oneself as doctrine, nor does the participant any longer view the elements, the celebration, and their meaning as usual. Rather the meaning of the Eucharist (Christ) becomes itself the lens through which one's own being, and being-itself, is viewed. Eucharistic lenses radically alter one's appreciation of

---

12. J. Macquarrie, *Paths in Spirituality* (New York: Harper & Row, 1972), p. 73.

the Word—as when one comes into an appreciation of a work of art—first from the outside in terms of one's own intentions, finally from the inside in terms of the Author's intentions.

This shift also suggests why it is so important that this central symbol of Christian transformation be a meal as well as doctrine and celebration. It has to be not only perceived with the senses and understood for its multiplicity of meaning but also quite literally "taken in" and made a part of one's physical being. This creates most tangibly the optional conditions for the existential figure-ground shift whereby that which is in one and reaching every aspect of one's nature from mind to body, both inside and out, may suddenly (or eventually) become the reality that encompasses and envelops one. If what one takes in were not so exhaustive of every aspect of human being, then the transforming moment in which one is turned inside out, so to say, would not be total, not so thoroughly convicting. It is with this understanding that I am suggesting that the Eucharistic transformation, or convictional knowing in the context of the Euchar-ist, is the supreme imaginative expression of the graciousness of being. Hence it is normative for convictional experiences, and indeed for all those ventures of the imagination that we have called imagina-tive leaps, whether they are conversions, illuminations, inspirations, visions, or insights.

Convictional experiences in particular put the convicted person inside a four-dimensional belief. This is the source of their overpow-ering convicting significance. Ordinarily, we are happy if we can "grasp" a multidimensional meaning and "hang on to it." So much the better, we say, if we can get it to become a part of us. However, all this which generally preoccupies Christian practitioners is valuable but not convictionally decisive; the four-dimensional transformation of the Eucharist requires that one be inside what is believed in order to "see" whatever is out there, in here, and everywhere in terms of Christ's intention for all creation, from the commonest bread crumbs to the Kingdom of God. Everyday Christian experience badly needs what the transforming moment does to place people inside their convictions, just as the transforming moment needs everyday Chris-tian experience as its substantive content.

In view of the plurality of possible transformations, it must be stressed here, as in the contrasts with Zen, that the key question raised by transformation is, "Into *what* is one thrust as a result of transformation?" Here, of course, the Christocentric character of the Eucharist is definitive. For instance, one does not simply know *about* the crucifixion and resurrection; one is able to enter into all that *is* in light of this tremendous dialectic. As participant in the sacrament, one is united not merely socially with the community, but now one's very being is united with others through the common ground of Christ as being-itself. One does not merely know about the body and blood of Christ, but his blood severs the priority of all other blood relationships, and his body becomes the family of God by which one's inherited kinship can undergo transformation and renewal. These and many other aspects of the new vision come when the Eucharist and transformation intersect.

The Eucharist as eschatology adds an important dimension to the normative character we are attributing to it. It is not only integral to the installation of the Lord's Supper that it be received in anticipation of the return of Christ as a foretaste of the heavenly banquet, it is also a substantive statement of that which is always implicit in transformation. As in the earlier quotation from Barth, the transforming moment at which one is "awakened" is an awakening into the ongoing and final transformation of all things. What we have tried to make explicit by use of the logic of transformation is that proximate transformations bear a figural or "sacramental" relationship to the ultimate transformation. Thus, all transformations are implicitly eschatological, but the Eucharist makes that implicit significance explicit and definitive. It is explicitly a celebration of and participation in a future climax, and it is definitive in that Christ Jesus is he who is to come as the climax of the history of transformations and as the finisher of all unfinished transformations.

PRELIMINARY PLACING OF CONVICTIONAL EXPERIENCE

We may pause at this point and ask where the understanding of convictional knowing has brought us so far. In Chapter 3 we say how fragile and flexible is the human self, open-textured and constantly in the process of composing its world, even while falling into dependency on the world it composes. Thus, the self is afraid of a transparent relationship with the Holy because release of one's self-contained existence seems to be surrender to alien forces containment was designed to keep out. It seems to be a collapse into an abyss of loneliness, anxiety, and despair.

Christian conviction claims, to the contrary, that Jesus Christ has plunged into the abyss and filled it with his nature. His Spiritual Presence, "the pleroma" of his being, has transformed the cross and void. Therefore, from a standpoint within Christian conviction, we do not have to be afraid of plunging in ourselves; we will be greeted not by empty silence but by relief, joy, and the recognition that he is there. Despair of human life and destiny are shadows across the face of Christ; they are too deep to be penetrated by two-dimensional vision; they are as forbiddingly dark as pain, guilt, and death. Yet for the one convicted they are deeper avenues into the knowledge of Christ's Presence. Even the "dark night of the soul," following in the type of Christ's crucifixion abandonment, becomes only that which temporarily obscures God's nature so that the nature of the one abandoned may be made even more like his. Relative to the transparent ground between our self and his nature, the threat of ultimate emptiness becomes ultimately an empty threat.[13]

Thus, it can be said that convictional experiences are invitations or moments of awakening into a transparency that has been in the making for some time. They are assurances that the void is not bottomless; they call us into the resurrected life of Christ, who, filling all in all, seeks to actualize that fulfillment through the transformation of all human life (Eph. 1:23, 4:13). The convicting experience is saying, "Don't be afraid—trust and live. Live beyond the boundaries of the shelters you have built up against the void. Live in the transparency of the self with the Holy." The transparent relationship between Christ's nature and ours is the vital nerve, the very heart of the truth so thinly disguised, or so nearly revealed, in the transforming moment.

What we have come to understand in convictional knowing is how the objective truth of the revelation in Christ may be subjectively known. At the heart of convictional knowing is a radical figure-ground shift that is not merely perceptual but existential, in which the truth of Christ's revelation transforms the subject from a knower into one who is fully known and comprehended by what he or she first

13. I am aware of the gnostic sound this may have, because it seems to speak as did Valentinus of the pleroma, the whole spiritual world, and evil (matter) as a shadow in relation to that spiritual reality. This would be a false construction of what I am saying. There is, to begin with, no degradation of matter, and no effort to set matter against spirit in this argument. By Spirit, I refer to the dynamic being of Christ's transforming Presence in every aspect of human nature whether visible or invisible, physical or mental, and whose Presence is in the process of transforming present human nature into a humanity that conforms to his nature. Understanding how this Presence works transformingly in very concrete terms is partly the function of the next chapters. The negative principle I have referred to as *void* is essentially that which is designed to reverse creation, to undo the "ex nihilo" of divine creation, making all that is into nothing once again. In him the drive toward nothing is repeatedly transformed and made to contribute to the furtherance of redemption, the inbreaking of his World.

knew. Convictional knowing describes the structural and dynamic link between knowing about Christianity and becoming Christian. As such, it supplies the necessary context for understanding those intense convictional experiences as the path of transformation from a life of two-dimensional truths into a four-dimensional existence governed by the unfathomable truth of God.

The essence of convictional knowing is the intimacy of the self with its Source. The breakdown of the eternal distance between them, the establishment of the internal dialogue, the illumination of Christ, the shared joy of Christ and the thrust into the people and culture of Christ, together constitute the shape of that intimacy. This is the form of the ongoing spiritual communion into which convictional experiences call the believer, not once but again and again throughout life.

Five

CONVICTIONAL KNOWING IN HUMAN DEVELOPMENT

➤ RELATING CONVICTIONAL KNOWING to human development will bring the theological claims of the previous chapter closer to everyday experience and answer certain questions that may have been raised in the discussion thus far. Basic concepts of human development are presupposed, because most of those I employ here are "common wisdom." The following paragraphs develop four theses that are of considerable importance in interpreting convictional experience from a viewpoint common to both theology and human development. None of these theses, I hope, will require more technical definitions than are given here, but if so I have set them down elsewhere.[1]

EARLY PROTOTYPES AND ULTIMATE SIGNIFICANCE

The first thesis concerns the relation of early prototypes to the ultimate significance of Eucharistic incorporation as described in the preceding chapter.

Take the following case as a focal instance for several converging observations. A little girl of five sitting in the garden one day

---

1. James E. Loder, "Developmental Foundations for Christian Education," ch. 5 in M. Taylor, ed., *Foundations for Christian Education in an Era of Change* (Nashville: Abingdon, 1976), 54-67.

suddenly became conscious of a colony of ants in the grass. Watching them running rapidly and purposefully about their business, she wondered how much of their own pattern they were able to see when all at once she realized that she was so close and so large that to them she was invisible. Later she wrote,

> I was gigantic, huge—able at one glance to comprehend, at least to some extent, the work of the whole colony. I had the power to destroy or scatter it, and I was completely outside the sphere of their knowledge and understanding.

Then, turning away from them to her surroundings she saw a tree not far away, and the sun was shining. There were clouds and blue sky that went on and on forever. And suddenly she was tiny, insignifcant before a limitless reality that she could see was far beyond her comprehension, so close and so gigantic it was invisible. As she described it,

> A watcher would have to be incredibly big to see me and the world around me as I could see the ants and their world. . . . He would have to be vaster than the world and space, and beyond understanding and yet I *could* be aware of him—I *was* aware of him, in spite of my limitations, at the same time he was and he was not, beyond my understanding. Although my flash of comprehension was thrilling and transforming, I knew even then that in reality it was no more than a tiny glimmer.

Running indoors, delighted and overwhelmed by her discovery, she announced, "We're like ants running about in a giant's tummy!" Although she lacked language to explain herself, and she was not understood by her parents, the power of her vision stayed with her so that at the age of sixty she reported,

> All my life in times of great pain or distress or failure, I have been able to look back and remember, quite sure that the present agony was not the whole picture and that my understanding of it was as limited as the ants in their comprehension of their part in the world that I knew.

This is one of 4,000 such experiences, collected by the Religious Experience Research Unit, Manchester College, Oxford, about 15 percent of which occurred in childhood.[2] In relation to this book, it is striking for several reasons.

First, the enduring significance of the experience for this woman means that the figure-ground reversal in her childhood awareness was no mere perceptual arrangement easily reversed by new stimuli. It was a change of enduring significance because it touched and expressed an internal order more profound than any change in circumstances, ideas, or maturation could alter. The episode suggests that there is in the personality an order of being and change deeper in its transforming movement and stronger in its staying power than any changes that take place in the developing ego. I will say more about this subsequently.

A second observation is that to reductionistic psychoanalytic eyes this is a screened memory of intrauterine existence and earlier childhood. This is explicit in the reference to the "giant's tummy," and it is implicit throughout in the interplay between big people and little people, in being at one with yet distinct from, and in the emotional ambivalence that moves between awesome respect and intimate feelings of being watched over.

For every creative insight, there are prototypes, which provide necessary patterns on which a genuinely new understanding may be constructed. In the context of creativity, however, prototypes do not *explain* anything; at best, they account for starting points or establish general models. Just as some of the earliest automobiles had reins instead of steering wheels, the prototype may provide encumbrance as well as insight. Prototypes not only cannot explain, but they also cannot show *significance*. Who would have foreseen, from looking at the horse or even at that reined vehicle snorting down a dirt road, the immense international automobile industry of today with all the power it exercises over those who invented it. Of course, analogies are not arguments, but perhaps the point is clear. It is important to recognize and accept the prototype as a point of departure (and even as a point of possible explanation in psychopathology), but in the context of creativity, governed as it is by transformational logic, *explanations* are to be made in terms of the relative success or failure of an insight in mediating the transformational process. Moreover, *signification* in Christian context is established by that ultimate horizon toward which transformation moves the universal,

---

2. E. Robinson, *The Original Vision* (Oxford, England: Religious Experience, Research Unit, 1978). See also A. Hardy, *The Spiritual Nature of Man* (Oxford, England: Oxford University Press, 1969).

united with and in the particular, yet without reduction of either: Jesus Christ, the logos as flesh.

Third, from a Christian standpoint, this experience is Eucharistic in its formal characteristics; clearly the child moves inside a vision of the "watcher" in a way that is both fascinating and awesome to her. A reductionistic explanation, playing out Nicodemian literalism as regards the second birth, cannot, as we have said, account for its enduring and redemptive power in this woman's life. It is rather its partial, "sacramental" participation in *the* sacrament of the Eucharist that gives it transcendent significance. By foreshadowing and indwelling our human participation in the reality of Christ, the child's experience acquires a staying power over against subsequent developmental changes. Indeed, the Eucharistic Christ is the same ultimate reality that gives power and significance to the prototype of "birth" in the notion of "new birth"—not the other way around, as we are wont to confuse the order of knowing and being.

Very early experiences, as I will show, generate awareness of and longings for an ultimacy great enough to establish their value forever, so there is no fundamental age limit on when one must undergo a "conversion" that has lifelong value. This episode, then, exemplifies in a formal and structural fashion how convictional experiences, at almost any age, may reach toward, even as they participate in, Eucharistic transformation as their final explanation and significance. Moreover, it shows that the sort of transformation celebrated in the Eucharist, rooted in the earliest and most primitive structures of self-awareness, is as much a matter of preserving a gracious continuity as it is a matter of introducing genuinely new and discontinuous moments of imaginative reconstruction.

TRANSFORMATION AS STAGE TRANSITION

A second major thesis is that transformational logic is rooted in and permeates every aspect of human development as the pattern that governs the stage transition process. As most of us recognize, human development is generally studied in terms of "stages," referring to levels of internal personality integration and the range of environmental complexity that the developing person is competent to manage. However, because most of life and growth is carried on not at stages but between stages, the stage transition process then is the most prominent part of human development, although it is studied, perhaps, the least. My thesis here is that this prominent aspect of development is transformational in its basic pattern.

Both Erik Erikson, the leading psychoanalytic interpreter of human development, and Jean Piaget, the leading structuralist, interpret the stage transition process as closely akin to the transformational dialectics of the nineteenth-century philosopher Georg Friedrich Hegel. The historical dependency here is not clear, perhaps even to Erikson and Piaget; however, systematically speaking, they both acknowledge the kinship. Because of their systematic use of an implicitly dialectical process, psychiatrist Peter Wolff was able to integrate both views of stage transition in the concept of orthogenesis that is more explicitly Hegelian.[3] Orthogenesis (*ortho,* "straight," and *genesis,* "development"), as worked out theoretically and empirically by Heinz Werner and his followers, is the tendency of a living organism, personality, society, or symbol system to unfold in a given direction with relative disregard for the constraints of the environment. Werner found the process to be a dominant force in the development of every cell tissue, fetus, and brain.[4]

As applied to the stage transition process, orthogenesis may be articulated (*articulare,* "to break into joints") as follows. Initially, a relatively *global* or less differentiated, equilibrated condition pertains. Then (first) this condition is confronted by new environmental demands and emerging organic potentials that disrupt the equilibrium of the initial condition and call for higher levels of integration and complexity management. Normal birth is an obvious example of a relatively well-equilibrated condition giving way to disruption under the combined pressure of internal and external demands. The one-word name for this stage is *differentiation,* although clearly, when applied to psychological birth, differentiation is conflictual for the newborn, who must face numerous harsh incongruities (Leboyer to the contrary notwithstanding).

Second, differentiation is followed by a period of *specification* in which the aspects of the organism or personality undergo specialization and maturation on their own. To continue the example of

3. P. Wolff, "The Developmental Psychologies of Jean Piaget and Psychoanalysis," *Psychological Issues,* vol. 2, no. 1, Monograph 5 (New York: International Universities Press, 1960). This monograph was Piaget's suggestion for connecting his view with psychoanalysis (personal communication, Sept. 1966).
4. H. Werner, *Comparative Psychology of Mental Development* (NewYork: International Universities Press, 1948). See also J. Langer, "Werner's Comparative Organismic Theory," in P. H. Mussen, ed., *Carmichael's Manual of Child Psychology,* vol. 1 (New York: Wiley, 1970), chap. 10.

psychological birth, the newborn child develops in a number of part processes such as grasping, sucking, ear-eye coordination, and speech soundings. All these parts, developing on their own schedule and reaching toward integration, come together in the next stage.

Third, *integration* is both a functional and structural coordination of the differentiated and specified aspects of the developing organism or personality. By about eighteen months under normal conditions, the newborn has reached an internal integration of elementary part processes and regularized his or her relation to the environment so that "basic trust," as Erikson calls it, tends to predominate over "mistrust," and those things that are "mistrusted" (such as the edge of the bed) generally serve further adaptation. This early ego-environment integration (a favorable balance of trust over mistrust) is a latent structural potential that emerges with regularity at this period. It will serve as a foundation and as the next "global" condition for subsequent differentiations and reintegrations of the ego.

Fourth, each new integration *generates* two *results:* (1) it makes possible a much more efficient use of energy; for example, energy need not be continually dissipated in the search for trustworthy patterns of behavior but instead be invested in new explorations, and (2) it generates its own reinforcement; that is, the efficiency of the more well-integrated behavioral pattern automatically gains the rewards of adaptational success. In the newborn, new energy is released *from* early struggles to adapt and *for* emerging new potentials such as the symbolic construction of reality, which dawns on the child at about the age of eighteen months. The dominance of basic trust *proves itself,* freeing the full expression of language and the other higher functions of the personality; the dominance of mistrust arrests development and tends to retard the full and rewarding use of higher functions.

It should be evident from this generalized statement of how orthogenesis governs the stage transition process, that the sequence described in Chapter 2 as transformational logic is a built-in part of human development. When you realize that it is repeated again and again as transitions in stage development are accomplished for the ego and for all its part processes (language, intelligence, moral judgment, and so on), it is clear why this sequence is so deeply ingrained in the personality. It is the pattern of new life by which we make disordered things make sense; it is the dynamic order by which we construct fixed or stable orders; it is the process by which we compose content.

As I indicated in the first thesis, prototypes derived from the basic, physical aspects of experience are often transposed with effectiveness to higher orders of human functioning, so this process is transposed to higher orders of behavior. The first transposition to be mentioned may already be evident in the way orthogenesis was here articulated for the stage transition process. That is, the process is transposed to the level of intentional acts of creation in any number of spheres (see Chapter 2) where established frames of reference are absent and transformational logic must be employed. In this transposition, certain aspects change: differentiation becomes more explicitly conflict; refining the differentiated parts continues as scanning in which the conflicted parts are clarified and tried in any number of combinations with each other and with other associated or bisociated connections. The latent structure that emerges in human development is replaced in creativity by imaginative constructs conveying genuinely new combinations of conflicted factors. In human development, the integrated functioning of the new competence releases energy for coping with greater environmental complexities as the "aha" in creativity expresses a similar psychophysical reaction. In human development, actual performance demonstrates the validity of the new structures of competence, and in creative behavior validity is established in terms of continuity (congruence) as well as the "public test" (correspondence). Thus, stage transition dynamics are transposed into conscious or intentional behavior as the creative process, with the logic of transformation maintaining the structural continuity from one position to the next.

Transposition takes place again as the capacity for creative behavior is moved from actual time and actual discovery into fictive time, thus becoming the plot for transformational narratives. That is, narrative forms that move from an initial lack, loss, or dilemma into a gain over the original conditions as a result of the lack are considered transformational. This distinguishes them from those that end in stalemate or disaster, or merely re-establish the original, disrupted state of affairs. All transformational narratives are mediated by the narrative equivalent of the intuition or insight. Thus fairy godmothers, genies, magic lamps, and the like all lend to folktales their spiritual quality, usually making it all turn out better for the hero than it ever was before.[5]

---

5. See C. G. Jung, "The Phenomenology of the Spirit in Fairy Tales," in *Psyche and Symbol*, trans. R. F. C. Hull (New York: Doubleday Anchor Book , 1958), pp. 61-112; V. Propp, *Morphology of the Folktale*, trans. L. Scott (Austin: University of Texas Press, 1968); E. Maranda and P. Maranda, *Structural Models in Folklore and Transformational Essays* (The Hague: Mouton, 1971). The essential point that can be made from all three of these references is that narrative forms may be recognized as a major variation on the transformational process.

However, transformational logic transposed into narrative is more than diversionary. As early as age five, and perhaps before, children can respond therapeutically to transformational narrative. That is, stories that have transformational plots and are integrated into the life story of the child can make a significant contribution to healing childhood depression and neuroses. By age nine, the child can recognize the essential structural components of a transformational narrative, and by puberty the young person is ready to accept as part of his or her self-reflection a transformational narrative or myth about his or her own culture, self, and society. If Levi-Strauss is correct in his major thesis on mythology, we develop a capacity to transpose transformational logic not only into stories we tell, but also into stories that tell us who we are, why we are, and what is our destiny. I must discuss the relation of Christ to mythic structure later, in the context of C. S. Lewis' conversion to Christianity.

Here, simply note that the logic of transformation becomes the basis on which we construct mythical "worlds." It is such because it is first and primarily the dynamic pattern by which all those elementary "worlds" with which we are genetically endowed (kinship relations, language, morality, and so on) take form and come into actual expression. Subsequently, confronted with the great dichotomies of existence, such as life versus death, male versus female, and corporate life versus the individual, it is natural that we attempt to resolve these dilemmas the same way in which the dynamics of development taught us all along to create those more elementary "worlds." Subjecting these great dichotomies to the dynamics of transformational logic yields myth, and mythology is so compelling partly if not primarily because it is a symbolic order generated by the same dynamic pattern that gives growth to the human personality.[6]

As already noted (Chapter 2), other transformations could be mentioned. What this link to human development may provide is an account of why it is that once we enter into a creative process or a narrative-like pattern, there is a compelling "sense of an ending" that drives us toward completion. Clearly, if the process has been exercised with completion for several years in the course of development and through several stage transitions, it continues to press toward comple-

---

6. For a full explication of this idea, see Chapter 6, note 1 (pp. 159-60), on Levi-Strauss. Generally, mythic systems, like developmental stages, are constructed as resolutions to dichotomies that threaten to break down the organization of the social and/or personality systems. The developmental process is ontogenetically primary and so forms a foundation for the process by which mythic systems are generated.

tion and closure when raised to the level of conscious behavior and narrative expression.

This thesis may also help to account for why one entering consciously into the logic of transformation at any one of the five major turning points of the logic tends to move backward and/or forward until the whole pattern is completed. The patterned process as a whole, laid down as such in the developing personality, continues to reassert itself as it has been learned and many times reinforced.

Of course, the point here is not reductionistic. It is not the point to reduce every transformation to the dynamics of growth, but stage transition dynamics are a powerful and pervasive force throughout life. Their influence—unlike, say, that of the birth experience—is not merely confined to one period of the life span but applies with accumulating power to all periods. Hence its transposition into cultural forms, even into the Holy Spirit's action in history, is all the more compelling for us. However, to keep the orders of knowing and being distinct, it is clear that the ultimate significance of transformation is not given with its roots in development but in its expression as Spiritus Creator, by which all proximate transformations are finally transformed.

TRANSFORMATION BEYOND STAGES

It is generally assumed that the transformational process is in the service of and dependent on the stages of development. This is surely true where ego development and inherited structural potentials are concerned, but it is not fundamentally true. The transformational process is more fundamental in that it may (1) transcend the stages, reversing arrested development and reinstating repressed structures; also (2) it may leap ahead by passing stages and establish an imaginative basis for development that incorporates but is not restricted to the so-called normal sequence. In effect, I am suggesting a figure-ground reversal with respect to stages and process. Whereas most studies of development are concerned to map the stages and leave process to itself, this discussion is concerned primarily with the integrity of the process. I want to let the stages emerge in the context of a primary concern for process, first, because we actually spend more of our lives in transition than we do in equilibrium, and second, because stages, as we will see, must finally become a self-liquidating notion if the transformation of human life is to be consummated in Christ.

In the first place, the transcendence of transformation over the usual stage sequence order can first be exemplified by "Little Hans," Freud's classic case for demonstrating childhood sexuality.[7] However, instead of showing evidence of childhood sexuality, a matter surprising only to a Victorian mentality, this case dramatically shows how the dynamics of transformation are capable of reconstituting arrested development. I have already shown this in the earlier case of Christina, but that was an unpublished case. Dealing with Freud's classic case puts the claim in more public terms. A reinterpretation of this case actually shows both the transcendence of the process over the stages and at the same time confirms the claim of my previous thesis that stage transitions are conformable to transformational logic.

The salient features of the case are that a three-year-old boy, Hans, was caught masturbating and was threatened with castration by his mother. He was told that a certain doctor would do it, and it happened that little Hans' father was also a doctor. During the period when Hans was age three to five, the mother gave birth to a daughter, and Hans developed overwhelming phobic reactions. The father began to write to Freud for advice, and eventually, with the help of advice through the mail from Freud, was able to help Hans formulate his problem in terms reminiscent of the Oedipus drama. When the problem was adequately formulated, Hans had two fantasies, one in which he was visited by a plumber and supplied with male sexual equipment as great or greater than his father's, and second in which he was married to his mother and they had children while the father was, at the same time, married to his own mother, Hans' grandmother. After these fantasies appeared, little Hans announced that his "nonsense" was gone.

What Freud saw in this case was the foundations of childhood sexuality and the Oedipal situation in particular. What I propose through a reinterpretation of the case is that Hans' story is as much a contribution to the dynamics of healing and development as it is evidence that children have sexual feelings and Oedipal struggles.

The essence of the healing process operative in this case can be described as resolution to an arrested state of development. In the normal course of things, Hans would have come to surrender his sexual longings for his mother, repress them through an identification with the father, and enter into a period of latency. The Oedipal

---

7. See "Analysis of a Phobia in a Five Year Old Boy," in S. Freud's *The Sexual Enlightenment of Children*, ed. Philip Rieff, trans. J. Riviere (New York: Collier, 1963).

struggle, however, generally reappears in middle adolescence. Until that time the repressed Oedipal resolution of childhood has been gathering force in the unconscious and erupts with the added energy of "the return of the repressed." If the early resolution has been relatively uncomplicated, the adolescent can yield to the incest taboo and redirect his (the male is the paradigm in this scheme) sexual desires toward members of the opposite sex outside his original family. In Hans' case, the trauma inflicted by the mother's threat could have disrupted subsequent development, but through the therapeutic process the little boy was led into a reworking of the developmental struggle, and his psyche produced a remarkable resolution.

We have further evidence that it worked from the fact that when Hans grew up and reached the age of nineteen, he met and spoke with Freud in person for the first time. Freud's follow-up indicated that Hans, a normal young man, remembered almost nothing of the sequence surrounding his development from age three to five. That one should not recall the early Oedipal struggle and its resolution is as it should be. Thus, we can conclude that the therapy effectively reconstructed the developmental process as suggested earlier.

If now we look at the dynamics of that therapeutic process it is evident that the critical turning points of the process and, by implication, of the developmental process, followed the logic of transformation. Summarily, the conflict was first felt but not articulated or "owned" by Hans until the conversations between the boy, his father, and Dr. Freud (by letter) began. The first critical turning point occurred when, after the rapport between the father and his son had been built up, the conflict could be articulated by the father (under Freud's instruction) to the boy, and Hans could readily accept it as an adequate expression of his feeling. The conflict as articulated was not pressed or confronted, merely borne. Second, an interlude followed during which time Hans slept—and presumably scanning and dreaming did their work. Third, on the following day he was visited by two remarkable fantasies that embodied resolutions to the specific conflicts of the situation and to the Oedipal conflict generally. That is, in the first fantasy, threatened with the loss of his penis, the plumber supplied him with an extra large one. In the second fantasy, threatened by the overpowering father and loss of his love, Hans replaced him and identified with him; threatened implicitly by retaliation from the father, Hans' second fantasy married off his father to the grandmother in a double Oedipal triumph; threatened with the loss of the mother's love and her making him impotent, he now possessed her in marriage and they have children; threatened at first by the rival sibling, Hans now was the proud producer of children, so new arrivals complemented rather than threatened him. The power of imagery to work out resolutions to opposites in conflict was here functioning with dramatic effectiveness. However, the net result of these resolutions is that a positive identification with the father was effected and apparently the positive affection for the mother was restored, although the sexual aspect was repressed and successfully redirected. Fourth, after having the fantasies and playing them out, Hans announced, "My nonsense is gone." This expressed the release of tension generated first by the situational conflicts but present at a deeper level due to Hans' failure to come to a satisfactory solution to the Oedipal stage of development. Fifth, the continuity between fantasy and conflict was interpreted to him at the time, and the resolution was verified by a relatively normal subsequent development, indicating that Hans was not bound in any maladaptive way to his developmental past.

First, here is evidence for the claim that therapy is redevelopment with transformational logic governing the connection between the two. Second, the fantasies, however bizarre or removed from the realm of actuality they seemed, were effective in restoring actual ego functioning at the appropriate level of development. Here the reader should keep in mind the distinction between self and ego as described in Chapter 3. The significance of Hans' fantasies is very far-reaching, but notice that in this case the distinction between bizarre images that erupted as symptoms (phobic fantasies) and those which worked a resolution lies in the difference between their respective structural compositions. Not only did the healing fantasies resolve surface conflicts, but they also brought forward the basic structure of the Oedipus complex, treating it as resolved. Because some positive resolution to the Oedipal structure is a necessary step in the development of the ego, it must be concluded that the dynamics of transformation have the power to call forth and reconstruct latent or arrested ego structures—even if that be done through bizarre phenomenon. Third, this process is a far better psychic analogue for the interpretation of religious experience than obsessional neurosis—the analogue Freud preferred. This is not to say that some religious experience does not follow the neurotic pattern. Surely Freud has been immensely helpful in analyzing and interpreting religious pathology. The problem is that Freud only understood sick religion, and even then he only understood the sick part of it. He did not recognize in the dynamics of this case and in the healing process generally (for example, the same sequence could be demonstrated for the working through of a trans-ference) a more appropriate psychic analogue for the dynamics of positive religious experience.

The basic assertion I am making is that the dynamics of this process, in some distinctive ways, are in control of the stage structures of the ego. The interplay between structures and process is here being given a reversal of the usual emphasis. Namely, instead of conceiving of stage structure as the basic controlling factor and this process as simply subsisting in the developmental matrix serving a fixed sched-ule of structural emergence, this case argues that the process can be exercised in a variety of ways to call forth structural resources from the substrata of the psyche in order to meet a great variety of conflictual situations, whether governed by or embedded in the developmental sequence or not.

Restoration of an arrested state of development is only one of the possible variations in this structure-process relationship. As indi-cated, redevelopment would most likely be performed in the context of therapy and deal with the personal unconscious. However, at a deeper psychic level, the process may cover a wider scope and involve much more of the life span.

In the second place, having described how the transformational process may transcend and correct arrested development, I now turn to the larger claim that it may leap over stages of development and incorporate them in an order of its own. By way of making this point, I will look in summary fashion at two figures, Carl Jung and Martin Luther. Of course we cannot do justice to these personalities except to show how transformation is related to ordinary development in each.

Carl Jung, the one-time crown prince of Freud's psychoanalytic circle, broke away during his middle years and eventually established his own school of analytic psychology. Jung's break with Freud's antispiritual pansexualism led him into a deep search for his own personal myth and its basic structures. His mistrust of rationalistic theory vis-á-vis the palpable depths of the psyche and his recognition of the gripping numinous quality of inner experience are at the very foundation of his life and work. Accordingly, he first applied all his psychological findings and theories, derived from empirical studies or his work with patients, to himself, and only later did he make them a part of the analytical method. In effect, he had first to discover in himself what his theory later explained.

It was through this in-depth search of himself and his patients that he discovered the "collective unconscious," its archetypes with their cross-cultural religious significance, and the transformational process that transcended the life span. The aim of this overall process was "individuation," or the fully integrated personality. As one might surmise from Jung's method and experience, "individuation" is not possible prior to one's middle years. One must have experienced a good deal of life, be over thirty, and be already well educated before entering the Jung Institute in Zurich. Individuation is an integration of the total personality based on the mediation of an archetypal form called the self and made manifest to conscious awareness in powerful images linking opposites (male-female, God-man, good-evil, and so on) in a dialectical unity. The self, the God image, and the mandala (a Sanskrit word for "circle"; here it means a mystical circle, usually divided into basically four quadrants, expressing the totality of the individual) are all interchangeable, although the basic structure always unites opposites around a center, mandala fashion. A rudimentary outline of the psychic structure might be drawn as follows:

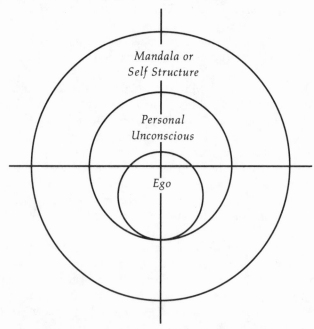

For Jung, "Christ" is an image of the self, as in the eleventh-century relief shown on the following page. Christ, seated at the center, unites by his nature the four equal extremities of a cross designed as a structure of wholeness underlying the four gospels. Conscious ego and personal unconscious are combined and transcended by this

"Christ Surrounded by the Evangelists." Eleventh-century relief in church at Arles-sur-Tech, Pyrénées-orientales (photograph: Archives photographiques, Paris). Plate LX from C. G. Jung, *Symbols of Transformation,* trans. R. F. C. Hull, 2nd ed., vol. 5 of *The Collected Works* (Princeton, N.J.: Princeton University Press, Bollingen Series XX, 1967).

archetypal pattern for which the glorified Christ serves as the definitive symbol.

For our purposes, it is important to note that the God image for
Jung is the mediator of a transformation that stretches across the life
span and beyond. Because a mandala-structured God image arises
from psychic depths beyond the personal unconscious and is sustained in the psyche as a governor and monitor of the relationship
between the conscious and the personal unconscious, it mediates a
transformation that moves the conscious ego out of the center of the
personality and replaces it with itself. Thus one might say Christ was
the center of the personality, meaning that Christ symbolized the
centered structure by which the personality was individuated. This
declares that another order deeper than the ego has made the ego a
peripheral although necessary aspect of the person. If the ego is
relativized, then so are all the developmental studies that concentrate
on the stages of the ego's development. Transformational logic here
has stepped completely outside the stages, and, employing a transcendental (that is, psychoid, not divine or revealed) mediator, it has
recentered the personality in a way that Jung would describe as
"spiritual." In fact, "individuation" for him is inextricably a religious
process; all therapy for people after reaching their middle years
requires a religious dimension. Overall, the transformation reaches
back into infancy and before (if the archetypes are indeed inherited as
a collective unconscious), and it reaches forward into a continuing life
with "God," all the while remaining centered in the self.

Jung's works are a feast of symbolic riches and a theoretical hall of
mirrors, yet for our purposes two crucial matters stand out. One, the
transformational process as described may be transposed to a transcendental realm and reach over the entire life span. Although related
to developmental stages through the conscious ego, transformation
depends on them only in a secondary way; that is, they increase the
ego's capacity to cope with its everyday environment and so establish
a differentiated counterpoint to the claims of the God image at the
center of the personality. Beyond that, they are not significant in
establishing and maintaining the centered wholeness of the person.
Two, such a recentering and overarching transformation requires at
least a transcendental mediator, for which Christ may at most by the
symbol. By this Jung meant that Jesus Christ had himself undertaken
the way of "individuation" and so established the goal of self-
realization. Thus is might be said that accepting self as Christ will
necessarily individuate the personality.

As with our discussion of Zen, we must pay close critical attention to the nature of the mediator because it has definitive significance for the quality of life and being into which one is transformed. Jung was particularly critical of views of the mediator other than his own; he found those who made the ego the center of the personality to be heading for egomania, of which Adolf Hitler was a supreme example. By implication, of course, Freudian psychology was wrong along the same imperialistic lines. Jung was a man of many visions, a kind of seer, and he claimed to have seen a vision of his wife after her death as a perfectly individuated person, perfectly balanced between opposites. There is something as impersonal and static about his description of her integration as there is about a structured circle falling into quadrants around its center. She had become mandalalike.[8]

Individuation after the pattern of mandala as self and as God leads to other possible distortions. Jung was once told in a vision that a figure named Salome was worshipping him, as she said, "Because you are Christ." Jung rejected the notion but this suggests the basic problem that his understanding of transformation in relation to Christ is not sufficient, because it implicitly confuses the order of being and knowing. Thus, in Jung's position the symbol "Jesus Christ" is one way of knowing one's self, but Christ's self-understanding makes Christ the revelation of being-itself. There is nothing in Jung that finally answers the question of ultimate truth, hence there is nothing in his understanding of Christ to prevent Jung from assuming that he, his self, is the answer. Here it is all important that the truth not get confused with a structure for knowing it. If one is to understand Christ at all, Jung's order of being and knowing must be reversed.

Reversing Jung's priorities and asserting the ultimacy of Christ with respect to the archetypes of the self is not just theological dialectics. It is a crucial matter whether one coming under the power of an ego-transforming process will be able to continue that process in love for Christ's World or will be arrested in an archetypal structure of personal wholeness. That is, if Christ is a symbol of the self, then self structures will define Christ (Jung), but if the self is a symbol of Christ, then Christ will define the nature of the self. If the latter

---

8. Jung's vision of wholeness here is not uniformly represented throughout his works, but in this vision of his wife he is claiming the clearest comprehension of wholeness that could be grasped. In another vision, he saw her continuing her work on *The Holy Grail* (a work she had not finished) after death. My point has not so much to do with Jung's wife as with his view of optimal human wholeness—see C. G. Jung, *Memories, Dreams and Reflections* (New York: Vintage Books, 1961), p. 296.

pertains, it will be marked not by anything resembling a static balance, but by sacrificial love, the form that transformation takes in Christ.

To arrest transformation, making the balanced self its goal, is to abort the process in a kind of gnostic salvation that tends to create a cultic group of elite people possessed of this particular sort of wholeness. Nevertheless, transformation as Jung envisioned it is a dramatic example of a transcendental version of transformational logic. It makes the point in purely human terms that the development of the ego may be relativized and recentered around a deeper psychic order. However, it does not meet the issue of Christ as Mediator in his terms. Otherwise it would have to take seriously his initative, his revealed mediation, and his destiny, not only for the individual but for his World, the Kingdom of God.

Martin Luther, whose view of Spiritus Creator I have already linked closely with transformational logic on the transcendent level of God's action in history (Chapter 4), is himself a personal instance of transformation exceeding the boundaries of so-called normal ego development. It should be a matter of record from the beginning that in Erik Erikson's interpretation of Luther, according to his own (Erikson's) scheme of normal ego development, he found that Luther moved off the "normal" scale. This was because, as Erikson said, he was a "homo religiosus." That is to say, his very nature was constructed around instrinsically and inextricably religious matters. His personal identity as a member of his society was taken over and shaped by the question of his existential identity as a human being before God. In general, this also means that the final stage in the ordinary course of development, namely confronting one's own death and the ultimate meaning of life in light of that death, is inextricably tied to the ongoing sense of void at every stage in one's life. Thus, the final crisis in normal people is the lifelong crisis for the religious personality, and the scale of normal development cannot contain, much less explain, a person who brings his or her solution to life's final stage into every intervening stage. In effect, this is to reverse development from a standpoint implicitly outside it.

Because Luther did not fit Erikson's normality scale, Erikson interpreted his behavior in a generous and sensitive fashion but as a special sort of psychopathology. The implicit imperialism of the stages is manifest here, and so I must briefly describe Luther's transformation on somewhat different grounds.

There can be little doubt that the lightning bolt that nearly killed young Martin Luther in 1505 and changed his career from law to the monastic life simultaneously released in him a powerful reservoir of repressed frustration, anger, and guilt. All through his monastic career, he was plagued by doubts, demons, and scruples—not merely moralistic matters of lust and pride, but existential matters as to who he was in relation to the one whom he feared God to be. The magnitude of his struggle is surely linked psychologically to the frustrations of his childhood. He had a highly verbal and intimate relationship with his mother. His apparent closeness to her was part of the frustration he felt toward his father, who rather brutally took him out of her kitchen and made him work and go to school as an extension of his own ambition. He obeyed his father, but it must be assumed that under the surface he despised his own submission and longed for a restoration of that apparently warm, nurturing relationship with his mother, who awakened in him both his sensuality and his angry rivalry with his father. The relationship to the father was profoundly ambivalent, however, because he clearly wanted his love and approval all the time he fought inwardly against him.

The relationship to his mother, which was more supportive and less fraught with ambition, was nevertheless also laden with ambivalences. Apparently she could be outraged, as when she beat him until he bled for stealing a nut. Also, because she had lost many children, she apparently felt possessive of Martin and resisted, even disavowed him, when he went into the monastery.

All these ambivalences and much more, repressed and expressed, were powerful forces released by the thunder bolt on the road that led to Erfurt. Yet the psychological history—the study of origins in personal prototypes—is not sufficient to account for the depth and persistence of his confrontation with nothingness at the hands of a God who would surely be justified in damning him, given, as he saw it, the guilty and distraught condition of his soul.

Luther was traumatized when he performed his first mass. Contrary to the psychoanalytic view, I want to suggest this was not merely because he had a father complex and the Almighty Father was about to minister grace through his hands, but because he had an intense sense of the Holy. The elements of the Eucharist were powerful instruments of the Almighty God, and there was no escaping his judgment as implicit in the Eucharist celebration. The Eucharist was traumatic for Luther because it was an awesome undertaking, and it was awesome first and primarily because of the nature of the Holy. Indeed, Luther may have been closer in his trauma to the reality of God's Holy Presence than the monks around him who found the mass to be a more familiar ritual. The dynamics of ambivalence toward his own father are involved in but they are not the cause of his awe; that ambivalence simply prevented him from having the usual sort of defenses against the sense of the Holy that a more "normal" development might have imposed.

This is not to say that Luther should not have struggled to find out who he was in relation to the awesome Father God, nor that he should not have come to some resolution of his disabling sense of being nothing in the presence of God who is all in all. It is to say he had the absolutely correct conflict, and it is well for the history of Western Christianity that a traditional Freudian psychoanalyst was not there to reduce that four-dimensional conflict to a two-dimensional question of how to deal with his ambivalences toward his father and mother and get back into law school. The ruptures in the family context, the "world" in which he was raised, gave rise to the crucial questions of human existence such that Luther's conflict went far beyond a matter of adaptation; it was for him a matter of "All or Nothing," as it always is when faith takes on a four-dimensional aspect.

Given these dimensions of his conflict, his resolution had to be equally titanic. As he saw it, he had to see God "face to face." The answer came when he saw that Christ was "the face of God." In his famous "tower experience" in 1512, he was "meditating on those words, 'the just lives by faith' [and] 'justice of God,'" and a figure-ground reversal occurred for him with sufficient power to eventually launch ninety-five theses and the German Reformation. It was then that he saw with great relief that the just God does not condemn but that "the just God justifies." The power of experience lies in the fact that at last Luther was taken into the presence of the Almighty God as one justified by Christ. As one justified, he could now see that God's face was open toward him; that is, Christ present in the Eucharist, in the Word of scripture, and in the church, graciously addressed him. The magnitude of Luther's vehemence in proclaiming the Gospel to a decadent religious world must be seen as the power of the reversal in his own immanent sense of damnation at the hands of a just and holy God. That is, all the awe and trauma he felt toward the awesome Almighty God, which threw him into the despair of nothingness, became, in its reversal, the power of God's Spirit in him and going before him as one "fired on the world with a velocity not his own!"

Writing later to Melanchthon, Luther said that theologians are made not by studying books but by "living, dying and being damned." The point was not that all theologians are in hell but, rather, that only when there is sufficient descent into a four-dimensional "inner conflict" can there be a proper sense of the transforming power of Spiritus Creator. Only then can grace set one into the new reality of the Gospel of Christ, who is "the Face of the Father."

As I said, this does not constitute "normal" development, and when a psychoanalyst looks at it he or she must argue that the developmental prototypes are definitive, that Luther splits his ambivalence toward the father: he submitted to the loving father to whom he is reconciled by his identifying with Christ, but he projects the negative side of the father into "the devil" and "the papacy." The "father of lies" and the papal imposter were one and the same. This allows him both to feel justified and to get revenge. The mother is restored to Martin through his relationship to the Bible. He was *"matrice scripturae nati,"* reborn out of the matrix *(mater)* of scripture and found there the generous flowing, verbal relationship with the scriptural "mother" that he had long desired since the earliest intrusions of his father. Psychoanalytically the overall process is one that hinges on Luther's identification with Christ, and thus he recovers from his early developmental aberrations like one emerging from a psychotic episode.

Departing from the scale of normal ego development inevitably means that new meanings must be constructed because there are no prefabricated ego structures to draw up and use as ready-made solutions for such a departure. Consequently, crucial experiences with the key people in one's life must be brought into play as prototypical grist for the mills of the imagination, but it does not follow, as I said earlier, that these prototypes serve to *explain* anything in the context of the truly creative act of human transformation. In particular they cannot explain the creative, imaginative construction of meaning that Luther generated to meet the agonizing four-dimensional struggles he persistently dared to engage. On the contrary, prototypes are remarkably weak when one considers, as I suggested in relation to Luther's first mass, that they were not the sole or even central cause of his agony. The Holy was a real fourth dimension for Luther, a genuine irreducible disclosure of God.

Moreover, early family prototypes tend to lead the psychoanalytic interpretation into distortions of the ultimate meanings that Luther formulated. The position based on prototypes must assume that there is an identification of the good son, Martin, with Christ who is the good Son of the Heavenly Father. This was the very opposite of Luther's own Christology in which Christ, he insisted, was always an "alien righteousness." By this he clearly meant ego alien, not ego identified. Here the explanation by prototype actually fails to account for the genuine creative nature of the new resolution because it cannot accept the one unique cause of Luther's behavior: namely, Christ, who becomes the ground of the self without absorbing the self, the living center of the personality displacing but not destroying ego identity.

Luther's condition is actually closer to what Jung described as transformed ego than to Erikson's interpretation. However, the impersonal Jungian mandala has been transfigured by the living Presence of Christ (in the Eucharist, in the scripture, and in the church by the power of Spiritus Creator). The crucial factor for our study is that in this condition Luther saw himself in terms of extreme, opposing totalities held together in dialectical unities; he was totally sinful and totally justified, both damned and blessed, both slave and free, both dead and alive. This suggests that the Spirit of Christ has transfigured and employed the mandala structure of self-knowledge to recenter all aspects of Luther's being on Christ himself.

Moreover, this dialectical unity of extreme opposites kept always before Luther, even in his early thirties, the final developmental issue: how "to affirm life itself in the face of death itself" (Erikson).[9] It is because of the ego-alien Presence of Christ that the final crisis of ego development is ever present (as one "dying daily"). In the hands of this Presence, Luther—like other people who are "homo religiosus"—leaped over the whole of his mature years from his prolonged adolescent struggle regarding *who* he was to the final struggle of *why* he was. With respect to ego development, Luther's transformation is as radical as anything Jung describes, but it is far more radical with respect to the nature and role of Christ.

Before turning to a more integrative statement of Jung's relation to Luther, I must note that explanations on the basis of personal prototypes also fail to account for the sweep of transformation that occurs in young Luther's life by the power of "Spiritus Creator." As mentioned, the standard psychoanalytic account must claim that Luther's

---

9. E. Erikson, *Young Man Luther* (New York: Norton, 1962).

transformation is recovering from a psychoticlike episode because its only frame of reference is the normalcy of stage sequence. Deviation is *ipso facto* pathological. However, if it is recognized that the logic of transformation establishes the norm, then it is possible to take Luther's self-understanding and his theology as seriously as the psychoanalyst takes stage sequence in human development. By that norm we can listen with understanding while Luther ascribes his transformation to the Holy Spirit: doing as he has always done, the Spirit enters into the nothingness of "inner conflict" and makes something new out of nothing, as in the original creation of all things and in the resurrection of Christ from the dead. Spiritus Creator acts from outside the stage sequence frame of human development, yet, as described in Chapter 4, that action follows the pattern of transformational logic that is so deeply ingrained in the dynamics of human development. Thus, what appears as psychopathology to the analyst is in a transformational perspective neither disordered nor degenerate; rather, it is a higher order and a regeneration.

Both Jung and Luther are figures whose lives and self-understanding transcend the "normal" sequence of development. This itself is not what is unique about them; this I count as a common phenomenon. Rather, their uniqueness lies in their genius for describing and interpreting from different perspectives the phenomenon and implications of ego transformation. Hence in different ways they disclose an order of the human personality that runs deeper than the study of ego development and is far more significant for convictional experience. Combining their perspectives will conclude my thesis on transformation beyond the stages.

Although Jung tended to confuse the order of knowing with the order of being, the inherited structures of the psyche with the revelation of God's nature, he nevertheless does show how the internal structure of the personality may undergo a radical recentering. By showing that the key to this recentering was a master image structured so as to combine opposites of existential proportions, he described what also became the self-understanding of Luther as he underwent transformation. Are they then talking about the same thing?

I think not; the apparent convergence between Jung and Luther suggests a structural analogy. That is, it is possible to see in both that the personality is recentered and dialectical opposites are held together at and by the new center. It detracts nothing from the transcendence of Christ to agree that such a structure resides in the psyche as an innate potential (Jung), nor does it diminish Christ to claim that he regularly makes himself known in the transformed personality; that is, not through the ego but by recentering the ego around himself. That recentering gives us the familiar "I—not I, but God" pattern of prophetic, messianic, and apostolic utterance.[10] It might be more difficult to say Christ *must* use this structure, but that he reguarly *does* use it seems unproblematic. It is of special importance to the understanding of convictional experiences that there be such a structure characteristically employed in the transformation of the personality. As such, it is analogous to the Oedipal structure that made possible the healing fantasies of Little Hans, making them not imaginary but imaginative. As such, decentering the ego and recentering the personality around a new center capable of integrating all the powers and extremities unleashed by dethroning the ego provides a formal statement of the properties for any image that might claim convictional significance for the personality. So much for convergence.

The point of divergence between Luther and Jung is on the question of priority and the distinction between being and knowing. For Luther, the formal structural pattern of extreme opposites held together in a dialectical unity is of minimal importance with respect to *who* gives that structure its identity. That identifying Person must be Christ and in him all opposites are united, but the unity of opposites in him is incidental to his living Presence as the Word of God. Through the Holy Spirit, that structural pattern may be the internal or psychic order we attribute to his Presence; that is, it may indeed structure our knowledge of him, but it does not confine or delimit his being. To put Jung in Lutheran terms (terms he might, incidentally, have obtained from his father, who was a Swiss Reformed pastor), the recentering of the personality by the Presence of Christ makes the centered self a symbol and sign of the transcendent being of Christ.

By putting it this way, I am suggesting that those psychic structures or structures of knowing that unite extreme opposites are fundamental to the imaginative vision of Jesus Christ. He himself unites God and humanity, the universal and particular, life of life and death of death, the depths of hell with the heights of heaven, sin and holiness, human wretchedness and divine glory, the beginning and

---

10. The full implications of this statement may be found in A. McElway and D. Willis, *The Context of Contemporary Theology* (Atlanta: Knox, 1974), pp. 194-205.

the end—the list could be continued. However, Christ's being far exceeds any analysis of opposites because no mere consequence of analysis is able to make the Christian difference; it is Presence, personal and transfiguring the dark face of sheer balance into the "light of his countenance," that makes the difference. The Eucharist as a union of opposites is intellectually interesting but it only has transforming power as the personal Presence of Christ, the very face of God.

However, putting it this way also implies a great deal more because if Christ identifies and transfigures the self structure then Christ is not merely the resolution to existential dichotomies but the One who initiates the in-depth struggle with those dichotomies, the One who provokes by the light of his Presence the blindness of despair over oneself before God. By his initiation, he defines the struggle for which he is the mediating Presence, and we know him by an imaginative leap. Responding to a sense of his Presence, we know intuitively, if not immediately in an image, as if lightning had flashed across the sky and illuminated his face, that this Presence unites all things without confusing or dissolving anything. As he initiates and mediates so he will bring to complete and final conclusion all things in himself; so mediation is not merely the way by which a human being is transformed but a disclosure to any who can "see" of all that is to come.

TRANSFORMATION AND CHRIST EVENT

I have spoken of personal prototypes and archetypes; now I must speak of transformation in relation to a particular sort of historical type, "the Christ event."[11]

In Chapter 2, I spoke of "event" as the way one experiences the logic of transformation. When we perceive God in Christ, undergoing in himself the logic of transformation in history, then we are perceiving what I mean by the "Christ event." During his earthly ministry, there were many transformations that Jesus Christ performed in individual lives, and there is an overall, historical movement of transformation (including his earthly ministry as its central turning point) that climaxes in the eschatological future that the Eucharist

---

11. I am aware of the continuing theological discussion of what this phrase means. However, I am confining my remarks to the way in which "event" as previously defined (Chapter 2) may have informed the early church.

promises. None of these is what I mean by the "Christ event" as a historical type; rather it is the way in which God himself appeared in history through the understanding of the early church. He does not appear as a merely momentary or episodic vision of light, nor does he take over political leadership and construct a utopian social system. He appears to the early church as one who by his own initiative enters into all "worlds" (incarnation): by the proclamation of his World, he exposes the deepest possible conflict (sin) and then takes it into himself (crucifixion). In an interlude, he enters into the condemned and buried past of world history (the descent into hell) with the intention to draw all things together beneath the earth, on the earth, and above the earth. Then he emerges as the bearer of a radically new being, or new being breaks in on the earth through him (resurrection): The inherent continuity of God's action in Jesus Christ is exultantly affirmed (glorification), and it corresponds with public life in history to the great gain of all who can "see" that continuity (pentecostal creation of the church).

Many scriptural passages support and highlight the parts of this event, but the most comprehensive and succinct account of the whole logic of transformation as it structures the Christ event is in Phil. 2:5-11. This passage, called the "Carmen Christi" (the song of Christ) because St. Paul based this part of his letter to the Philippians on a song they sang, follows the essential turning points of the logic of transformation. His claim for the Philippians was that they already had in them and sang about the essential pattern that was Christ's way; they only needed to "let it be." In the context of his concern for humility, his plea to them was that they let Christ's way become the way that defined them. "Let transformation after this pattern unfold in you," might be a paraphrase of his plea that the Philippians have the mind of Christ.

Although a discussion such as this could be greatly extended, I must let it rest here. What I have just described is a structural statement of a historical event. Structure and sequence are combined just as they are in grammatical speech; neither the sequential flow of speech nor the structure that patterns it are dismissable if there is to be language. Similarly, the Word of God is spoken in history via the Christ event, in which structure and sequence are combined. This is not the only way in which the Word is spoken, but it is one way that is extremely important for connecting contemporary experiences of human transformation to Christian history. Examples of this are, in some respects, evident in Luther's case and in subsequent cases I will describe, but one well-known case is especially worth discussing here.

C. S. Lewis' biographers have provided a clear-cut connection between his conversion and the Christ event.[12] I will take his case as exemplary of the general thesis that the Christ event calls forth and gives historical concreteness to the transformational potential of the personality. To put it succinctly, the Christ event is the historical paradigm of transformation.

In order to use Lewis' biography to explicate this thesis, some brief background information will be necessary. As most religious readers know, Lewis was an Oxford don who converted from atheism to theism and eventually to Christianity. The nature of his conversion is especially interesting, because he went from sensing "the steady unrelenting approach of Him whom I so earnestly desired not to meet" into a reluctant submission to the divine mercy and humility that accepted him, even though he was "the most reluctant convert in all England." Thus, he was first overtaken by the actual Presence of God; only subsequently did he name or "see" the connection between that God and Christ—or Christianity.

For understanding the deeply personal nature of Lewis' conversion, note that he was raised in a happy, nominally Christian home. However, when he was almost ten, his mother died, and at that point "Atlantis sank" into the sea. There were, as he said, "islands of satisfaction" after that, but he was personally and emotionally cut adrift from the center of intimacy and his deepest source of security. His brother was closer to his father than he, and he felt increasingly estranged from his father as he matured. He continued a very close relationship with his brother, but he was now, in effect, on the periphery outside the family nucleus of brother and father. It is impossible to exclude Lewis' Christian background, his deep losses, and his consequent unresolved encounters with personal emptiness as prototypical factors in his subsequent struggle with atheism. In his conversion, Lewis found that the depths of his negation of God, no doubt quickened and deepened by the loss of his mother, were at first gradually and then suddenly reversed. He found in the Presence of God the undoing of his negations not only of God but of other negations as well. Affirmation of God yielded new affirmations of self, love relationships, and eventually, with the help of proper circumstances, even heartfelt affirmations of his father. In some sense, Atlantis was restored, but, transfigured by joy, it looked more like new Jerusalem.

---

12. R. L. Green and W. Hooper, *C. S. Lewis, A Biography* (New York: Harcourt Brace Jovanovich, 1974).

The point here is not reductionistic but transformational. Here we have a personal prototype (the mother) who provides the terms and the occasion for Lewis' confronting the deepest human dichotomy of all, life against death. Death and exclusion intruded and anchored subsequent absences, emptiness, oppression, and atheism in his personal history. Of course, there was more to his atheism than this, but ultimate negation found an experiential root at this point. I will say a good deal more about negation and its transformation in the following chapter.

Here I want to point out that the childhood crisis that first set Lewis' life in the overarching shadow of death was exactly reversed by his conversion such that death was now set in the overpowering light of the Divine Presence. Such a sharp reversal as Lewis experienced—as is characteristic of Paul, Augustine, Luther, and Kierkegaard—tends thereafter to shape one's perspective on the very nature of being-itself and how one best understands it.

One needs to make only a cursory review of some of Lewis' literature to see how many of his basic insights depend on a striking figure-ground reversal. It is evident in his science fiction when outer space becomes the stronghold of grace against the hideous evils that prevail on earth, "the silent planet." Thus he reverses our usual, fearful assumption of an invasion from Mars and hideous creatures taking over the benign earth. Again, *The Screwtape Letters* are so striking not merely because the position of evil is both so accurately and surprisingly depicted, but because it is portrayed as implicitly, and therefore humorously, as the perverse reverse of grace. Reversal of figure and ground is also a key to his understanding of miracles and the resurrection of the body, but perhaps the most explicit articulation of this approach to interpreting the relationship between God and humanity is in his sermon "Transposition." Here he discusses the movement from lower to higher and conversely higher to lower orders of being. In contrasting human development to transposition (suggesting much the same thing as I have described in the notion of a divine transformation of human transformations), he writes,

> I am not saying that the natural act of eating after millions of years
> somehow blossoms into the Christian sacrament. I am saying the
> Spiritual reality that existed before there were any creatures who ate,
> gives this natural act a new meaning, and more than a new meaning:
> makes it in a certain context to be a different thing. In a word, I think

that real landscapes enter into pictures, not that pictures will one day
sprout out into real trees and grass.[13]

The normal order of development is reversed as grace intrudes on
given conditions to make them what they could never, otherwise,
become. This I suggest is a mind set that has special strength for
Lewis because of his own experiences of conversion and the undoing of
what seemed to be irreversible losses. But more than than, it was
precisely this mind set that put him in a position to respond to the
Christ event.

To his lifelong friend and correspondent, Arthur Greeves, Lewis
wrote of the second phase in his conversion to Christianity as follows:

> I have just passed on from believing in God to definitely believing in
> Christ—in Christianity. . . .
>
> What Dyson and Tolkien showed me was this: that if I met the idea
> of sacrifice in a pagan story I didn't mind it at all: again, if I met the
> idea of God sacrificing himself to himself . . . I liked it very much and
> was mysteriously moved by it: again, that the idea of the dying and
> reviving God (Balder, Adonis, Bacchus) similarly moved me provided I
> met it anywhere *except* in the Gospels. The reason was that in Pagan
> stories I was prepared to feel the myth as profound and suggestive of
> meanings beyond my grasp even tho' I could not say in cold prose "What
> it meant." Now the story of Christ is simply a true myth: a myth
> working on us in the same way as the others, but with this tremendous
> difference that *it really happened:* and one must be content to accept it
> in the same way, remembering that it is God's myth where the other are
> men's myths; i.e., the Pagan stories are God expressing Himself through
> the minds of poets, using such images as He found there while
> Christianity is God expressing Himself through what we call "real
> things." Therefore it is true, not in the sense of being a "description" of
> God (that no finite mind would take in) but in the sense of being the
> way in which God chooses to (or can) appear to our faculties.[14]

What this account explains so pointedly is that there is an innate
structure in human nature that responds to transformation wherever

13. C. S. Lewis, *Transposition and Other Addresses* (London: Bles, 1949). Also
published under the title *The Weight of Glory.*
14. Green and Hooper, pp. 116-118.

it appears, even in pagan mythical systems. One may be personally well prepared for an existential transformation by having suffered irreversible losses for which transformational narratives suggest an undoing. That is, if one's defenses against the deeper-than-ego structures of personality have been loosened, broken down, or opened up, then there may be a greater readiness to respond personally to transformational structure written out in historical terms by the action of God in Christ. The reasons for this will be discussed in the following chapter.

Lewis' spontaneous reaction to a variety of mythic transformations was to be "mysteriously moved." In effect, he took them into himself. What he finally "saw" was that they are proximate forms that themselves are in need of transformation following the same logic. Thus, in coming to Christian conviction he could perceive that in Christ, God performed on them the transformation that they performed humanly in mythical and poetic terms. Thereby transformation was transposed into an action of God "in history"; moreover, all history, including Lewis' own, became subject to redemption in light of the Christ event. By this perspective, he was able to see himself and those other proximate forms as inside and a replication of the transformation of all things. Thus, his own transformation became fully Christocentric and Eucharistic.

It is one thing to say that humanly the structure of transformation is an innate potential that needs to undergo transformation by the initiative and Presence of Christ; however, Lewis' emphasis on the concreteness of history is stronger than this. He is saying that "the actual incarnation, crucifixion, and resurrection" constitute the most adequate possible expression of God's Word to humankind. All of our efforts to restate the actuality behind scripture, doctrine, or any Christian literature are "less true" than the actuality itself. Yet as described by the early church, the Christ event resonates with the transformational potential in every personality and enables us to comprehend obscure historical actualities, contemporary personal transformations, and the overall transformation of history under his initiative.

Developmentally, what I have suggested is that Lewis was more able to respond convictionally to this resonance because of his personal history. However, as I have argued all along (and as his own view of transposition states it), the lower order—that is, the personality prototypes or even the archetype of rebirth—is not able to give human transformation its meaning, much less explain it. When

Atlantis was transformed, Lewis was not regressing to the lost mother; it was a transformation into the reality toward which all mothering—indeed, all parenting—points, and from which all parenting is derived: the God of the Christ event who, as the ultimate progenitor, "lets all beings be" through his transforming power.

CONCLUSIONS

From this study of transformation in human development, certain conclusions may be drawn that will help focus the approach to convictional experiences in the final chapter of this book.

First, note that there are several strata of the developing personality within which transformation unfolds. At the biological level, the transformational pattern is most clearly expressed in orthogenesis. As stage transition process, it is expressed both at the level of part processes (such as language and intelligence) and in ego development. Then, transposed to the level of intentional conscious behavior, it is expressed in the act of creation and in narrative forms. Transposed again, it is the internal pattern of the healing process in the context of redevelopment. As indicated earlier, it also transposes into development in interpersonal, social, and cultural contexts. Most significant for our concern here is the origin of all its transpositions in the pattern of God's action as Spiritus Creator. However, the Creator Spirit transforms all transformations in the course of effecting his purposes at all levels of human development.

Second, given the pervasiveness of transformation in human development and creativity, its reflection of the pattern of Spiritus Creator, and its transcendent relationship to every aspect of human experience, it is now clear why it may be called the guiding pattern of the human spirit (see p. 56, n. 13). As indicated earlier, it is this aspect of human being that is addressed analogically by the Holy Spirit, and it is this aspect that is transformed by the work of that Spirit.

Third, transformational logic as guiding pattern of the human spirit creates new meaning on the basis of prototypes, archetypes, and mythical types. The typological basis for transformation does not in itself explain or establish meaning, but it does anchor transformation in the elementary forms of human experience. The human construction of new meaning depends in part on continuity with previous personal experience and on what existential dichotomies are implicitly engaged, but it depends, finally, more on the integrity of the guiding pattern, its interweaving of continuity with discontinuity so as to generate something that is spiritually satisfying. That is, the creation of new meaning depends finally on satisfying the demand for transformational integrity and completeness.

Fourth, the stages of ego development that are generated by the dynamics of transformation may be thought of as both the fruit and grist of the human spirit. The transformational work of the human spirit both generates new stages and it transcends and reworks them for the sake of generating new "worlds." Under the transforming work of Spiritus Creator, the new "world" is his World, the Kingdom of God, which breaks in on development at all levels and stages with apocalyptic suddenness. No doubt one must be fixed at a certain stage to be preoccupied with stages at the expense of the spirit and the Spirit, but, on the other hand, no one will doubt that stages of development are part of the Spirit's work.

Fifth, the dialectical unity of existential opposites characterizes the structural impact of the Divine Presence of Christ, but the Divine Presence is far more than a "composito oppositorum"; as the face is beyond its flesh and bone, as the transfiguration is beyond the normal figure, so is his Presence beyond the oppositions united in him. It is a useful and interesting study to examine the rich plurality of oppositions that are united in the Eucharistic Presence of Christ, but it is a violation of the spirit and the Spirit to rest assured with the new balance. What Christ's Presence calls for is ongoing transformation through participation in his transformation of all things. This calls for "works of love," which begins to move us toward the next chapter.

Sixth, paradoxically one of the most significant contributions that the stages of development make to the transformational work of both the human spirit and the Holy Spirit is their repeated failure and consequent disequilibrium. For the earlier years of life, this generates new competence, but it also brings about an accumulated sense of void and inherent meaninglessness that climaxes usually in the middle years. This heightened sense of nothingness underlies development and finally exposes the ego as a truth-producing error. That is, the ego is exposed as unable and insufficient in the face of death to center the personality; the ego, in all its accumulated stages of competence, is eventually recognized as incapable of embracing its own negation. For the first half of life, the ego does in some sense center the personality, yet its very competence eventually makes for a keen awareness of its absolute limitations. Thus the ego stages are, in relation to the transformational character of the spirit and the Spirit, a self-liquidating notion that finally must give way to a deeper sense of psychic order and the transcendent Presence of the Holy One in the face of Christ. In order to explicate these last two assertions, I will turn to the final chapter of exposition and to a description of the aim of convictional knowing.

Six

FROM NEGATION
TO LOVE

➤ TRANSFORMATIONS CENTERED ON the convicting presence of Christ implicitly reach across the whole life span. Although conversions such as C. S. Lewis' or Luther's can be illumined by examining parent-child dynamics, the transformation actually goes deeper than family. Moreover, by conversion one is enabled to affirm life itself in the face of death itself through all intervening stages of development, but the transformation implicitly reaches beyond one's own death. How does this all-encompassing transformation occur, and why or to what end is it accomplished?

THE THEOLOGICAL DEFICIENCY OF NORMAL DEVELOPMENT

The hypothesis I will be developing is that the key to how and why convictional transformation must overleap the normal course of human development lies with the developmental history of negation. Putting it in broad outline, something is inherently wrong with so-called normal human development. Normal development is psychologically constructed, socially supported, and culturally maintained so that people are drawn out of the full four dimensions of their being. It is preeminently two-dimensional, aiming at the comparatively meagre values of survival and satisfaction as determined by socially accepted norms. Restricting the range of human being has severe consequences; most fundamentally, there is a death of conscience and a loss of ultimate concerns. When in the relativity and pluralism of personal and social life nothing deeper is known than the two dimensions of human existence, just the self and its "world," then conscience is no stronger than is necessary for successful adaptation, and ultimacy is irrelevant. Where definitive values and the concern for ultimacy disappear, people will deplete their own being and destroy each other, ironically, in the name of survival and satisfaction.

There is nothing new in this general claim and its predicted outcome. It seems to be an inevitable—although, I would claim, not necessary—human potential for individuals and groups to restrict themselves to patterns of life that eventually prove self-destructive. The compulsion to such restriction does not originate outside us but inside us; however, it accumulates power as we develop "normally," according to social standards, toward the ultimate restriction of death. This pervasive and powerful tendency is the opposite of transformation and is its enemy, but it can be ferreted out if we examine some of the labyrinthian turns in the developmental history of negation.

Four Negations

Recognizing that negation is an extremely elusive notion to pursue, I will begin with the premise that negation is always negation *of something*. Types of negation will be determined, then, by what is negated. In other words, negation will be given its experiential shape by that on which it works a limitation, refutation, contradiction, diminution, denial, perversion, or annihilation (to mention a few of the ways in which negation operates). Negation as fundamentally derivative and qualifying may be divided into four general types: *calculative, functional, existential,* and *transformational.* Although subtypes might be constructed, they would add unnecessary complexity to the basic distinctions made here.

Calculative negation articulates and preserves objectivity and refers primarily to the negation of subjective or egocentric distortions of presumably objective or universal truths. For example, when one prunes or purifies a concept, it must be stripped of any imagistic, emotional, or otherwise unexplained subjective aspects. As such, calculative negation is generally a cognitive and intellectual matter, applied as a principle in empirical, propositional, critical, and systematic contexts.

I have already said a good deal in Chapter 2 regarding the perils of "objectivity," particularly as it tends to be exercised absolutely in conventional science and technology. This is not to disregard the need to take an objective perspective on matters, qualifying one's own position by bringing it into "public" view, but to strive for calculative negation as an absolute aim in any area of life is an eikonic eclipse distorting the very truth that is supposedly preserved by being objective. Because I have already discussed this at some length, I will not pursue it further here.

Functional negation is negation in and of psychological functions, including both intrapsychic and interpersonal relationships. Repression is the most common form of intrapsychic functional negation. In interpersonal terms, Erikson's description of shame may be understood as the functional negation of autonomy within the second stage of ego maturation. Correlatively, autonomy may be seen as the functional negation of shame. I will say more about this in the next section. The possibilities here are, of course, diverse, but all functional negation is contained within the psychic or the interpersonal spheres of experience. Moreover, it has to do not with the content of experience but how content functions vis-à-vis the personality and its "world."

Existential negation refers to the negation of one's own being. An experience of nothingness as that which forcibly confronts one with one's own nonexistence is as close as one can come to existential negation. Existential negation may also be understood as the ultimate negation of the capacity of the ego to construct its world, sometimes called "ego shock." All negation in some measure points toward the void, but in existential negation the person is immersed in it.

The term *transformational negation* refers to the negation of negation such that a new integration emerges, establishing a gain over the original negated state or condition.[1] Double negation, as accomplished by a mediator, establishes a new state of being that includes the

---

1. The deep structure that underlies our human construction of the Christ event, as well as the structure by which we comprehend the work of the Holy Spirit as "Spiritus Creator," can be put most concisely in the terminology that Claude Levi-Strauss uses for the construction and analysis of myth. However, as with Carl Jung, the structure is important but it is not a saving reality until it becomes "God's myth."

Levi-Strauss' formula ("design" might be more accurate) for the deep structure of transformation is: $f_x A : f_y B : : f_x B : f_{A-1} Y$ where B is the mediator by which an initial negative condition $(f_x A)$ is negated, and a new transformed condition $(f_{A-1} Y)$ is established. The terms are analogous to the noun *(A and B)* and verb $(f_x$ and $f_y)$ components of a kernal sentence in most language systems, but here we are dealing with mythic systems. Specifically, *A* and *B* designate agents and f_y and f_x designate

first negation as an essential element of the gain. Transformational negation, although a distinct form of negation, occurs only in relation to some other type of negation.

Calculative transformation occurs in scientific discovery when new insight negates a conceptual problem by reintegrating its elements so as to establish a new order of higher complexity than had hitherto existed. Here the imaginative insight generated from the subjective life of the discoverer provides a negation of negation by mapping a new situation in and beyond the very context and substance of the problem. Einstein's transformation of the Newtonian universe is an example.

Functional transformation occurs regularly as the stage transition process that begins as a given stage of ego formation or one of its part processes (such as language or intelligence) proves to be ineffective in meeting the demands of its context. New competencies (such as grammar or elementary structures of logic) emerge, drawing together the elements of the original frustrated or ineffective condition around the newly emerged configuration, thus multiplying the capacities of that function. By functional transformation, stage transitions are accomplished; discontinuity and continuity are dialectically interrelated so as to bring forward the latent competencies of the personality. Examples of this have been given in the previous chapter.

---

positive and negative functions respectively, performed by or through those agents. The proportionality notations signify continuity and suggest that this pattern refers to relationships among comparable magnitudes. The working out of the formula in human action depends upon a mediator (B) that has a dual function, one positive or constructive (f_y), and one negative or destructive (f_x). The key factor in this structural model is a built-in double negation $(f_x B$ negates an original negative situation $f_x A)$. The f_x of B must be of the same or sufficient magnitude as the f_x of A if the double negation is to be effective in freeing the redeemed state $(A - 1)$ to live in and become a function of the positive function of the mediator $(f_A - {}_1 Y)$. Double negation by the mediator is the condition for establishing not only a redemption of but a gain over the original situation. The extremeness of Levi-Strauss' structuralism is to be avoided because for him meaning depends strictly on the structural patterns that govern symbolic behavior. The formula helps us to focus on certain essential variables in a transformation process, but my view takes diachronic meaning seriously as well. See C. Levi-Strauss, *Structural Anthropology* (New York: Doubleday Anchor Books, 1967), chap. 11, especially p. 225. Also see E. Maranda and P. Maranda, *Structural Models in Folklore and Transformational Essays* (The Hague: Mouton, 1971), p. 30 ff.

An example of how the formula is being applied in the context of this chapter is as follows:

• $f_x A$ represents the double-bind condition of original sin (A), whereby every effort (f_x) to extricate oneself only intensifies the condition.

• $f_y B$ represents the redemptive activity (f_y) of Christ (B).

• $f_x B$ represents Christ's (B) "becoming sin (f_x)."

• $f_A - {}_1 Y$ represents the transformed condition as: sin-canceled human existence $(A - 1)$, which is a function (f) of the redemptive activity (Y) of Christ.

Existential transformation refers to the negation of the "experience of nothingness"; one's potentiality for nonbeing is ultimately negated. This is most common in a religious experience, but the form and substance of such experiences vary widely. Existential transformation in the context of negation is, of course, essentially the same as what I have described earlier as convictional knowing. However, I want here to stress the level of human experience on which convictional knowing must take place if it is to be truly convincing; hence, I refer to *existential* transformation.

The Christ event — the historical sequence as appropriated by a believer and as discussed in the foregoing chapter — may be taken as a paradigm of transformation at the level of existential negation. In that appropriation, Christ becomes the adequate mediator for contemporary existential transformation because in his crucifixion he takes ultimate annihilation into himself, and in his resurrection that ultimate negation is negated. In Christ, death dies; by his becoming sin, all sin is canceled. Christ thus creates an ontological gain for those who are in his nature. The crucifixion is a sine qua non of the new being in Christ, lest transformation be truncated in a fantastic aberration from or elevation of one's human existence. Likewise, resurrection is a sine qua non as the opposite side of crucifixion, lest God become preeminently an executioner.

You will recognize in this classification of negations matters I have discussed earlier, now being discussed from the standpoint of their inherent dependency on negation. It is important to take up this standpoint so that the *how* and the *why* of convictional transformation may be seen more clearly and comprehensively.

DEVELOPMENTAL PERSPECTIVE ON NEGATION

The main argument of this section is that the prototype of religious experience, potentially manifest in a three-month-old-child, sets up in subsequent human life a cosmic loneliness. Human development beyond this period may be understood as a series of circumambulations expressing this longing and implicitly searching for a transcendent centering of the personality. What follows is a developmental account of the source of this loneliness and the reason it is so difficult to satisfy.

In setting up the prototypical basis for this position, I will assume a psychoanalytic view regarding the origins of life and its negation.

The "birth trauma,"[2] so-called partly because in the normal course of a birth the child comes near to suffocation, is the primal existential negation. This experience of negation ramifies through the whole organism and lays down the foundation for interpreting subsequent experiences of negation. If this psychoanalytic type of assertion is correct, then, ontogenetically, existential negation precedes all other forms of negation for the newborn child.

The effect of this original existential negation is that a series of apparently random activities are set in motion as the newborn child seeks postnatal equilibrium. These activities such as sucking, grasping, focusing, and a variety of "primary circular reactions" (Piaget) all contribute to the adaptational struggle. However, what the child is seeking intuitively (as opposed to consciously) is a center around which to integrate this multiplicity of new activities and emerging competencies. The child is looking for an inclusive alternative to living in the random uncertainty of the postnatal world. Ultimately, of course, the solution to this *existential* negation cannot be met by any emerging *functional* competencies.

René Spitz in *The First Year of Life* has made a series of observations regarding this search for a centering of the child's personality. The search goes through four phases. The first is the oral stage, in which the mouth serves as "the cradle of perception" and the receptive cavity by which the child learns to incorporate his or her world. This standard psychoanalytic observation is considerably elaborated by Spitz, but then he goes on to show that this general physiological orientation shifts toward the love object, a person present. The standard indication of this focus (some even say "imprint") of the child on people is that at three months he or she seeks and learns to respond to the presence of a human face — even a schematic design of a face will do — and give a smile. So regular is this smiling recognition of the face and so marked is the shift from a physiological center to an interpersonal one that Spitz calls this facial mirroring the primary organizer of the personality.[3] This capacity is obviously not as instinctively inevitable as vision or sucking, but it is more like

---

2. The emphasis here is not on "trauma" as such but on the existential negation implied in the radical transition from the life-supporting dependency of intrauterine existence to the independence of postnatal life. That this is an existential negation without necessarily being a "trauma" should be evident.

3. For further information regarding this phenomenon, see D. W. Winnicott, *Playing and Reality* (New York: Basic Books, 1971); A. Rizzuto, *The Birth of the Living God: A Psychoanalytic Study* (Chicago: Chicago University Press, 1979); and R. Spitz, *No and Yes* (New York: International University Press, 1957).

language; that is, a developmentally innate structure that, if it is presented in an appropriate environment, will be learned and used as a decisive, formative power for future growth within and even against that environment.

Translating this observation into Erikson's terms, this is a nucleus of trust as it begins to emerge and establish itself in the child from twelve to eighteen months of age. The face, then, is the personal center that is innately sought by a child and the focus of the earliest sense of one's humanity. The smiling response focuses primal wholeness. Perhaps wholeness is experienced most primitively at the fetal level, but here the undifferentiated "cosmos" of the child becomes personal and interpersonal, focusing on the face.

The "face" here is to be taken as an interpersonal reality and as a primal symbol of wholeness. Many varied studies have pointed to the unique physiological, personal, and interpersonal significance of the face. This view partially reflects a Jungian notion that the face represents an archetype of wholeness because it is generally round and its center bears a cross. Jolande Jacobi quotes Justin Martyr as follows: "The Cross is imprinted upon man, even upon his face" *(Apologia)*.[4] The cross in the face represents "man in his contradiction" unified by the circumference of the face. This image of the self archetype is a promising integration of Jung's concerns with the ontogenesis of the human personality.

I suggest that what is established in the original face-to-face interaction is the child's sense of personhood and a universal prototype of the Divine Presence. In the face-to-face interaction (whether actualized or remaining an innate potential), the child seeks *a cosmic-ordering, self-confirming impact from the presence of a loving other.* Some Jungians may want to say the archetype is an independent and impersonal structure beyond any facial or personal presence, and Freudians will want to say that the Divine Presence is nothing other than the screened memory of the mother. However, in Christian context, the self-understanding of the convicted person combines the sense of personal presence and transcendent order. Thus the primal experience of the face as actual presence and in its significance as symbolic expression provides a prototype for the convicting Presence of God.

In the developing child, however, cosmic integration focused on the face-to-face interaction is short-lived. At about six months, the child

4. J. Jacobi, *Complex, Archetype, Symbol* (Princeton, N.J.: Princeton University Press, 1959), p. 172 n.

begins to distinguish the mother's face and to react regularly with anxiety to her *absence* and to strangers who appear at the crib. This reaction, the third phase in Spitz's scheme, is so regular that at six months an anxiety reaction to the sense of the absence of the mother's face becomes the second organizer of the personality. During this same period, the child is learning to respond to "No!" in verbal, gestural, and affective form so that during this time he or she is sensing an inner absence together with an increasing awareness of external *interdiction*. It is as if the primal, integrative experience of fetal existence, which is lost in the separation of birth, were now being relived in the interpersonal outer world. By nine months after birth, the child has relived the integration and separation that occurred during fetal life and in the act of birth itself.

The developmental solution to this overpowering sense of absence, combined with the external threat of punishment or abandonment (perhaps reliving the original existential negation of birth), is to shift the center of the personality from an integrative to a defensive posture. That is, the child's gathering sense of negation is gradually suppressed by his or her increased competency, activity, and mobility. However, the inevitable "No"-saying of parents (in gesture, word, and effect), which inhibits action and mobility, triggers anxiety and the deep sense of absence beneath. Trapped between inner absence and outer inhibition, the child takes the initiative to turn the inner sense of absence against the negating environment, and thereafter *incorporating* and *presuming* negation in all personal relationships, he or she seeks to set them up on his or her own terms. Thus, as the child moves into the fourteenth month of life, the emergent (in this case "emergency") center of the personality becomes his or her determined use of *negation*. This persistent use of "No," regardless of the issue at hand, is built on a dynamic pattern that in a more developed form would look very much like a reaction formation. In this defensive maneuver, one does just the opposite of what one wants to do with all the energy (and more) one would like to do the first thing. This, the fourth phase in Spitz's outline, establishes the dynamic foundation of the autonomous ego. It is constructive for the purpose of repressing hurtful or potentially destructive inner longings and to weigh outer considerations with appropriate objectivity, but it is destructive to the true centering of the personality.

The ego autonomy emerges as an outgrowth of the child's learning to function as the agent rather than the victim of negation. Thus, negation creates the foundation of the autonomous ego, and the personality is thereafter effectively divided. This is not to diminish the constructive capacities of the ego that emerge at this time, but the developmental solution to the loss of the face and primal absence is only functional. As a *functional* negation of an existential condition, it cannot affect transformation of the *existential* condition; the necessary double negation does not occur. The constructive capacities of the autonomous ego are necessary for survival and satisfaction, but in an existential sense they are all peripheral; the integrative center, that primal longing for the cosmic ordering, self-confirming presence of a loving other, is split off and buried when ontogenesis turns in the direction of autonomy.

This split is evident in that the innocent, wondering look of the infant increasingly shys away from face-to-face interaction — interaction that in adults inevitably generates profound ambivalences. Sartre sees it one way in the category of "the gaze," and he makes lidless eyes, whereby we may not shut our eyes to the other one, a crucial part of hell. Dietrich Bonhoeffer, noting the commonplace experience of shame whereby we all know we must look away if we catch someone's eye on the street or in the marketplace, sees it another way. This, says Bonhoeffer, is evidence of our original sin. Genesis (the J writer, at least) may have been working from a similar prototype in moving the woman from the face-to-face relationship with God into a felt absence (the woman was "alone") matched by the environmental negation, God's command ("do not eat"). That the woman responds to this situation and the stranger's (serpent's) face with anxiety is evident in that she overstates God's command ("don't touch"; note the psychology-mindedness of the J writer) and finally falls into an incorporation of the negation trap, resulting in an inner division of herself against herself (fig leaf concealment) such that face-to-face interaction could not occur thereafter without shame. Notably, the Genesis account parallels the ontogenesis of shame.

The infant does not experience shame at staring, wide-eyed and searchingly, into the faces of all kinds of people of all ages. This shame-free look of the child is gradually abandoned during the first five years of life, but while it lasts it is often a powerful antidote to inner divisions and concealments of the adult mind. The longing for the face that will not go away seems to persist through life as we see how the hardened, weary faces of elderly people so readily warm to a child's innocent look. Something like this primal nostalgia may be behind our own response to the compelling account Martin Buber gives to the "I-Thou" relationship and to the "Thou-I" of Emil

Brunner when he speaks of God's addressing us. Luther's powerful longing to look God in the Face was the desire not merely to be rid of guilt and shame but for a fundamental recentering of his personality on a Face that would not go away.

It should be reiterated that the longing is not for the actual situation of the mother-child relationship of three to six months, but the *impact* of that experience in which *one is given a place in the cosmos, confirmed as a self, and addressed by the presence of a loving other.* To say this is "nothing but" regressive wishing is purely reductive; rather, the prototypical impact is set by the first encounter. The longing is for a loving other to address the whole person (as before), including the differentiated ego with all its competencies, and to set that whole-differentiated person into the cosmos as self-affirmed and beloved.

DYNAMICS OF EXISTENTIAL TRANSFORMATION

The pattern of reaction that grounds the ego in negation typifies a prominent distortion of the human spirit. It is often repeated in subsequent stages of ego formation, and it is a widely exercised dynamic in socialization systems from the achievement-oriented family, the public school classroom, and American business practices to any number of other contexts in which "the ritualization of progress" (Ivan Illich)[5] is fostered. This pattern, built on the negative foundation of the ego, implies that in any context where the developing person may encounter ego failure, the underlying sense of void intrudes, compelling the threatened ego into developing further competencies, sharpening those already available, or achieving new goals and reward, all to the end that the ego's "world" may be not only recomposed but extended, and the sense of void once again repressed. This results in a distortion of the human spirit not only because there is an unwillingness to recognize that human being is essentially four-dimensional, but also because the void will inevitably overshadow the ego's "worlds," as does the nostalgia for the more deeply repressed longing for the enduring Face. Yes, the four-dimensionality of human being will express itself anyway, but the question is whether the intentional efforts of the ego cooperate with or distort what it means to be fully human. This is fundamentally the question of whether the personality will in fact undergo a recentering that displaces the ego,

---

5. I. Illich, *De-Schooling Society* (New York: Harper & Row, 1971), chap. 3.

or will, in quiet desperation, persist in its addiction, distorting and tearing two-dimensional life by attempting to stretch it over the four dimensions of human existence.

Clearly, the so-called "normal" course of development puts the ego into a double-bind situation vis-à-vis the existential condition that underlies it. It cannot transform or displace itself, and it cannot ultimately deny its need to be replaced as the center of the personality. Its existential condition is analogous to the functional condition of the neurotic personality. Thus, it may be useful to construct a parallel between transformation in therapeutic knowing and transformation of the ego itself. This will place convictional experiences in their mediating position and indicate how ego transformation, like therapeutic redevelopment, is a fundamentally healthy approach to recentering the personality.

As indicated in the previous chapter, ego transformation should be understood not as destruction to the ego, but as decisive recentering of the personality around a transcendental reality that points to the invisible God. The net effect actually enhances ego functioning, because the ego has less need to control or limit perceptions or understandings of self, world, or others. The ego-as-center constricts its vision lest the underlying existential negation come into view and the centripetal force of nostalgia for the true center draw it back into nothingness. However, once the center is invested with God's Presence, the ego's anguish at absence and abandonment is dissipated, and its defensive energies can be poured into its competencies. As described earlier in reference to "mundane ecstasy," decentering the ego liberates and empowers its functioning even though and precisely because it is no longer the presumed center of the personality.

The analogy with the undoing of a neurosis might be laid out as follows. First, let the original condition of neurosis be seen in terms of its double-bind character such that no matter what the neurotic does to extricate him- or herself from the neurosis he or she further entrenches it because the neurosis is precisely a pathology of choosing and of doing. The double bind of the ego is the same, because it cannot discover the enduring face without undoing itself as ego: it cannot embrace its own negation and displacement.

Second, the source of mediation in therapy is the therapist, who on the one hand works analytically to expose the basis of the neurosis, but who on the other hand supplies the personal reality to which the neurotic may relate constructively as the neurosis abates. The key to successful mediation through the imaginative reconstruction of the client's "world" is sufficient externalization of the causes of the neurosis through the cooperative effort of therapist and patient. Externalization combines both affect and understanding, but once "out there," rather than embedded in the neurotic's own system of choice and action, he or she can choose against it and by implication choose for the new reality represented in the therapist but as imaginatively reconstructed by the client him- or herself. The mediating factor in religious experience is the image or vision itself. Usually such experiences have a transcendent quality that makes them unique, so one must infer that they begin and end in a supernatural Presence. The work of the mediating image is both to externalize for the personal ego the underlying threat of nothingness and at the same time supply a new context of meaning that embraces and transcends it. Thus the image becomes the Face of God, relativizing the ego and at the same time setting it free.

Third, the appropriate outcome of therapeutic mediation is a new confidence in the process of self-understanding, self-acceptance, and self-affirmation—in effect, confidence in the dynamics of therapeutic knowing. Confidence is not supposed to rest in the therapist per se (otherwise the therapist has made the client dependent, and the client is not well but merely identified with the therapist). Accordingly, the outcome of existential transformation is not that one is simply absorbed into the Divine Presence, nor that one worship the experience itself, but rather that the transforming process is to be trusted. That is, what the transformed person will most likely call "the Spirit," or the ongoing transformation that continues to express the Nature and Source of such experiences, is the new milieu in which the transformed ego lives.

We may presume, then, that the ego is constructed over a deep sense of void, and all its competencies, from intelligence to its culturally contrived world views, bear the marks of a defense against an awesome nothingness. The most competent defense the ego can employ is, in repetition of its origin, to incorporate all those negations that are seen, heard, and experienced and to make them the premises of its interactions with the world. However, the void is too vast and cannot ultimately be incorporated, so the developmental history of negation teaches us this ironic lesson that the study of ego development is the study of mounting futility. Some who are "fortunate" enough to have experienced trauma early in life already know this, and do not have to wait for the middle or later years of life to teach them. The seed of the solution, however, is sown early; before the child is trapped into recognizing the void, there is the primal experience of a cosmic ordering, self-confirming Presence of the loving Other. This remains the source of hope with which development has endowed the personality. Convictional experiences are the fulfillment of that hope because they present in manifest terms the presence of God; they become his Face for the believer. As such, they free the ego for a reversibility of the negation dynamics on which it was founded.

CASES OF EXISTENTIAL TRANSFORMATION

The following cases from my own counseling practice provide substance to the claim that transformational negation may occur at the level of existence and effectively raise the ontology of the Face to the level of a living Presence.

The Case of Willa

Willa, a middle-aged woman, came from a home in which she had always lived as an intruder. She was the child whose birth forced her mother and father to marry. She was chronically neglected and mistreated, and after her second year in college suffered a schizophrenic breakdown. While getting treatment in a state hospital and not making any progress, she was, as she described it, "too depressed to make myself distinguish between dreams and reality." Her head nurse told me that the staff was resigned to Willa's never leaving the hospital. She would sit for hours, hold her stuffed doll, "Tony," and wish for death. One day, after being in the hospital for some time, she felt a Presence come up behind her, embrace her, and "tell" her, "The silence is not empty. There is a purpose for your life." When she turned around, there was no one there, but the silence remained full of affirmation for her. The experience was remarkably effective in motivating her back into life. Complete health was not instantaneous, but whenever she felt stronger in her ego functioning she felt more convinced about this experience. Moreover, she said the experience "made people appear as people" and established meaningful boundaries for subsequent relationships. The experience clearly had intervened to establish the center of the personality at a level deeper than ego functioning but consistent with its development. For Willa, this was the Presence of a loving Other, giving her a place in the world and affirming her worth; the latent symbolic power of the Face had been actualized.

Interpreting this case, it is evident that Willa's ego had already collapsed into abandonment. She had fallen into what the ego dreads most; she had surrendered the boundaries of the ego to the experience of nothingness. The convicting experience had a transforming effect because the mystical Presence of a loving Other did the work of mediation. The silence was simultaneously negated and filled; her sense of absence or abandonment was simply canceled. At the same time, she was implicitly told what she should choose if she wanted help: namely, the reality represented by that Presence and the ego strength that came with it.

In both this case and the one that follows, it is especially remarkable how the experience opened up the repressed past history. Horrendous stories of her childhood came pouring forth in Willa's newfound capacities to "put things together." The point is that the ego had surrendered itself in the schizophrenic break, but was not liberated for seeing things from the past and piecing together her story until the primal longing to be centered in God has been satisfied. Once the defensive structure of the autonomous ego had been negated, it was free to cooperate with the integration that recentering promised.

Another way of saying this is that a reciprocal relationship between the ego and the divine center of her personality was instituted. By "reciprocity," I mean the figure-ground reversal whereby the ego and the Divine Presence are alternately the center of action, but the center of identification remains the Divine Presence. Thus, as mentioned earlier, the Old Testament prophets said in effect "I, not I, but JHWH"; Jesus said, "I, not I, but the Father"; and Paul said, "I, not I, but Christ."[6] Recentering the personality means that identity ceases to be irreversibly univocal and becomes instead reversible and reciprocal between the center and the ego. This case is important not only for the sharp focus it gives to the reciprocal character of this woman's identity but also because she would say she lives increasingly "in the Spirit"; that is, in the ongoing transformational process that so suddenly altered the center of her life.

The Case of Norma

Some years ago in Boston, I had as a counselee a young minister whom I will call Norma. She chronically passed out at the end of our sessions. My response had been simply to leave her to pull herself together while I took the next client in another office. I tended to assume that she was suffering from some separation anxiety and that

---

6. See A. McElway and D. Willis, *The Context of Contemporary Theology* (Atlanta: Knox, 1974), p. 194.

her behavior was manipulative. Finally when, in a moment of inspiration, I told her I wanted to work spiritually rather than in a more conventional way, she said she was relieved to hear that. Now she said she could really tell me why she passed out like that. "You see when we start going back into my personal history that way, I get all confused, the world turns to cardboard, and I start to hear screaming in the back of my head. It gets so loud I can't stand it, so that's when I pass out."

We talked about this a bit, then I suggested that I put my hands on her head and pray for her. This I did sitting on the arm of the sofa beside her. I prayed quietly, asking Christ's Spirit to enter her life and take the screaming out of her head. Suddenly as I prayed, she turned and hit me again and again as hard as she could. Fortunately, owing to my position, the blows fell on my shoulder and back, so I could continue to pray. At last she stopped and began to cry, sobbing deeply as if greatly relieved. Then she began to laugh. Her tears up to now had been practically nonexistent and her laughter very strained, but this laughter was free and full of relief. She got up, picked up her things, and said, "I am not going to see you anymore," and she left *me*. She went home and began to read the Bible and "pray in the Spirit," without any prompting or earlier experience of such a thing.

The voices never returned. However, she came back and told me of a dream she had following her experience in the office. It recalled an episode in her childhood after her grandmother, the dearest person in her life, had died. As a young child, she had gone to the crematorium where the grandmother's body was to be cremated. Sensing the austerity, gloom, and threat of the place, she had tried to run outside, but she was suddenly pulled back and a huge door was slammed to secure her in the room.

Until the time of this dream, even though she was a practicing minister, she had dreaded funerals and had never done one—always managing to get someone else on the staff to cover for her. After the history prompted by this dream had been worked through, both with me and with another counselor, she was able not only to live through the long, cancerous death of a dear friend of hers, but even to conduct her funeral with a sense of confidence and spiritual integrity. This transforming moment was the beginning of a long spiritual journey. Eventually, she served on the staff of a hospital where she regularly contacted the terminally ill, and she is now the pastor of her own congregation.

The mediatorial role is clearer here than in the first case, since the double negation implied in continuing to pray while receiving the externalized attack (a result of grace, not good management) is what finally makes the positive claims of Christ's Spirit a real choice for her. Her sense of having had existential negation negated was sufficient to change the course of her development, but repeated return to the Source of that change was required in order to sustain the remedial work necessary for restoration of the crippled ego.

The psychodynamics of this case reveal an unresolved grief process in which Norma came to struggle not only with the loss of the grandmother but also with the larger existential question of death's meaning and personal nonbeing. The screaming voices represent a thinly veiled attack by an unincorporated sense of separation and annihiliation directed at her conscious life. When the defensive work of the ego is weakened or damaged, then the negation that it usually enlists as aggressive support of its autonomy splits off into demonic forms. Christ is the key to Norma's dealing with grief and the existential despair it produced not only because he provides care in the context of rapport, but also because he is able to deal with the demonic in a way that is beyond human agency.

Further observations may be made here. First, the counselor's role may become parabolic with respect to Christ, who is perceived as a true mediator. This suggests that the mediatorial role may have both a proximate and an ultimate form. Second, the double negation also has both a proximate and an ultimate form because the dream revealed an experience in which the infant's primal fear of abandonment was brought forward into the child's experience of the grandmother's death. Here the ultimate is experienced first: namely, abandonment is abandoned through Christ's intervention, so that the proximate abandonment inherent in the grandmother's death could also be abandoned as a subsequent and derivative consequence. Third, the gain that results from this existential transformation is that, in spite of some arrested ego development, the personality is centered in such a way that remedial efforts of the ego may be made in a reciprocal (rather than defensive) relationship to the center, Christ's Presence.

In general, these cases reveal by their very extremity the personality's structural potential for being transformed and recentered on an effective vision of God. When the experience of nothingness, felt as a threat to the developing ego, is embraced by God's own being, then even cases of extreme abandonment may undergo transformation.

Thus the sense of cosmic loneliness may be satisfied by existential transformation.

CONCLUSIONS ABOUT NEGATION

The following conclusions focus themes and/or implications of the foregoing discussion.

One, probably the most painful human experience is nothingness in its many forms (loneliness, meaninglessness, death). No one overcomes this by any defensive or emergent competencies of the ego. This is because the ego is constructed on the principle that absences, although a necessary part of existence, are to be denied and inflicted on the environment through objectification and control, but, from the egoistic standpoint, if possible they are to be "managed," not embraced and suffered through. The constructive aspects of the ego, creative in themselves, are nevertheless built on its defensive structure, and they presuppose negation throughout the ego's valiant, prepossessing concern for survival and long-term satisfaction.

Two, if the hypothesis regarding negation incorporated as the foundation of the ego is correct, even in principle, then developmentally the defense against primal absence is an accumulating force that eventually (at least by the middle years) becomes an overbearing burden to the constructive powers of the ego, and the accumulated pain of nothingness slowly begins to draw the ego back toward that primal absence. As ego competence declines, the rate of the descent increases. The corrective is the intentional turn inward and renewed seach for the lost face. This was the process, mentioned in the previous chapter, that so interested Carl Jung and why in his practice there was no healing that occurred for middle-aged people that was not religious in nature.

Three, there is no possibility for recovering the lost face through the impact of convictional experience without eventually encountering nothingness. The impact of the convictional experience reaches back under the defensive structure of the ego and restores the same conditions for the mature, differentiated personality that the prototypical facial encounter introduced for the emerging child ego. Thus the ego is enjoined by the convictional experience to discover that, by trusting God, its defensive maneuvers are reversible and that the primal absence is now bearable. Indeed it is even gracious because it haunts the self-sufficiency of the ego with constant reminders of its conflicted origins, calling it back again and again into communion with the Face that endures, the Face of God.

Four, if this overall hypothesis makes sense theologically, then it does so because the patterns and dynamics of human development are prototypically related to basic theological concepts; such patterns and dynamics are original but deficient expressions of ultimate categories of meaning. The face of the loving parent is prototypical of the Face of God; the early sense of absence is prototypical of the ultimate void, "outer darkness" and abandonment of God. The transforming impact of a convictional experience on the mature personality, in which negation incorporated becomes a reversible process, is a prototype of the transformational work of God's Spirit in history.

Five, what is wrong with normal development is its inherent loss of the Face, hence its denial of person-centeredness. The dynamics of negation incorporated compensate for that loss stressing not people but personal survival and satisfaction. To be sure, people are worked into the ego's "world," but they are secondary to survival and the satisfactions that can be built on the dynamics of negation incorporated. Convictional experiences restore the original impact of the Face and make negation dynamics reversible. This is the basis for claiming that, if convictional experiences do what they are intended to do, they will generate a person-centered life of four-dimensional proportions.

CONVICTIONAL KNOWING AND GIVING LOVE

Love's Enemies

I have said that convictional experiences reach across the life span from beginning to end; they reach deeper than family into the archetypal structures of personality and farther forward than one's own death into the transforming work of God's Spirit in history. This is accomplished for the individual by reversing the ego dynamics of negation incorporated and reconstructing the primal facial encounter for the mature personality. If this is *how* the transforming impact of convictional experience occurs from the standpoint of negation in human development, then it may now be asked *why* this is to take place.

The answer is "for love's sake." There are two fundamental enemies to giving love. The first is the fear that acceptance become absorption, and the second is the fear of rejection, abandonment, and, in effect, dying.

The first is a perversion of the opening scene and the primary object relationship between the child and its mother. As Jung pointed out, it appears over and over again in marriage that one partner will become dominant and absorb the other into his or her style of life. This arises because we try to do just what the psychoanalyst tells us is "normal." That is, separated from the parent of the opposite sex, we attempt to make another person satisfy our need. We know it is not "adult" to make the spouse into "a parent," but the transference of affection from the parent of the opposite sex to the spouse is the "normal" order of development. Even though we bring expressions of that affection under the control and direction of the adult ego, the underlying developmental drive is still to acquire the permanent presence of the face that will not go away. Thus, eventually many marriages give way to absorption, a deeply ambivalent satisfaction of that primal need. It does not matter which side of the absorption pattern you are on; either way, as the absorber or as the one absorbed, you apparently satisfy the need. The only defense one has against absorption is the distancing powers of the autonomous ego, but the ego is so constructed that it *prevents* face-to-face intimacy. Therefore it puts the personality in a double bind: without the defensive ego, absorption follows; with the defensive ego, no real intimacy is possible.

Most of us opt for one side or the other, but there is a third alternative. Because it is clear that another person cannot satisfy the primal longing for a face that will not go away, a convictional experience can provide a convincing sense of the Spiritual Presence of Christ, the Face of God. In this case, the double bind is broken, because if the primal longing is satisfied the person is free to give the quality of love that does not try to make the other person into the missing face. I must discuss that quality of love further, but first I must consider the second major threat to giving love.

The second enemy to giving love is an intrusion from the other end of the life span. Surely rejection, abandonment, and dying inflict the deepest pain we know. These are faces of the ultimate void that we can not ultimately overcome by any effort of the ego. The fear of suffering this way in a love relationship has deep roots in the personality because our primal association with a genuine face-to-face intimacy is absence. If the impact of the face first gives us our place in the cosmos and self-confirming love, then absence means that the whole order of the cosmos in which one experiences confirmation from the loving other can simply disappear at any time. The resultant anxiety built into us as a result of this early experience can be overwhelming. As I have said, our defense against that anxiety is an ego that does not let us get too close lest we experience that primal loss with overpowering force once again. Here is the second double bind that prevents intimate love giving: if one lets go of the defenses, the primal pain is overpowering, but if one keeps the defenses it is impossible to find the quality of love one so deeply wants, and wants to give.

Again there is a third alternative. The convictional experience is, as we have said, built on a double negation. That is, there is already in such experiences a confrontation with the experience of "death" to the ego. It is just precisely at the point where the ego's defenses collapse, via inner conflict, into the underlying void that the Spirit of God can act graciously, as Luther so vigorously and repeatedly said. Thus, what we have as a prerequisite to the assimilation of any convictional experience is a reentrance into "death," "loss," and ultimate abandonment. Some people have convictional experiences without coming to the point of "death," but they do not know how to assimilate their experience nor do they fully grasp why it was given until they undergo such a "death." Then convictional experience becomes the face of the Holy, which endures through abandonment. Ultimately one becomes grateful for the "death" because only in light of that does one see the full power of the convictional experience to satisfy the need for a Face that will not go away. Once "dead," one need not fear "death" again because the convictional experience, presenting the Face of the Holy, is always experienced as an immutable reality; not something that passes away, although passing moods or powerful human needs may make it seem so.

Now it may be clear why I had to emphasize the range and depth of the transforming conviction. It is its depth in reaching backward and its range in reaching so far forward that frees the personality to give love. If the depth is lacking or the range curtailed, then love will to that measure be deficient. Thus the capacity to give love is directly related to the power of a convicting experience to make developmental time reversible.

Assuming that the convictional experience succeeds in reversing the negation dynamics that conceal both the fear of absorption and the fear of abandonment, it will release the capacity to give love in a new way. What is this "new way"?

THE WAY OF LOVE

In convictional knowing, the ultimate way of love has been brought to the convicted person by the Convictor. That way is expressed in the pattern and dimensions of Christocentric transformation, but as an act of love it has prototypical roots in the most rudimentary forms of human existence.

First, deeper than consciousness, is the longing to give love and a willingness to give it sacrificially. The child's response to the mother's face is a unique gift to the mother even if the mother knows the three-month-old child will respond to a cardboard face on a wooden stick. The gift, in a primal form, is the gift of sacrificial love because it celebrates or calls forth from the mother the repressed longing *in her* for the face that will not go away. Her response to the smiling child is implicitly a religious one, and the child's unwitting gift of grace is a sacrificial one. The etymology of the word *sacrifice* has nothing to do with blood, death and martyrdom; it has to do with "making sacred." The bloodier aspects of sacrifice are only means to that end. Speaking ontogenetically, before the emergence of the ego and the decentering of the psyche, a child's sacrificial love is not a death-ridden thing; rather, it is a matter of drawing the other one into the Presence of God. However, as an adult, such caring is dangerous business. To re-present the Presence of God is after all the point of witnessing *(martureo,* "to witness") and martyrdom, but if the recipient of the witness is locked into an ego-structured existence, witnessing to the Presence of God becomes a much bloodier matter, and the usual meaning of sacrificial love emerges. It is the untransformed ego that is the bearer of alienation from the face of God and the repressive preserver of guilt and shame. As the psyche's own primary response to victimization, the ego reenacts its origins, making victims of birds, animals, people, and God, all in a perverse attempt at self-preservation.

Combining the primal level with the ego level, it seems that a child's innocence provokes both religious longing and a sense of condemnation or judgment. Hence, a profound motivation for child sacrifice in some primitive cults would be expiation for distance from God and extinction of the innocent accuser or the accusation always implicit in innocence. The archetypal significance of the slaughter of infants in association with the birth of an infant God may, similarly, have roots in fundamentally ambivalent religious motivations engendered by the underlying defensive structure of the ego. If the infant *is* God as in the birth of Christ, then the others who are slain become scapegoats; they take on themselves the negative side of the ambivalence engendered by the appearance of innocence that *is* divine. This yields the net result of freeing the believer for a less ambivalent adoration of the innocent Divine child. The religious martyr would be one who, re-presenting the face of God, stands in opposition to the egoistic construction of existence, and calls for a recentering of the personality; coming against egoistic negation, the martyr is extinguished while the ego of his or her executioner reenacts its original "crime" against the true center of the personality. The deep longing behind all this, expressed ever so briefly in the child's act of giving love, is, ironically, the desire to give love and hence to draw the other one into the Presence of God. Its perverse opposite, engendered by the shamed, negatively based ego, is to destroy what a person most wants: that is, to give love *sacri*-ficially.

To be sure, giving love is not the only motive in the developing child, nor is it the strongest. Sheer survival demands are louder, more constant, and insistent. Nevertheless, if it is true, as many psychologists and ethologists argue, that altruism is a built-in aspect of human nature, then this would be the primal locus of its religious significance. That is, if altruism is to have religious significance, then the facial mirroring and the archetypal power of a child's innocence to portray a loving Divine Presence (as in the incarnation) is a most likely locus. As a motive, altruism may be quieter, but its link with religious experience makes it more enduring than all the others, because in Christian martyrdom, even death gets its meaning from self-sacrificing love.

This hypothesis regarding the primal need to give love is only the summary of a position, but its thrust should be clear. The way of love is deeply and enduringly rooted in our nature, but it must inevitably live in an ego-oriented social order that either denies those roots or else subordinates them to incidental expressions in and around the supposed "real business of life": namely, ego survival and satisfaction.

A second major prototypical source of convictional knowing, understood as the way of love, would be the sexual act. In scriptural language, *knowing* is a sexual matter, and as such it reveals an important prototype for the ultimate nature and way of love. It is not that sexual knowing is the "real" thing and all else is a sublimation, as Freud claimed. It is rather that sexual knowing in human beings, and as it extends into the lower orders of nature, is designed to be the antidote to species death. It perpetuates the species and is thus a physiological demonstration of love's power over death. Moreover, in human nature, as distinct from the lower species, the mating act is characteristically—though not necessarily—conducted face-to-face.[7] This further explains the value of this prototype; this primal order of human experience in which death is overcome by love is also an act of knowing in which one comes face-to-face with the knower. Finally, the conception and generation of a new human being from the union of two lovers makes this a remarkably striking pattern for the higher order of convictional knowing in which the sexual act finds its meaning.

The modern "sexual revolution" has attempted to dispel the false significations so often attached to the sexual act. However, its true meaning or ultimate significance is more obscure than ever. Its significance is obviously not in itself, because left to itself it grinds down into boredom, takes off in rapturous unreality, or turns into an act of aggression against the higher transformational potential of a human being. For all its power and excitement, sexuality has no significance of its own; it must always eventually seek a context of meaning outside itself, either in the self-destruction of the personality or in its transformation. As a prototype of convictional knowing, it may be seen as a face-to-face act of supreme satisfaction in which transformation of the life span, explicitly bringing new birth against death, is accomplished. As definitive for the way of love, it is obviously lacking both four-dimensionality and divine intentionality, but as a prototype it anchors convictional knowing in the deepest matrices of human affection and in our ongoing love for the next generation.

To understand Christian convictional knowing as the way of love is to recognize these prototypes and others already mentioned as participating in the highest act of personal transformation by which all other transformations are transformed; it is to understand that in its ultimate form, convictional knowing is primarily a free and gracious act of love. The Holy One is the Knower, and it is the convicted person who undergoes transformation in the process of being known. First, to be known is to be disclosed in one's central self-contradiction, in one's incapacity to compose a world that does not feed back magnified self-contradiction, and in one's silent half-ignorance of the void that envelops and permeates the whole self-world composition. Second, to be known is to find this very condition indwelt and suffused with the potentiality of new being; to be known is to be supported in awaiting

7. J. Z. Young, *An Introduction to the Study of Man* (Oxford: Oxford University Press, 1971) p. 483.

its consummation with expectancy. Third, then, comes the consummation, and with it a new integration of the self-conflicted fragments of the original disclosure: the Knower, who repeatedly brings something out of nothing, resolution out of dissolution, beauty out of chaos, and healing out of brokenness, constitutes the self in *himself* and the self's world as *his* own. Fourth, to be known is to experience the deep release of self-destruction destroyed, and the positive power of new being. Fifth, to be known is to affirm and celebrate with others the self as spirit, the "World" as the Convictor's composition, and the void as the dark chrysalis of new being in the face of the Holy One whose love persistently "lets be." Thus, under divine initiative, convictional knowing is an inherently four-dimensional and transformational act of love.

It would be fruitful and interesting to pursue the ethics of love as a duty to love the other one as the self has been loved: namely, with a four-dimensional transforming affirmation of human particularity. However, this is a very far-reaching topic, and it must be concluded here with a brief comment on the pattern of convictional knowing.

Its definition resides in Christ and its power in his Spirit, but its enactment is the particular "duty" of each one who has been so loved. I say *duty* — the word suggested by Kierkegaard for the motive that lies behind "works of love" — not to inflict moral conscience on a gracious act of the Spirit of God. Rather, to continue to love as one has been loved is the only way to abide in the transformation effected by his Spirit. This is what gives ultimate sanction to our claim that convictional knowing is the way of love; the only way to participate in it is to give love as it was given. To fail to give love is implicitly to participate in self-destruction or in destruction of the self as spirit.

To answer questions concerning strategies of love and the context of love would take me into a long discussion of the types of love (eros, phileo, caritas, agape, and so on) and their signification. The logic of transformation has, I believe, established a pattern of continuity among them, but differences, as they pertain to different contexts, must remain here undeveloped. However, in the following chapter I will deal with a specific type of case based on this issue.

In terms of my original quest for a context within which to view and interpret convictional experiences, I have completed the circle. What remains is to make bridges from the theoretical viewpoint I have developed to specific cases. This I do in the next chapter, in the form of guidelines. These are designed to help answer the question,

"How does one integrate what one has come to understand about convictional knowing with the actualities of case experience?"

Seven

GUIDELINES INTO CONVICTIONAL KNOWING

INTRODUCTION

➤ AFTER SEEING HER convictional experience in the larger context of convictional knowing, one woman told me, "For all these years I thought I was temporarily insane." Not only had she suffered the unnecessary affliction of debilitating self-perception, but also she had lost the redemptive quality the experience might have added to her and others' lives over the intervening years.

Convictional knowing as we have described it is a process patterned after the logic of transformation. As such, it supplies a larger context within which seemingly bizarre experiences may be interpreted for the contributions they make to faith and spiritual development. It has been argued that many seemingly bizarre experiences open up dimensions essential to being fully human. Further, the position has been taken that what we consider "normal" human development is actually abnormally narrow when the full range of being human is taken into account.

I have been less concerned to develop this process in general than to show how it might be understood when it is identified and governed by the Spiritual Presence of Christ. I will continue to be concerned with Christian convictional knowing in this final chapter.

What follows are guidelines for reflecting on convictional experiences. They are lines of convergence between the composite of all the cases and the Christian understanding of transformation that we have been discussing in the previous chapters. Of course, certain of these lines are more prominent in some cases than in others; hence certain ones have been selected as exemplary of each particular guideline. Yet all guidelines are important, at least implicitly, for all cases. Similarly, the understanding of Christian transformation is important for, and implicit as, the systematic interconnection among all those guidelines. These propositional guides, then, are rather like middle axioms or mediating principles between the broad spectrum of transformation and the particular case.

As to the cases themselves, they are presented here as composites. That is, each one as presented is a composite of at least three or more cases that structurally and dynamically exemplify one of the guidelines. Presenting the cases in this way serves two purposes: it reminds the reader that the guidelines cut across several discrete instances, and for that very reason are general guidelines rather than mere abstractions from a single instance; also, identifying aspects of the cases have been altered without changing the essential point of each case involved.

These exemplary cases may be taken as models of how key aspects of the transformation process operate in the re-creation of human lives that for one reason or another have lost their spirit. The guidelines should not be taken as merely a kind of checklist for measuring convictional experiences but as points of entrée into the ongoing transformation of Christ's Spirit in the world. The transforming moments that constitute the key to these experiences are moments in which the subject glimpses, however partially, this ongoing transformation. The guidelines are attempts to widen the vision glimpsed in that moment, to unfold and expand the significance of such avenues for intentional participation in the humanizing of humanity according to the nature of Christ.

This is not an attempt to establish "spiritual laws" to which the Holy Spirit must conform. It is rather an effort to focus, in propositional form, certain crucial themes that characterize a transforming encounter with the Spirit of Christ. These propositions do not diminish the freedom of Christ's Spirit any more than do other themes that characterize human nature or than do our understandings of God's self-revelation in Christ. Thus, these propositions thematize the impact of convicting experiences on the human personality and the personality's response to the impact in light of God's revelation in Christ.

My general aim is to deepen spiritual formation by enabling people to indwell the transforming moment, let it unfold its content, and let it move the person into an unfolding of Christ's transformational work in personal life and World history. Correlatively, these guidelines help draw the line between subjective intoxication and the Spiritual Presence of Christ. They should not inhibit but free the convicted person for the fullness of the particularity that these experiences characteristically bestow, and so strengthen faith's capacity to give love.

I have divided these propositions into two major groups: those that emphasize aspects of theology and those that emphasize aspects of psychology. Both groups are governed in some measure by both disciplines; however, the transformational logic in certain guidelines is more immediately related to the revealed action of Christ, the Divine Knower, and in others to the response of the transformed ego to his action. Thus the distinction is not between transformed and untransformed considerations but between revelation's claims regarding convictional experience and the convicted person's own response to the experience.

GUIDELINES: THEOLOGICAL EMPHASES

1. *Convictional experiences are to be seen as initiated by Christ, not by any human effort, spirits, or departed souls.* It is antithetical to the Christian view that one lifts him- or herself into a spiritual realm so as to "contact" some supernatural being or so as to become more "spiritual."

In the following case, a young minister was working with a fourteen-year-old I will call Merle, who had been visited in the night by a friend returned from the dead—a sixteen-year-old high-school cheerleader and honor student who had committed suicide, apparently in reaction to a broken love affair. She and Merle had never dated; but their families were close, and the suicide was a terrible shock to Merle's family as well as to the girl's. She had appeared to him a month after her death, telling him that he would be dead from cancer by December—only four months away—so that he could come and be with her. He had been both frightened and pleased, but his fear finally led him to talk to the young minister.

Looking at the broader context, it was evident that Merle tended to be withdrawn, the chronic loser in a competition with his older brother, and not very close to either of his parents. Clearly, there was a deep, unsatisfied need for intimacy, usually buried in withdrawal and guilt but now manifested in his grief reaction. The young minister, the only one in whom Merle would confide, took this shared confidence with a keen sense of its worth. He helped Merle become involved in youth activities and eventually prevailed on him to share the matter with his parents.

Meanwhile, the suicide victim appeared to Merle two more times on monthly anniversaries of her death. A bit obscured in the shadows the last two times, she reiterated her promise. When Merle asked her, as the minister had suggested, what God thought about this, she became uncertain and evasive. Her pleas for her own plausibility led away from any focus on divine interest, to say nothing of divine initiative. Arguing that people often appeared after death to direct others' earthly lives, she claimed this should not be a cause for alarm.

The young minister continued to strengthen his relationship with the boy; in prayer and conversation he emphasized God's loving invitation in Christ. Merle was gradually making high school friends. When a medical examination in December showed no signs of cancer, he was reluctantly able to accept the results and move back into his family and into the church with some satisfaction. At last report, the nighttime visitations had ceased altogether.

Obviously, Merle's was not a transforming convictional experience, because it was clearly not at God's initiative that the girl appeared. It was also not convictional because, although it relieved several personal needs, as hallucinations and occult experiences often do, it did not heal them. Merle's intimacy need was relieved by his being with an attractive friend he had always admired. The situation provided him a way to be rid of, and have vengeance on, a painful family situation and rejecting friends ("They will be sorry"). Furthermore, Merle would not have to commit suicide or take any responsibility for the anticipated vengeance in the afterlife, so his buried guilt would not be intensified.

God's initiative toward Merle was in meeting his need for intimacy through living people, especially those in relationship to Christ. The young minister responded to the intimacy need by keeping the trust Merle had placed in him. By working with him in terms of God's initiative rather than by crying "hallucination" and having him put under psychiatric care, he salvaged the positive consequences of the nighttime visits.

Something in Merle's psyche cried out for a *spiritual* solution. He pressed toward a resolution to the intimacy struggle, presupposing that a transcendent spiritual reality could supply the missing satisfaction better than any other source. To have had this immediately identified in psychoanalytic categories would have frustrated his longing for a solution "from beyond." The spiritual longing was telling the truth; Merle was confronted with a situation in which there were no latent structures of meaning able to bring forth an explanation. That is, his genuine longing for intimacy was not finally for merely human warmth. He longed for intimacy with God, who could account to him not only for his personal needs but for the absurd death of his admired friend. Psychoanalytic referral in this case would have abandoned a four-dimensional struggle to a two-dimensional solution. However, had the visitor reappeared after the medical examination, even after the allaying of Merle's anticipations of cancer, referral would have been appropriate. Yet constant ministerial cooperation would still have been necessary, so that Merle's genuine spiritual longing would not have been lost to his pathology and treatment.

What did occur kept a spiritual longing in a spiritual context, a four-dimensional question where it could receive a four-dimensional answer. Accordingly, Merle was able to grow in his awareness of the nature of all four dimensions implicit in his experience. Moreover, he was brought into a context where the Eucharist and Christian community could begin to replace his visitations as a means of grace.

Occult practices thrive on such visitations as Merle's. Essentially, they occlude the personal needs of the self and the intentions of Christ. The occult practices by which transitory states of mind are induced to call people from the dead, to receive advice, or to determine destinies are systematic manipulations of dynamics that are latent in most of us but which appeared spontaneously in Merle. Even when the purpose involved seems more congruent with virtue and the extension of this life, occult practices are fundamentally faulted on implicit concealment of real human needs. Also, they attempt to replace divine initiative with human intention (conscious and/or unconscious). The outcome of such practices is not freedom and a desire to give love after the pattern of Christ but a sense of spiritual power over oneself, others, and all "worlds." What does not begin with Christ's initiative, either directly or by implication, cannot end in him.

2. *Transforming experiences initiated by Christ are characterized by a resulting sacrificial love in the one transformed.* This, more than any other result (such as spiritual powers, healings, prophecies,

tongues, or visions), marks an experience as being "of Christ." Sacrificial love is effected at least partially by yet another aspect of the experience initiated by Christ: his entering into brokenness and conflict with the power of resurrected life. This I have called the Eucharistic Christ.

One of the most common and painful needs for counseling arises in marriages that are breaking down because one partner "has God's Spirit" and the other does not. Often, the one who "has It" becomes extremely attracted to another person also "in the Spirit." What follows is a composite case bringing together different elements from several cases of this type.

The "spiritual couple" — a husband and his newfound friend "in the Spirit" — seemed, at least to themselves, greatly enriched personally by their relationship, and growing in spiritual sensitivity. Each knew where the other "was coming from"; he loved her poetry, and she loved his mind; they found themselves sensitive to the other's inner life, so much so that one would frequently know the condition of the other even when they were hundreds of miles apart. Scripture was "coming to life"; prayer was increasingly powerful in their individual and corporate life with God; worship was enriched as they shared life in the Spirit. Small wonder that the man, then a practicing minister, wanted more of it and had begun to be discontented with the demands of married life, not so spiritually blessed.

The two "in the Spirit" were sure that this was "the koinonia," because they were "gathered" by God's Spirit and were reflecting in their common lives the fruits of the Spirit (Gal. 5:22-23). To be sure, the man found greater inner strength for relating to his wife and her needs, but he became far more removed from her at the level of emotional and spiritual intimacy.

The pattern here is very familiar, but unfortunately often dealt with in terms of criteria external to the self-understanding of the people involved. Some counselors invoke the "no divorce for clergy" absolute; others take the opposite extreme: "Let them work it out separately in terms of personal fulfillment." I think, contrary to both these approaches, that we need to invoke the positive power generated in and by the spiritual relationship itself so as to bring about a response to the situation that is both therapeutic and ethical.

When the "spiritual couple" came to talk to the counselor, he did not assume that spiritual intimacy was *only* sublimated sexuality; he felt that the case could not be rightly handled by disregarding the religious connections nor by merely getting down to a "gut level."

Rather, all three started with the assumption that the Spirit's power to confirm the relationship between God and each of these two people was *the* reality.

Eventually the counselor talked also to the wife. She disclosed considerable interest in theological matters, but found spiritual matters too intimate to discuss. It was not, as the husband had supposed, that she was rigidly insensitive to the spiritual realities through which he was finding such renewal of life.

The "spiritual couple" and the counselor had stressed and agreed all along that the practice of love was to follow the dynamics of transformation in which the void, however it showed its face, was to be embraced by the strength of the spiritual companionship that was God's gift to them. This premise, I contend, was a genuine product of the spirituality in which they were involved. Being able to act on this premise was the crucial reason for taking spirituality seriously as the key to whatever solution might appear.

The marriage relationship, as it turned out, was the point at which the void appeared, and it was there that the power of the spiritual life had to become manifest if it were to be true to its Christomorphic nature. The spiritual couple had to forfeit plans for a "great ministry together in the Spirit" and find the reality of Christ's Spirit in breaking up their relationship so that the husband might embrace the brokenness in the marriage and learn to nurture his wife's spiritual sensitivity—a thing she genuinely desired.

Both members of the "spiritual couple" had to confront their respective contaminations of the Spirit. The minister who had lost his father at age five and had an adoring mother needed to confront his tendencies to envision God's action in the image of his own adaptational strategies. His spiritual companion had to reenter her growth process and establish there capacities for self-acceptance that would make her respond to God's Spirit with a stronger sense of her own self-worth.

It was an agonizing process for all concerned. The ability to embrace the pain, and to bear with it, was a gift of the Spirit to all three people. They came through the process not doubting their experience of God. Rather, he was confirmed to them in their realization that his Spirit is not an airy or vacuous positive feeling, but a power to engage them dynamically in transformation.

God's Spirit, understood both biblically and experientially, is ethical, or just. The release of God's Spirit within the convicted person is often accompanied by his pressing to the fore unresolved conflicts. He then enables the sacrificial love necessary for the resolution of these conflicts and for interpersonal reconciliation. God does not effect new relationships that would seem to obviate the need for such resolution and reconciliation, nor which, like the counterfeit occult experience, relieve personal needs without healing them.

3. *Consistent with the continuity of Christ's initiative, transforming moments, subjectively sensed to be from Christ, will go in search of objective expressions about Christ.* Hence scripture, sacrament, worship, and theological writings take on fresh life and become extremely vital in establishing the meaning of transforming moments. They are what make traditional meaning personally significant; but a personal transformation is also an awakening to the larger context of what Christ has done, and continues to do, to bring his World into our "worlds."

The episode I want to recall here was told by one of a small group of college seniors in a workshop on interpersonal conflict. This group, which was "gut-level" confrontive, driving very hard toward the personal core of vocational issues, pressed him to account for his interest in the hospital chaplaincy. Why didn't he want to be a counselor or psychotherapist and chuck the religious baggage? He finally mustered sufficient courage to account for himself with the following experience.

During his late high school years, he began talking with a minister because he was lonely for mature, adult companionship; he needed to talk himself out. He said he did not understand much the minister or the Bible said, and the service of worship was meaningless. His need kept him in contact with the minister for a while, however, then he dropped the relationship.

His father, probably alcoholic, fought with his mother frequently. One night, not too long after he had decided to discontinue the discussions with the minister, he was awakened by his parents' loud arguing. He went downstairs to find his drunken father approaching his mother, ready to strike her. At that point, he did what he had never dared to do before. Stepping between them, he faced his father and demanded, "Leave her alone!" The father was dumbfounded. He stood motionless for a long, tense moment. Then he wheeled around and stormed out of the house. The boy said nothing to his mother but went back to bed.

The next morning he arose with a new awareness of himself and his world. He could not wait to get to a Bible; he read it like a starving man at a feast. Overcome by enthusiasm, he restored his relationship with the minister, and in the renewed relationship learned that the language and life of the church was what described his new state of being.

This is a remarkably sudden, highly condensed connection between experience and theological language. Such a connection distinguishes the boy's transformation from a purely psychological resolution (as of an Oedipal conflict) and illustrates a hallmark of true convictional experience: the longing for closure toward which the initiative of Christ moves, in and through the experience.

Thus the normative convictional experience occurs in relation to the Word of God. This is the Christ-instituted way of placing such experience in context. The convictional experience is gracious in itself, but it goes in search of a manifest expression of grace as given by Christ, as the mind seeks closure in the definitive argument or the paradigm case. What is satisfied in such closure, however, is not our need for fulfillment but the completion of Christ's act on us.

4. *Convictional experiences are to be seen preeminently as a breakthrough from the future.* Prototypical factors in one's personal history are not definitive, because such experiences are transformational; they bring the past forward into a new future made possible by the transforming event. This proposition works against a reductive use of personal history in interpreting convictional experiences, and it insists that where the experience is confirmed as being of Christ, it carries a promise to the recipient regarding who Christ will continue to be for him or her.

In the experiences cited earlier from my own personal history — my father's death and the accident — continuity in the Divine Presence from one to the other is evident. In both events Christ entered my personal suffering, bringing forth new being where before there had been a sense of nothing. Both times transcendence was manifest in assurance that defied desperate circumstances. Each time, within the range of my own relationships and influences, personal history was decisively, although not immediately, altered. For me, each new experience was at Christ's initiative. However, because of his constancy and transcendence over time, it seems possible to revisit a memory of his Presence, and find that his Presence is no longer a memory but a living reality in the present, the future of time past.

A seminary student, Rita, discussed with a counselor her plans for dropping out of school at the end of her middle year. When asked why she had entered seminary in the first place, Rita told the following story.

During her senior year in high school, she played the organ for revival services in her home church. She did it with relative indifference until one night the evangelist's invitation to grace became irresistible. She was warmed and so deeply moved that she stopped playing, arose from the bench, and went forward in what she described as "the Presence of God."

The experience was decisive enough to alienate Rita from a circle of close friends and from her boyfriend, who thought she had become too holy. She said she had tried only to communicate her experience, not to elevate herself. However, he perceived that she had changed, and he could not have the same sort of intimacy with her as before. The transition into college further alienated her from her friends, but she attributed the main break to her encounter with God's Presence.

Now approaching her final year in seminary, she was encountering a similar set of circumstances. Her closest companions in seminary did not believe in the "mystical stuff." She had grown quite close to a man (with whom she had not shared her spiritual experience); yet the relationship was dying, partly because she "couldn't feel anything" when she was with him. Although the high school experience seemed pretty well buried, she acknowledged it as the source of her original commitment to enter seminary. Now, facing her senior year and the imminent responsibilities of ministry, she felt as though the whole experience had amounted to nothing—or as though, if the experience had mattered, God had abandoned her. She wanted out, but of course the issue was not closed; she had come to talk about it.

The counselor ventured back into her memory of the past in general, and to the significant high school experience in particular. Then he asked the question of Christ's initiative and God's intentions for her insofar as she could understand God within that experience. After some rather perfunctory answers, she was able to see that she was the recipient of a long initiative that sought not her alienation from the group but integration within herself and the continuation of what had been initiated in high school. She was to live in that Presence as the bearer of her future. It was in the context of God's continued action and purpose that she could see matters afresh. It became evident that even before the experience her high school group had been a self-alienating influence; the boyfriend had not been an unmixed blessing even when she was not "too holy." With these understandings she could make the leap forward into the present and future. The same God who had lovingly intended her integration then intended it still. The experience had been not only an act of mercy but also a promise that mercy would follow—indeed, precede—her into the future. At this point, prayer began to be meaningful, because now she ascertained the nature of the divine initiative she was addressing.

The story ends with Rita's determination to complete her seminary career and with the discovery that her seminary colleagues did not despise prayer and religious experience as much as she had thought. As for the new boyfriend, she discovered her real feelings for him, and they were negative; the separation from him could take place with integrity.

The story might have ended any number of ways, assuming that God's initiative was real and that the rediscovery of it in prayer established new directions and renewed conviction. In any case, the initiative that convicts us promises by that very conviction to remain a living Presence. The convictional experience is a breakthrough from the future even as it is a transformation of the past. The same God who becomes decisively present in the transforming moment precedes the convicted person into the future. The eschatological significance of the Eucharistic Christ implies that one is being met all along the way in preparation for a "final day." Such continuous, available Presence is summed up in the ingenuous prospect that on that final day we will say, as C. S. Lewis supposed, "So it was *you* all along."

5. *Convictional experiences call for a social context whose inner and outer structures sustain and celebrate the continuities of Christ (especially the Word and sacrament).* As mentioned in theological guideline 3, outer confirmation for the private experience of Christ's Presence is necessary.

The convictional knowing context, supportive of personal growth, is marked by the same characteristics that support human creativity within social contexts generally. However, insofar as these characteristics are embraced by the Spirit of Christ, they themselves undergo transformation. Following are these general characteristics, interpreted as transformed.

One: There is *no absolute human authority*, because authority rests with the Author of the convictional experience. By the same condition, there are absolute human limits in that no one in and of oneself can be the author, or initiator, of such experience.

Two: There is an emphasis on *complexity rather than superficiality.* Superficial formulas and pat answers quench the vitality of transforming experiences, whose inherent nature opens new realms of being and meaning that call for richer, deeper understandings. This is not to rule out the sort of simplicity that masters a wide range of complexity ($E = MC^2$; "the Word became flesh"); but it is to discourage cultic formulas, clichés, and trite Christian language, which foster partial truths, curtail thinking, and obviate attention to the uniqueness of the individual.

Three: There is an emphasis on *accepting the inner life* of the individual (dreams, images, and intuitions) as that without which the outer expressions and structures of the Christian faith cannot become personally meaningful. This is to support the development of imagination, lest the eikonic eclipse result from an external imposition of authoritarian systems rigidly overemphasizing right doctrine and moral order.

Four: There is a *positive value placed on stress* insofar as it reveals concealed differences in or between people, or as it reveals latent resistance to the Spiritual Presence of Christ. By engaging conflict in the context of the koinonia, new vision appears, both for individual and for corporate self-understanding. Convictional understandings are thereby drawn into the full four dimensions of human being.

Five: There is a *recognition and acceptance of personal differences* as manifestations of the divine interest in particularity. Thus individuals with differences of opinion may well be content, at least for a scanning interlude, with an agreement to disagree. Unity in the koinonia does not depend on conformity or on any other socially constructed reality. It depends solely on the Authority of Christ to gather and sustain his people. Strategically, unity (not uniformity) is more desirable than difference, except where difference may commence the dynamics of convictional knowing. In such cases, confronting difference (Point Four) is in the service of unity, driving it deeper into the underlying life of Christ.

Six: There is an *instrumental or activist axis* built into the inner structure of the social context; otherwise, the context tends to become exclusively engaged in internal and subjective concerns. It needs to support doing something about one's convictional experience. The relation of this contextual feature to the others mentioned above is as an emergent outcome; the instrumental orientation is not an antecedent purpose or a sufficient measure of the inner work of the group. The action that grows out of convictional experience must emerge freely, integral to the experience's power and complexity and to the context in which it is interpreted.

Illustrations of all six of these features in action could be lengthy, so I will only discuss the overall pattern of Christian life called the koinonia. I have in mind the notion developed by Paul Lehmann in

Ethics in a Christian Context,[1] where he defines koinonia as "the fellowship-creating reality of Jesus Christ" and establishes concern for the continuities of Christ. Although koinonia is not absolutely bound to Word and sacrament, they are the optimal expressions of this fellowship. This definition also makes clear that there can be no absolute authority except Christ, whose present reality constitutes the social unity of koinonia.

This is, of course, a unique social reality, because people enter it by grace, not by socialization patterns. They have roles and functions, but their particularity is heightened rather than diminished by the corporate reality. This does not limit the corporate power of the koinonia; yet it does limit institutional power to dehumanize through an imposition of role structures and status systems. Clearly the koinonia is not to be identified with the institutional church; neither is it to be separated from it. The dialectic between the koinonia and the institutional church is precisely what the preceding six points identify, insofar as that dialectic provides the growth context for convictional experiences.

Beyond its definition and location, the koinonia is also the context of responsible ethical behavior in a world so laden with ambiguity that good and evil often seem inextricable. Superficial thought and language are ruled out; yet the parable and metaphoric speech are examples of the profound, mastering simplicity that the koinonia cherishes.

What the koinonia does in ethical concern for the outer world it may be expected to do in its relation to the inner worlds and experiences of Christ that spring up in its midst. Namely, it takes the inner environment with all its ambiguities as an occasion for humanization. Indeed, making this concrete in a fashion consistent with the humanity of Christ is what I am attempting to do with these guidelines and cases; but of course actual application must be conducted in the living presence of other convicted people and in the Presence of the Convictor.

It goes without saying that the complexities rupturing all our "worlds" will also potentially divide the koinonia; the difference lies not in the absence of stress, nor in the obliteration of difference, but in the affirmation of both stress and difference as the potential beginning of a new process of growth. It is just such a social reality that

---

1. P. Lehmann, *Ethics in a Christian Context* (New York: Harper & Row, 1963).

makes it possible to act responsibly with respect to what God is doing in our "worlds" to make them his World.

Thus the ultimate context for the growth and development of convictional experiences is the sacramental community from which ethical conformity to God's action in all "worlds" is to emerge. Convictional experience, then, may be said to go in search of the koinonia as its context for growth, interpretation, and ethical expression.

GUIDELINES: PSYCHOLOGICAL EMPHASES

1. *Convictional experiences are revelatory of the self, world, God, and evil.* They do not occlude vision but widen and deepen it. Thus, the convicting experience that is of Christ will open up the self to itself, put one deeper into the world, and expose evil even as it reveals God's nature.

The first case illustrative of this guideline concerns the void and a side of life the client regarded as evil. The client, Steve, found himself repulsed by talk of the void. He had had a series of spiritual "highs." In their aftermath, just he, God, and his spiritual brethren were quite enough; one should "remain innocent of evil."

One had to have great respect for Steve and his wife, because both of them had broken out of the New York drug scene. One evening, desperately afraid they could never come off drugs, they had prayed together. Then each had had a vision. Steve said it was as if someone had poured "liquid peace" over his head; he was given an overwhelming sense of serenity and a spontaneous restoration of sanity. His wife's vision was of the virgin mother, whose outstretched hands promised forgiveness and love. The effect of the visions was ongoing and, because the couple were mutually supportive, it looked as if it would be permanent.

What they were not willing to confront, however, was their need to entrust the repressed anguish, heartache, and hatred to the same Spirit that had saved them from drug addiction. They wanted to do great things spiritually but did not want to examine the unfinished business in their own psyches. When they went to a counselor, it was with problems that concerned in-laws, but their conversations eventually touched on aberrant sexual behavior they still practiced. Finding the topic difficult at first, they discovered, as they submitted this "brokenness" in their human spirit to the Spirit of God, that he effected not a sudden wiping out of their problems, as they had hoped, but a genuine peace; he endured with them and affirmed their worth in the face of the aberrations. It was as if the Spirit refused to intensify self-destruction with divine condemnation. Moreover, they were eventually able to see the virtue buried in their vices and to reappropriate the love that had been lost to perversity.

What they experienced was the deepening, healing power behind their convictional experiences. They had felt it necessary to protect their spirituality rather than let the Spirit protect them. Their vices they attributed to the devil, so they never really had to engage the matter of evil as something to do with them. Surely they never expected to see the "good" buried in their vices, although they eventually did. They even came to be thankful for the struggles, without which their deepest needs for the Spirit of God would never have been made manifest.

The second illustration does not concern embracing the void so much as it does embracing the world. The two cases may be interpreted in somewhat the same way, but in this second case the manifest denial is of a shared "world," not of any darkness threatening the person from within. Luis, a truck driver with a large family, told of having had a nervous breakdown under the influence of a spiritual ecstasy that forced him to lie on a frozen pond during below-zero weather. He lay there, in the middle of a public park, for six hours, waiting, as he said, for the "light" to tell him what to do next. Finally he was picked up and hospitalized. Released after a brief stay, he returned to the pond. While there he experienced "a renewal"; this time, however, he simply saw people differently and "felt blessed" wherever he went.

Luis went to a counselor because he had begun to experience a persistent depression and could not get back "into the spirit." He struggled for words as though he had trouble concentrating on what he was saying. His eyes were shrouded with worry, his face empty.

For Luis, there was something decidedly wrong with every "world" he was able to compose. He wanted to be disembodied. As he saw it, "the world is a filthy, dirty place." His counselor assumed he wanted out, or at least wanted to embrace the imaginary world he lived in rather than "reality." He had tried reading scripture, contemplating Christ, and praying. His efforts to unite with a church and to worship were futile. Of course, the Christ Luis was praying to, as it turned out, was more a projection of the dubious ecstasy than the transforming Christ of the Emmaus Road.

Eventually conversation with the counselor established the Christ who loved "the filthy world," and Luis' need for that Christ, rather than the one who would disembody him and restore "ecstasy." His own thinking led him to see that his "Christ" was not the Christ of the New Testament. At this discovery, he and the counselor prayed together.

He did not return to the counselor, who was surprised to meet him one day in church. Beaming quietly, Luis took him aside to say that everything had "come together" for him since the last session. Skeptical because Luis had never pursued with him the significance of what had taken place, his counselor nevertheless perceived that Luis was beginning to embrace "the filthy world." Moreover, he had aligned himself with the church and had attributed his new life to the world-embracing Christ. Evidently Christ had not been absent from the previous ecstasy, but his presence had been contaminated by Luis' need to escape the world.

The third illustration concerns "the self" and tries to make it clear that convictional experience is designed to increase one's sense of self-worth without decreasing one's capacity to give love.

I am not as concerned as I used to be when people allege that God has helped them find a parking space, or some such thing. There is a fine line between superstition and faith in the gracious love of God; his love does indeed precede us, and we are free to follow. What I usually want to say in response is, "God must care very much for you." If God did help someone find a parking place, I am convinced it was because of that person's worth and God's appreciation of the particularity of the individual. If God didn't find the parking space, the fearful approach to the world that conjures up such assurances needs to hear that God's kind of love, not merely convenience, is the point of the spiritual walk.

Generally, convictional experiences like those I have described throughout these pages make possible a sense of self-worth and release those defenses that indirectly give rise to a superstitious outlook. Projectivity is actually made unnecessary; the internalized sanction of God's love does not need magic control over the threatening, dangerous world. It is a habit of mind hard to change, but with increased self-worth it becomes increasingly unnecessary. "Signs" become a burden and a bore as the Spirit of God grounds and expands the spiritual self.

The larger significance of the concern for self-worth is not to diminish superstition but to save the person from self-destructive tendencies. The case that comes to mind concerns Kendrick, a very competent student who had graduated from Harvard as a physics major. An unusually fine poet, he was also politically astute and had campaigned actively for John Kennedy's presidential election. Having entered law school, he was now chronically depressed and uncertain about vocational goals. Family factors were important because his father and mother had been divorced; his father had died two years before Kendrick began law school.

The grief process was long and difficult because Kendrick had been raised never to cry. In counseling he began, piece by piece, to ascertain his feelings for his father, from whom he had felt estranged. Still he had no tears. This time the convicting experience came to the counselor on his behalf.

They were talking about a powerful dream Kendrick had had, working it through in traditional categories, when the counselor was overcome by what can only be described as the thunder of silence within the Presence of God. They both stopped talking. The counselor then perceived for the first time that before him was a very young boy who needed primarily to be affirmed and loved. The counselor put his arm around Kendrick and told him what he had perceived. Finally, the tears began to flow.

The point is not merely that ostensible grieving was accomplished but also that it must be attributed to the illumining Presence of God. After this, Kendrick and his counselor began to pray as a regular part of their sessions, and Kendrick's Christian commitment as well as his vocation soon took definite shape.

Kendrick had been the victim of an obsession with success from childhood; both his parents reinforced early independence training, top grades, athletic competence, high-level artistic expression, and implicitly made love contingent on achievement. The little boy never had a chance for unearned warmth. The resulting resentment smoldered under his surface competence and finally expressed itself in vocational confusion. Now he was finding a sense of personal worth in and through the Spiritual Presence of Christ, and the repressive dynamics that characterize the achievement-oriented personality became reversible. The result was not that he could "not achieve" but that now, in the satisfaction of Christ's Spiritual Presence, achievement was unnecessary for his sense of personal worth. This in turn made it possible for him to step out from under the oppressive control of parental teaching and relate to his mother in freedom. "I have begun to see her as a person, and she is asking *me* how to deal with *her* needs for a change," he observed.

The deepening sense of the Holy is such an obvious outcome of convictional experiences that it may not seem to need illustration.

However, it is evidently the case that the Convictor takes on a quality of Presence that continually invites deeper intimacy even if this also implies threat. Where conviction is the effect of a supernatural force that does not invite a deepening personal relationship, there is considerable doubt about its Christian character. Knowing God only as an archetype, Idea, metaphysical process, or political ideology may turn one's life around, but none of these alternatives suffices to present the personal God revealed in Christ.

The case that makes this most obvious is that of a brilliant student who had completed medical school but decided not to practice medicine. Having subsequently been in two or three graduate schools, where he was periodically "converted" by Whiteheadian metaphysics and Marxist philosophy, he was in the throes of a Jungian immersion when he requested counseling. Furthermore, he was entangled in an agonizing love affair with a woman who he thought had divorced her husband on his account. Now, however, she had grown tired of him, and it was evident that he was not as important in the divorce as he had supposed. It was the first time he had ever lost anything he really wanted. He was left with guilt for contributing to her divorce and with a tragic sense of his own incapacity to give genuine love.

The great moan and semiconscious state into which he fell when he directly confronted his failure were evidence of a narcissistic shock. However, this dark moment was the very ground in which he began to approach a postnarcissistic sense of the Presence of God. "This was," he eventually said, "something that had a life of its own," something that lived in him anew and gave him vitality. Although he spent a year or two exploring the implications of this inner life, it was finally sufficiently convincing to him that he turned away from his earlier introspective delights and struggles. He eventually began doing cancer research and was able not only to set his former lover free but to enter a new romantic relationship that was honest, and free from his earlier imperialism and self-indulgence. The autonomous life of the Holy in him had worked a release into what we have called "mundane ecstasy." His awareness of God advanced from an opaque narcissistic reverence for his own powers, through a shattering of his false self-image, into the inner sense of new life, and finally into a transparent personal relationship to God that freed him to embrace the world.

Overall, this proposition claims that a convictional experience initiated by Christ characteristically opens up all four dimensions of human being. Exactly how that occurs will vary from case to case, because content is person-specific, but in general the experience should make all dimensions of existence more available to conscious exploration, engagement, and growth.

2. *Regardless of how sudden such experiences may seem to be, they have a personal history in the individual.* Most commonly, this history begins in a four-way struggle among the individual's sense of the holy, of void, of self, and of the world.

What has already been discussed in relation to young Martin Luther makes the best analytical illustration of this principle. Luther's lightning bolt experience was a bolt not just from the heavens above but also from the psyche beneath. Psychoanalytic observation, however, is only one way of noting that convicting experiences have a history in the individual. That is, one frequently finds the whole record of one's memories reordered by the convicting experience, and many forgotten events, persons, and meanings are illuminated as surprisingly significant.

It should be clear from the several cases cited in Chapter 6 that a reductive causal connection from past experience to present transformation is not being made. Psychoanalytic connections, which tend to be reductive and do analytical violence to the self-understanding of the transformed person, are partially rather than ultimately decisive. Experiential recall at least brings relevant associations to bear on the transformation, but deducing causality from associations is equally reductive. Some generic account of factors contributing to a convictional experience is essential; yet it cannot do justice to the experience's originality, integration, and power to open the future. Correlatively, convicting moments that work simply to seal off the past, making it a closed book, are likely to be repressive not only of future growth but also of all the meaning that may be in the experience for others. Reopening the past is an important latent potential that nearly always needs support and encouragement in one's personal appropriation of convictional experience. This, I think, has been sufficiently illustrated in foregoing chapters.

3. *Consistent with the principle that convicting experiences are revelatory of one's personal past is the proposition that the so-called normal sequence of human development may become reversible.* That is, convicting experiences may encourage reliving periods of early childhood and/or the anticipation of death. Much of the health that comes from such experiences derives from this unique transcendent relationship to the ordinary course of human development.

The issue at stake here is not merely the discovery that past factors had some bearing on contemporary convictional experiences but rather that this past may actually undergo a healing change, directly or indirectly as a result of convictional experience. The future also may be anticipated and profoundly affected through convictional experience. Even one's physical death may be anticipated and relativized by an analogical "death to the ego" as center of the personality. This is borne out by the fact that some form of sacrifice, or even martyrdom, commonly follows an experience of conviction. It is as if the struggle for survial and satisfaction becomes totally relative to the center of one's conviction.

"Reversibility" has two closely related meanings. The first is that the meaning of past experiences and of inevitable future experiences such as death may be automatically or subliminally altered. The second is that one's self-consciousness is liberated to revisit the past or to anticipate the future with increasing flexibility and freedom. Thus the linear unfolding of life through a prescribed sequence becomes, in effect, reversible for future development and self-understanding. God's action in effecting both forms of reversibility is decisive.

A common version of the healing move backward in developmental time is emerging in a contemporary Christian emphasis on the "healing of memories." Popular Christian literature abounds with accounts of people revisiting previous traumatic experiences through an imaginative reconstruction of the past (similar to Carl Jung's view of "active imagination"). In the healing of memories, Christ, preferably as the one who has initiated conviction in the rememberer, is invited to enter the trauma, to remold the memory, or to do whatever else may be necessary for wholeness. This often brings quite unexpected results.

One very intelligent young woman, whom we will call Georgia, had in childhood often been abused by a domineering older brother. Now she dreamed repeatedly of an approaching, threatening monster. Georgia and her Christian counselor assumed this to be a reliving of the fear of the brother's abuse. However, this understanding did not prevent the dream's recurrence, nor did it heal the childhood fears.

Later, with the counselor, and in the context of prayer for Christ's healing of the memories, Georgia deliberately tried to reenvision the monster of her dreams. When she was able to do so, her counselor prompted, "Now *love* the monster." Out of her remembrance of the loving Presence of Christ, which had previously effected for her several transforming moments, Georgia was able to muster some affection toward the fearsome image. This gracious accomplishment effected yet another: the monster she envisioned cracked open like a hollow shell. Inside, quite apart from her conscious intention, and even to her surprise, she saw a little boy curled up in a fetal position, crying.

For the first time she had made a move toward forgiving the childhood enemy; for the first time also she was able to see behind her fear of her brother into his own deep childhood needs. Now she could understand some of what had engendered his abuse toward her. Her understanding thus transformed, she was able to progress even further in her forgiveness of him. The dreams did not recur, and her fear of her brother was healed to the extent that she could at last enjoy being in his presence.

What is true of the past may also be true of the future. One young woman, a seminary student, described a repeated dream that first occurred when she was about eight years old. In the dream, she moved forward through life, grew old, and died; at death the whole of her life was entrusted to God. The Source of the dream, she said, was the Source of her strength as she moved, in later life, through a series of tragic losses. After each loss, the memory of the repeated dream restored her perspective on life, her faith, and her sense of self-worth.

The life of Sergius Bulgakov, late professor of dogmatics and dean of the Russian Theological Institute in Paris, draws together all the implications of reversibility. The story of his conversion and several of his writings are included in *A Bulgakov Anthology.*[2]

As a young man Bulgakov lived in a poverty-stricken Russian Orthodox family. Prospects were too black: his father lost heart, eventually becoming a drunkard; two of Bulgakov's brothers did the same. His mother—generous, kindhearted, improvident—was a woman whose congenital nervousness was aggravated by the tragedies of the family life, including the death of several of her children in infancy.

Surrounded by pain, the personality may retreat inward, and with the shrinkage often comes compensatory outward aggression. This is the redirection of energy described in Chapter 6 as negation incorporated. Young Bulgakov, by sheer force of determined brilliance, became a dedicated Marxist and a professor and author in political economics at Kiev Polytechnic. The conflict in his case was that

---

2. S. Bulgakov, *A Bulgakov Anthology* (Philadelphia: Westminster, 1976).

Marxism provided no personal meaning for his existence; his spirit was not freed but forced into a depersonalizing philosophy of history and humankind by the Marxist ideology.

As a child, Bulgakov had been impressed by the symbols, poetry, and color of the Russian Orthodox Church; yet at age fourteen he lost faith in Christianity. His faith did not begin to return until one spring evening when he was twenty-four. Driving across the southern steppes of Russia, smelling the strong-scented spring grass gilded by the rays of a glorious sunset, he caught his first sight of the blue outlines of the Caucasus. The sight so overwhelmed him that the emptiness of his Marxian outlook (which demanded that he see nature as a lifeless desert and surface beauty as a deceptive mask) fell out in sharp contrast to the rich, vital assurance he received then and there that nature without God was impossible. He recognized with sudden force that his negative identity—the counteraggressive Marxist he had become at age fourteen—was the repressed, reverse side of the devout life he had experienced earlier in childhood. His Marxist attack on oppression had been a one-sided ideological solution in which he had unwittingly wrought yet another kind of oppression on his own spirit and against the wholeness he sensed to be the promise of Christ.

A subsequent turning point in Bulgakov's conversion from Marxism reaches back even further into his personal history. At the age of twenty-seven he encountered Raphael's "Sistine Madonna" in a Dresden art gallery. He wrote, "The eyes of the Heavenly Queen, the Mother who holds in her arms the Eternal infant, filled my soul. I cried joyful and yet bitter tears, and with them the ice melted from my soul and some of my psychological knots were loosened."

Although he was still a Marxist, Bulgakov for a while went back to the picture every day to pray and weep in front of the Madonna. The cathartic effect of reuniting his repressed emotion with a sense of his body, and with that unifying sense of touch by which he first knew his own mother, restored Bulgakov to a deeper sense of his selfhood.

On yet a later occasion, he found himself in what he termed a state of absent-mindedness followed by a state of trembling and tears as he made confession, received pardon, and "partook of the Blessed Body and Blood of my Lord." This convictional experience united the first two with it, for it was a return to the "mother" church at sunset just as the evening bells were calling to prayer. The Spirit of God had freed the inverted Marxist ego in a "moment of absent-mindedness," or momentary interlude, to yield to the transforming image of Christ.

This prepared him to return to the body of Christ by which he ascertained the meaning of his selfhood, so that in 1908, at the age of thirty-seven, he made a decisive return to Russian Orthodoxy and entered the priesthood. After that he wrote several theological works, developing a unique doctrine of the Holy Spirit based on the figure of Mary.

This culminating experience of his return to orthodoxy he later spoke of a "spiritual death" to himself, repeated in his ordination and again in his anticipation of surgery for throat cancer. His profound sense of "dying before death" in and with Christ is a superb example of the fashion in which a previous conviction may move a person into death with an illuminating, indwelling, and transforming awareness: death is already familiar to oneself and also to Christ, who goes through it ahead of, and with, his people.

Bulgakov indwelt both extremities of his life span, deriving the deeper understandings of faith that contributed so much to his influence as a theologian. In this he not only exemplified the way in which conviction makes one's own life span reversible, but he also used that reversibility to articulate the Lordship of Christ over all of life.

4. *Reversibility of human development does not imply absorption of the psychological ego.* Rather, it means that *freedom to choose* for or against what God is doing in the world is actually enhanced, because fewer of one's choices are subject to unexamined psychological influences.

As mentioned earlier, Freud claimed that the aim of psychotherapy with neurotics was to free the ego to choose for or against neurosis. This too is the impact of convictional experience when the life span becomes reversible. However, it is important to make this explicit, because it is often assumed that experiences of convictional impact are the *product* of a neurosis rather than its undoing.

Neurosis in general is characterized by a symbolically distorted world in which one sees realities overladen with incongruent meanings that must be consciously rectified or accounted for. Thus the classic example of ritualistic handwashing as a symptom of repressed guilt may be understood in symbolic terms as the neurotic's "seeing" dirty hands when there is little or no suggestion of dirt. The dirty hands are a perceptual distortion stemming from the neurotic tendency to create external symptoms out of internal conditions. When the reality of everyday life is distorted from the moment of perception, there is no freedom of choice; all choices are inherently misconceived. Thus, under neurotic conditions, all choices are bound to repeat the past and relive the distortion endlessly.

In the case of Norma, cited in the previous chapter, her convictional experience freed her to recall the traumatic childhood experience of being forcibly held in the crematorium when the body of her beloved grandmother was to be cremated. The recovery of the experience in a dream was simultaneously the recovery of the power to choose against the neurotic fears that had accumulated around the long-repressed trauma.

In another case, a counselee, Phil, described to me his indirect involvement in the suicide of a girl friend. He said he had fallen in love with her while studying abroad but had broken off the relationship. When she killed herself with an overdose of heroin, he felt it was because of his rejection of her. Now he was distraught, guilt-ridden, and plagued with thoughts of taking his own life. A repeated manifestation of the guilt was that he feared "you can see right through me," and he recounted his story only with great anguish.

After a few sessions without much progress, I suggested he pray, explaining what might be involved in that. Before the next session, he had experienced so much peace in private prayer that he was ready to tell me everything. He admitted that the story was mostly trumped up. The girl was not dead but living in another country. He had been trying to deal with her rejection of him and his urge for revenge; but now all thoughts of suicide and chronic depression had disappeared. The prayers and confession were so healing that prayer became a major and powerful source when he went into the ministry. Not surprisingly, he was particularly effective with potentially suicidal patients.

The neurotic pattern was broken in this case by what Freud, in self-contradiction, would have called the "neurosis of religion," but what I would prefer to call the "transcendent reality of a convictional experience." The psychological result was, after all, therapeutic, not neurotic. The student was freed to choose against the perceptually distorted world that he had fabricated for me and for countless others. When he was freed by prayer, he entered with great relief into the reality of straightening things out with all whom he had deceived.

The liberating effect of convictional experience need not be restricted to correcting neurotic situations. It may also work against corporate myths and social distortions, which can be equally debilitating to the individual's capacity to choose for or against what God is doing in the world.

The American success mystique, classism, sexism, and racism are all distortions of such social magnitude that no one would call them *neurotic* in the usual sense. Yet they bind freedom and accordingly come under condemnation when convictional experience is allowed to unfold its full and proper meaning. Martin Luther King, Jr. is probably the outstanding example in recent history of one whose convictional experience freed him to choose against the perceptual distortions of racism.

Obviously, the list of examples could be multiplied, but the central point is that the convictional experience nurtures one's capacity to choose against perceptual distortions that bind to a repetition of the past and frees one to choose for a genuinely new future that continues to enhance a similar freedom for others.

5. *The transformational process facilitated by a convictional experience calls for continuity of expression,* contrary to the tendency to put experiences of convicting power into authoritarian frames of reference. What is experienced as transformation is designed to call forth further transformation. As Christ's Spirit seeks continuity in the transforming experience, so also does the human spirit.

I recall the case of a young seminarian, Don, who sought counseling because he could not preach. He could not say anything about his faith because, as he put it, there was "nothing in here [pointing to himself] to say." He did not lack mental ability and could do fine academic work, but he was convictionally void.

Don traced the roots of his call to a revival service he had attended at age twelve. There he felt compelled by Christ's Spirit to leave his family and go forward at the conclusion of the service. It was obviously a powerful experience for him, one in which he felt free, cleansed, and truly happy.

The revivalists gave him some literature that told him how to stay Christian by conforming to certain moral principles. As a result, his attention was diverted from the Source of transformation to the moral principles. He tried to abide by the principles all the way through high school, but finally in college he gave up. There followed a long series of escapades, then depression.

Internally empty and seeking something he knew he had lost, Don came to seminary through the help of friends. Although scholastically competent, he could not break out of his depression and finally sought counseling. It became more and more clear that he really had come to the seminary because of the impact of that early conversion experience. He and the counselor did a number of things to indwell his experience, but the most decisive help came in seeing that those authoritarian moral principles imposed from without actually violated the creative power of the experience within. The discontinuity between the "laws" and the spiritual movement of personal transformation had finally broken his spirit; he could not cooperate with the way of the Holy Spirit.

Nevertheless, the convictional experience had had a lasting effect on Don; the vitality of it still lived within him, although it had been completely repressed. He and his counselor talked about the experience, about its creative power, and about the spiritual love he wanted to give. He began to have a series of dreams in which he saw himself wrestling with someone (usually a woman), at first aggressively, then playfully. Deep, frustrated, angry motives were gradually unpacked; he began to sense the positive joy of God's Spirit, which had already been released in him but which moralistic rectitude and subsequent frustration, aggression, and depression had repressed. The long hours he had spent depressed and staring out the window came to an end. One day he found himself arguing about controversial issues while actually loving and caring for his antagonist. Indeed, he claimed to have "tremendous love" for all people. He had no further trouble preaching, and after graduation committed himself to a job that required preaching several times each week.

Don's story illustrates the basic principle that the convictional experience must be seen as the central turning point in a creative act performed by God's Spirit. The liberating consequences of that act need to be celebrated and affirmed. Moral principles fearfully imposed to prevent backsliding draw the person into an authoritarian regime, violating the transforming work of the Spirit and inviting a perversion of the love the Spirit inspires. The transforming work, once begun, will continue, and the process through which the Spirit takes the person is a sequence he or she may go through many times again. What needs to be understood is that the Spirit, who is the Teacher, intends the wholeness, freedom, and joy of the one who comes under conviction. There is nothing vacuous or uncertain about this; the initially convicting process, moving from conflict through resolution, is the same sure process by which God's intention operates in subsequent periods to generate wholeness after the pattern of Christ. Continuity, then, implies a recognition of the nature of the process by which Spiritus Creator acts on human lives and a willingness to trust God's sovereignty to initiate this process again and again in the course of one's spiritual formation. Furthermore, it implies that human agents in this process do well to understand and cooperate with its nature, not distort it.

Don's case is not unusual. Often people who have undergone remarkable experiences of transformation become authoritarian about scripture and spiritual laws. The incongruity between the freeing transformation and the rigid aftermath is so striking that I have summarized some of the basic causes underlying this distortion.

One: There is fear generated by convictional experiences — fear stemming from the awesomeness of the Holy and from the suspicion that one is not quite oneself afterward, fear of losing the good thing that has happened, and fear of aspersions cast on the experience by other people (often the closest friends and relations). These fears employ an aggressive, authoritarian posture to defend the authenticity of the Holy and to drive away all detractors.

Two: It is also the case that people who experience God convictionally frequently assume that now *they* have power. This may well be compensatory, and part of the fear, but in any case the power one receives becomes more important than the Giver or the intention behind the experience. When the Presence of the Spirit begins to wane, one tries to keep it or retrieve it, resulting in the temptation to substitute personal power for the Power of God. When the Spirit's Presence continues vital, the temptation is to give it one's own direction rather than to let the Spirit of God do what he will do. In attempting to possess the Power of God, one misses the creative action, which is convictional and liberating but not deifying.

Third, the general lack of thoughtful language about God's Spirit and his action on us and the world leaves people who "experience the Spirit" bursting with a desire to speak, equipped with little more than clichés. Fear and uncertainty often prevent departing from trite words and reflections about what has happened. Yet if we do not think about the Spirit and do not attempt to formulate new ways of speaking about his action, we stifle our own spirits and develop in no way commensurate with the potential offered by such experience. Lack of growth entrenches a position, and as a result the position is defended dogmatically. One wants to say more but, not knowing how, says the same cliché three times, with ever-increasing volume.

We do not attack someone who is frightened, weak, and at a loss for words, so why attack the authoritarian Spirit-filled Christian? In part because such people attack us first; but our response to their attack should be in accord with the Spirit's way with us rather than in self-defense. The inner life behind the dogmatism we are confronted with longs for creative renewal. It is often our disinterest in, or aversion to, this renewal that evokes attack. Of course, our disinterest and aversion may also be based on fear, weakness, and lack of understanding. I do not underestimate the difficulty of altering an authoritarian stance, but neither do I underestimate the Spirit in such Christians. Their attack is a temptation to miss the point, but the importance of continuity seeks to hold us to spiritual transformation as the inherent and overarching pattern of development.

EPILOGUE

➤ IF TRUTH IS stranger than fiction, as we sometimes say, it may be that we live in a state of estrangement from the truth. Suppose it were all turned around and the fictions by which we live were suddenly and starkly thrust, as on the Damascus road,[1] into the light of a Truth so splendid we would cringe and hide our wounded eyes from it. Suppose we can only bear one glimpse of the Truth at a time. Then the Truth would be wonderful and terrible, and we would cherish our moments before it and long for more—yet we would be afraid lest we get too much all at once.

But suppose further that the Truth took on the nature of our fictions making—incredible!—our fictions bearers of the Truth. Who could conceive such a thing, even in retrospect? Perhaps only those who have once been partially blinded by the Truth—whether suddenly or gradually—come to the breath-taking realization that the One who sits at table and breaks bread and drinks wine with us[2] is the One through whom and for whom all ten billion light years of creation, including our own come-lately, here-and-now existence, have their being. To sit at table with Him is more wonderful and terrible than a blinding light since it allows us no fictional existence in

1. Acts 9:1-19; 22:3-16.
2. Luke 24:13-35.

which to shroud ourselves, no place to hide from the relentlessly gracious claim that our very existence, fractured and fictionalized as it is, is of infinite worth, potentially a bearer of the very Truth which we fear could so easily crush us under the weight of its glory.

But suppose, finally, that this awesome condition in which we may find ourselves has in it a kind of comprehensive intelligibility we had not dared to consider before, a reason above reason, a *supra rationem*,[3] that is so inclusive of us and the universe that we couldn't see it unless it were shown to us in a gigantic mirror. If even cosmic chaos has in it a hidden order, as we are surprisingly coming to understand, how much more astonishing and compelling is that greater intelligibility which unites all creation—even the turbulence and unpredictable upheavals of natural and human existence—to its creator. Such a union would have to be fully God and fully human. Yet this remains ancient text and obscure doctrine until, in that breathless moment, we see *ourselves*, the full dimensions of our existence, reflected in the Holy One at table with us. In the broken bread and wine He becomes the mirror in whom we see simultaneously the embodied chaos of human existence in a vast and meaningless universe, and the hidden order and sacred destiny which He by His Presence—and not separable from that Presence—in a moment of *epiclesis* would beget in us. Then—though we could never say how—we see that the fragment could contain the whole, we are captivated by the intelligibility of His nature which we long to embrace, and it draws us to the edge of the abyss of uncreated light, the inner life of God.

But alas—to lay hold on that remarkable intelligibility by which one's fragmentary existence becomes bearer of the whole, that intelligibility through which all things have been made—to lay hold on that by faith is to touch the ark of the covenant, it is to hear "the sound of a mighty wind," as "the roar of the New Jersualem," and it is to die. Who wants to die so that the uncreated light and life of God may indwell human flesh and turn everything we do into the work of God's Spirit?

Holy in its nature, the life of the Spirit is stunning in its impact; the depth of its mysterious centered silence remains unmoved, intensely personal, even in its rush through the walls of the upper room, its pause to console, its power to disclose and to heal, and its provocation to joy and exuberant praise. This is marvelous and dangerous; ordinary human flesh should not have to consider such alternatives.

3. 1 Cor. 2:6-16.

If we do die, then all that we saw in Him and in ourselves because of Him as He sat at table with us, now becomes in our death the transformation of ordinary existence. We become in our individual and common life the outer expression of His invisible nature, including the darkness of dereliction as well as the light of the transfiguration — that by which condemnation is condemned, false light is itself falsified, and daily life is a continuing intra-mundane ecstasy. Who will die to bear witness to the inner life of God, to become an expression of this higher order? Not many — or perhaps, in another way, somewhere inside, all of us know we are supposed to die. In moments of deeply centered reflection we know the death instinct is not biological but teleological — we have been given life so as to die for what is so much more important than our own lives. If we just knew a bit more — if we could just put out our hand and touch it, to be sure we are not being deceived. . . .

Now we must say a word of appreciation for Thomas.[4] All that we have said thus far has been in the subjunctive mood. But what if — the subjunctive that ends all subjunction — it is actually so. This, I think, is the dreadful realization that has made Thomas the most quoted empiricist of all time.

THE SOURCE OF THOMAS' DUBIETY

It is to Thomas' great credit that he knows a problem when he sees it. That is, I see in Thomas' famous dubiety not so much a problem of *whether* He lives, but *if* He lives — for *that* presents the problem. His doubt is rooted in a profound sense of the implications of such a claim and an unwillingness to take that step easily.

It is a problem to have the presumably dead Jesus, radically reversing the universal tendency of matter to disintegrate, appear before you in a form of tangibility you've never seen before. It is a problem so great that it may violently awaken you from a deep Newtonian slumber and put you into the world in a new way — yet without any sense of direction . . . perhaps, all you know to do is wander off and go fishing.

To be sure, the language of modern physics is not Thomas' language, but you might sense from the very way he demands empirical evidence that he is not about to give up his familiar three-dimensional world of cause and effect for the sake of anything that will radicalize space and time or finally alter the nature of what he has

4. John 20:24-29.

always assumed it means to be human. I imagine that he sees all too clearly that *if* He lives, the apparent and assumptive world we have always tended to take for granted is not actually definitive of us after all.

Of course, if Thomas had really wanted to avoid the implications of the claim his companions were making, if he had really wanted to avoid changing anything, he made a big, tactical mistake. He should have just walked away, left the scene so as not to be associated with marginal persons who thought that way. Short of that, if he simply wanted to stay in the group, the way to avoid the implication of that sort of groundshaking claim would have been to agree with it cheerily—"Oh, that's wonderful. That's really great! Yes, something surely did happen there." It's like what Sartre suggested for those who had bad faith: "Just say you believe in God, then you won't have to think about it anymore."

In either case, if you want to avoid the implications you don't, like Thomas, get impassioned and say, "I'm never going to believe this until I have the evidence right before me!" You don't start caring and demanding evidence in your life. Because then, sooner or later, you will surely walk headlong into the incarnation resurrected. The presence of Christ upon the earth and in human lives is very tangible.

Oh, yes, I know—"Blessed are those who have *not* seen and yet believe." Cynically, one can say, "Thank goodness he said that. I haven't seen anything and I don't want to, so I can *say* I believe, and by this saying, I can be better than Thomas and still not have it make any difference!"

No, in praise of Thomas, he knew a problem when he saw it, and he had the courage to say so, and the tenacity not to let go of it until he had an answer. Thus we learn from him that the abuse of invisibility for the sake of complaisance is vastly different from the "believing without seeing" of which Jesus spoke. The invisibility of which Jesus spoke *included* the resurrected body; the invisibility of which he spoke included a transformation of the visible world, included material impact upon human lives—healed bodies and restored relationships. The invisibility of which he spoke made a tremendous visible difference.

Yes, sooner or later, when you get passionate about this you will walk headlong into the resurrected incarnation. When that stunning moment occurs or when that astounding realization gradually dawns upon you over a considerable length of time—since it is not the "moment" as instantaneous but the "Moment of Truth" that counts—

when you say "My Lord and my God," without actually having to touch Him after all, you know you have been struck an immortal blow, you have been permanently wounded by the sheer awe and wonder of this grace. Once wised up, you can't wise down. Your condition in relationship to Newtonian normality is forever altered.

REDEFINING THE NATURE OF EXISTENCE

Thus we become, as Thomas dreaded, wonder-wounded heirs of grace. This is a problem to be taken seriously because it thrusts us into the world with a profound sense of lack of fit. And if we ask why He couldn't do it in some more ordinary fashion more in keeping with common sense and prudent management of interpersonal relationships; if we ask why he couldn't do it in a more "I'm Ok, you're Ok" sort of way; if we ask why it had to be too good to be true—or in the more impassioned biblical language, why it had to be so good they "disbelieved for joy"—then we are reminded that there are those here and around the world who experience life not as ordinary but as too profoundly agonizing for words. There are those whose hurt is so great or whose emptiness is so vast and silent that they want nothing more than to find a way to get out of this life, to drop the course with dignity, if possible—a simple "withdraw" stamped on their cosmic transcript. Such agony may not ultimately have anything to do with political oppression, social status, education or the lack thereof, or living conditions. For such persons the silence behind the silence is too deep for words—they just long, as one woman told me, "for blessed oblivion."

In actuality, though, perhaps this condition is not just for some few wretched souls; perhaps it is, however obscured, the actual case for us *all*—it's just that for some that ultimate loneliness has punctured the surface of cheery, spritely, everyday consciousness, and then the silent desperation of our natural human existence is permanently visible. Perhaps it is not just *people* either, but all *creation*, this entire cosmic order and disorder, groaning and in travail like a woman giving birth, waiting for the fulfillment of the promise that was thrust into history in that proleptic period of the resurrection appearances.[5]

Perhaps that is at least one reason why it had to be too good to be true: there had to be a Word spoken from the other side of a situation that was too wretched for words. From the other side of the silence.

5. See W. Pannenberg, *Jesus, God and Man*, trans. Wilkins and Priebe, second edition (Philadelphia: Westminster Press, 1977).

So, then, a word of appreciation for Thomas—who believed the empirical test was necessary but found, like so many after him in all fields of human endeavor from mathematics and physics to the life sciences and the human sciences, that the truth always exceeds the proof. This was spectacularly the case with Thomas; but wherever the Christian faith is concerned, the truth challenges even the ground upon which proof was constructed, as well as the purpose for which it was first conceived. Where Thomas was concerned it challenged the ground and purpose of his very existence and compelled him to reexamine not only his frame of knowledge but his presumed reality, the ultimate intelligibility by which he valued knowledge itself. Here was a new answer to the question, Why know anything at all?

What holds our account together, I believe, is not merely narrative form, cultic memory, and the like, but that higher intelligibility which includes but transforms the narrative quality of experience and cultic archetypes, however deeply they may be embedded in the past or in the center of the human brain. Such an intelligibility includes our human nature—and far more of it than resides within the limits of reason alone—but it also includes how we through that nature come to a knowledge of the physical universe and even to a knowledge of God, all in response to first having been known and thus having yielded to the irreducible necessity of self-involvement in any knowledge of that higher intelligibility which Paul called "the mind of Christ."

Self-involvement implies self-knowledge, but as I have tried to suggest in the preceding paragraphs, knowing ourselves is no easy task primarily because we do not really *want* to know ourselves. Tacitly, we suspect that we will find human nature too devastatingly empty in itself and at the same time—perhaps in the same breath— too awesomely close to God. This unyielding truth about us beyond what we would ordinarily choose to know is nevertheless the key to our knowledge of everything else. That is, we know that sooner or later the boundaries of our best-conceived worlds, as with the best-lived lives, must yield to destruction, so we challenge those boundaries even where they seem secure, buffers against apparent chaos. Implicitly, we seem to know that the only order we can ultimately count on must exceed the boundaries of the known universe—the infinitesimally small as well as the infinitely great—and we know that knowing itself must yield to a higher intelligibility because knowing cannot be its own reason for being. Thus, it is from beyond

such boundaries that insight — sometimes of revolutionary proportions — *comes upon us*.

Yes — there is an inevitable and decisive shift somewhere in every
act of creation and discovery from the active to the passive mode: in
the moment of insight the knower is being known; the self is caught in
the act of knowing. From such experiences where we discover the
unreasonable workability of mathematics[6] as well as the incom-
prehensible realization that we have been fully comprehended by a
loving Other, we sense deeply within ourselves that under the right
conditions and because of how we are made and in spite of how we
have come to our present state, we have access to that higher intelligibility which directly or indirectly has addressed us. Nevertheless,
our access to that higher order always means some kind of death: eros
must be crucified and transformed,[7] because that order is by definition *not* something within the bounds, or an extension, of the
ordinary as ordinarily conceived. Most of us — Thomas-like in our
inclination toward survival and satisfaction — do not and probably
cannot *choose* to die. Only a far-greater consciousness than ours
knows how, as an act of freedom and integrity, to lay down its life of its
own accord, how to set its face toward Jerusalem — a consciousness
paradoxically greater than life or death, since the life it lays down it
also takes up again. This is so far beyond us that even to glimpse it we
may need to have it thrust upon us — or we ourselves must in crisis be
thrown to the very edge of it, so we can actually make the choice that
allows us to see and appropriate some measure of the mind of Christ.

THE JOURNEY OF INTENSIFICATION

To choose for what I have described here and throughout this book is
to begin the journey of intensification. Biographies of convicted
persons — persons who have been conquered by a vision and have died
to everything else, persons who in their confrontation with the
intransigency of everyday events have totally exhausted life's energies, and for whom only the vision was a source of new life — reveal to
us the ones who have undertaken the journey of intensification. Often
they have shortened the ordinary course of living, packing more of life

6. For a discussion of this point see E. Wigner, "The Unreasonable Effectiveness of
Mathematics in the Natural Sciences," in *Symmetries and Reflections*, pp. 222-237.
7. C. Williams, *The Descent of the Dove* (New York: Meridian Books, 1956), pp. 115,
173.

into less time, so as to be, above all else, "faithful to their vision." It has been said of these persons — the artists, the heroes, the saints, the scientists, the prophets — that with the luck of talent and opportunity, they have produced the classic[8] — the classic text or the classic life.

We admire these convicted ones and we are glad they paid the price, but we set them apart from ourselves as a special type. Yet in a deeper sense that higher intelligibility implicit in such lives belongs to everyone by virtue of the essential nature of human existence; in the classic we are given pause to listen, as if to some distant voice, vaguely familiar, supremely important — if we could just hear it distinctly, it would be the ultimate solution to our vast sense of cosmic loneliness. To be sure it is much easier if we do not have to undergo such extremities and die ourselves, but still something within us is awakened when the classic appears, and then the power of that higher intelligibility comes — however obliquely through the artistic or literary or scientific or personal medium — in upon us. This happens because of the way we are made; the dynamics and dimensions of human existence, from the outer boundaries imposed by human emptiness and the Holy to the inner struggles and coherence of human development, are made for — indeed are supremely suited to — that higher intelligibility, and we long for it.

That higher intelligibility, manifest somehow in all realms of human endeavor, is definitively and transformatively revealed in the incarnation — in the One fully God and fully human. Whether at the cross-sectional extremities of human pain and joy, or at the longitudinal extremities of the human life span from birth to death, the transforming Spirit of Christ precedes and seeks to refashion us according to His nature — indeed, according to Him whose outstretched arms are simultaneously crucifixion and liberation. The loving embrace which crucifies us, and the crucifixion which frees us, disclose a grandeur of design and an ultimate contingency far greater than the universe itself embodies because they include us and the answer to our relentless question, *Why?*

No wonder Thomas was afraid. In Him we have to do with ten billion light years of creation, quite specifically at a given point in time made conscious, personal, and accountable to its Creator — who is also the Creator of our consciousness for which it is essential that accountability be established. The frightening and wonderful thing is

---

8. David Tracy, *Analogical Imagination* (New York: The Crossroad Pub. Co., 1981), pp. 133-34.

to find in the depths of one's own existence, from whence the question *Why?*, the answer already given by His Spirit.

Thus the ordinary becomes extraordinary, and the commonplace becomes the place of communion with the awesome God who comes into us, sits at table and takes food and drink. Who would have suspected such a thing if it were not disclosed to us in the mirror of Jesus, the Christ, the Face of God, the Holy One . . . fully human and fully divine. Yet if we step away from that mirror we do not know who or whose we are. Thus it is as utterly gracious as it is essential that His image should indwell us and we Him, by the presence and power of His Spirit.

RECONCEPTUALIZATION AND RENEWAL

In the journey of intensification the major issue resides not in our experiences per se, but in Him, the reality in whom they find their ultimate intelligibility. As most persons who have had such encounters would acknowledge, convictional experiences do not belong only to those who have them, but to anyone who is willing to wrestle through to a dawning of the new sense of reality they disclose. To rethink and reconstruct the view of reality in which we live is to open ourselves to new and wider ranges of intelligibility and so to thrust our existence more deeply into the nature of Him in whom all things cohere.

The main goal of this book is not merely reconceptualization but renewal of life in the Spirit of Christ. Perhaps the mutual enhancement of mind and Spirit will yield up new ways of conceiving the life of God in our midst, so that the communion of saints may again—as at its Pentecostal inception—be ultimately defined by no other reality than the Spiritual Presence of God in Jesus Christ at work to restore an anguished creation to its Creator.

GLOSSARY

➤ *Terms are defined as used in this book; bracketed references following entries are to related texts rather than sources. Words set in* SMALL CAPS *within definitions are also listed as entries elsewhere in the Glossary.*

ABSURD. That which nullifies the ego's two-dimensional construction of ultimate meaning. There are two types: the negative absurd, which nullifies the ego's meaning in the direction of ultimate VOID; and the positive absurd, which nullifies the ego's meaning in the direction of THE HOLY. In both cases, the ego's best efforts to construct an intelligible and meaningful world are presupposed, but proven intrinsically insufficient—thus "absurd." [S. Kierkegaard, *Fear and Trembling; Philosophical Fragments*]

ARCHETYPES. Elementary forms of the collective—as distinct from the personal—unconscious, believed by Jung to be inherited from the collective history of the race and providing formal solutions to universal human dilemmas. Although Jung hypothesized a neurological root for these archetypes, he nevertheless believed in their trans-historical scope and overpowering impact upon the ego. Thus they cannot be directly ascertained by the ego, but only indirectly via symbolic disguise. [C. G. Jung, *Two Essays on Analytical Psychology*]

AUTHENTICITY. A genuine expression, or mode, of human existence that exposes its inherent Christocentric four-dimensionality.

AUTHORIZATION. The establishment of one's being under the authority of God, thereby making one the author of his/her own existence in response to Divine initiative. As distinct from authoritarianism, authorization respects PARTICULARITY in SELF and in others, and affirms a transformational relationship between that particularity and its specific historical context. [S. Kierkegaard, *Fear and Trembling*, esp. "Problem I" and "Problem II"]

BEING-ITSELF. Being is the implicit assumption behind everything that is and that occurs. The self-referential usage speaks of the Holy nature of God through the language and concepts of being. The inner nature of God becomes knowable only as God reveals God's self to us. [J. Macquarrie, *Principles of Christian Theology*]

BISOCIATION. The surprising convergence of two incompatible frames of reference to compose an original and meaningful unity. Bisociation is the basic unit of an insight, which may include several bisociations to form a complex new meaning. [A. Koestler, *The Creative Act*]

CATHEXIS. Investment of psychic energy in an object, situation, idea, or person. *See also* DECATHEXIS.

CHRIST EVENT. Shaped by the five steps of TRANSFORMATIONAL LOGIC, the definitive TRANSFORMATION of being and history in which, mediated by the Presence of Christ, all personal CONVICTIONAL EXPERIENCES participate; and it is the transformation to which these experiences refer as the basis for their meaning. [S. Kierkegaard, *Philosophical Fragments*; P. Tillich, *Systematic Theology Vol. II*; T. F. Torrance, *Space, Time and Resurrection*]

CONFLICT. Refers, proximately, to incompatible forces or frames of reference that hinder coherent interaction between SELF and WORLD. Ultimately, conflict refers to any incompatibility among forces or meanings that hinder authentic existence in Christ. In the proximate sense, psychoanalytic conflicts pertain; thus Freudian literature (*The New Introductory Lectures on Psychoanalysis*) or Eriksonian literature (*Childhood and Society*) are relevant. In the ultimate sense, existential conflict is at issue; thus Kierkegaardian literature (*Sickness unto Death*) is most relevant.

CONGRUENCE. An occurrence in which an insight fits the terms of a CONFLICT and resolves it with maximum sufficiency and without excess. Congruence thus establishes CONTINUITY among discontinuous instances in the unfolding of TRANSFORMATIONAL LOGIC. In contrast to CORRESPONDENCE, this is an internal test of truth. *See also* DISCONTINUITY.

CONSTRUCTIVE ACT OF IMAGINATION. Insights, intuitions, or visions that appear— usually with convincing force—in the borderline area between consciousness and unconsciousness. They convey, in a form readily available to consciousness, the essence of a CONFLICT resolution [B. Lonergan, *Insight*]. *See also* IMAGINATIVE CONSTRUCT; SPONTANEOUS IMAGE.

CONTINUITY. In two-dimensional terms, the intentionality of consciousness to seek an object and to resolve incoherence in the SELF-WORLD relationship. In four-dimensional terms, continuity involves two-dimensional DISCONTINUITY, but drives toward existential wholeness relative to the universe and the universe's ultimate purpose and meaning [T. F. Torrance, *Divine and Contingent Order; Transformation and Convergence in the Frame of Knowledge*]. *See also* INTENTION.

CONTRADICTION. A form of CONFLICT stressing incompatibility among cognitive frames of knowledge, and breakdown of, or exception to, logical coherence. As used here, it includes contrary as well as mutually negating statements.

CONVERSION. TRANSFORMATION of the ego which may or may not be mediated by the Spiritual Presence of Jesus Christ. If mediated by Christ, it is unto the ultimate transformation of all things; such outcome is essential to His nature. *See also* METANOIA.

CONVICTION. The state of being thoroughly convinced—as in judicial imagery, when the case is incontestable and will stand as part of the permanent record. As used here, such incontestability has three aspects: a convictor, the convicted person, and the endurance through time of the convictional relationship between them. [W. Zuurdeeg, *An Analytical Philosophy of Religion*]

CONVICTIONAL EXPERIENCE. A four-dimensional experience in which all three aspects of CONVICTION are condensed into a single moment. The depth and power of such experiences are as a guarantee to the endurance of the relationship between convictor and convicted.

CONVICTIONAL KNOWING. The four-dimensional unfolding of TRANSFORMATIONAL LOGIC leading up to, through, and beyond a time of CONVICTION.

CORRESPONDENCE. The public test in which a subjective ascertainment of truth—such as insight, intuition, or vision—is examined by the judgment of one's peers as to whether it fits the reality about which truth was allegedly ascertained. In contrast to CONGRUENCE, this is an external test of truth.

DECATHEXIS. The withdrawal or release of psychic energy from a previously cathected entity (*see* CATHEXIS). This is a psychoanalytic term; much Freudian or neo-Freudian literature elaborates its implication (e.g. Freud, *The New Introductory Lectures*).

DIMENSIONS. A geometric metaphor referring to unique aspects of human existence. These aspects are essential to the structure of human existence, and in their mutual relatedness they remain distinct but interdependent in the construction of the whole. In this study, the four dimensions of human existence are SELF, WORLD, VOID, and HOLY.

DISCONTINUITY. In TRANSFORMATIONAL LOGIC, the moving beyond a given mental set within which a CONFLICT is first addressed but within which it cannot be resolved.

DISINTEGRATION. When used with technical significance, this may refer to the loss of the integration, or of the integrative powers, of the psyche. Such loss means psychic illness unless what was thought to be integrative was actually false, defensive, or diminishing to psychic wholeness; then, disintegration may introduce higher integration.

DOUBLE NEGATION. The intervening and confrontational work of mediation in TRANSFORMATIONAL LOGIC. The existing CONFLICT (NEGATION) must be confronted (negation of negation) by an intervening mediational figure or insight (see MEDIATING IMAGE); the confrontation is made within the terms of the conflict, not as a radical removal from the conflict. As distinct from pure cancellation, double negation keeps the original negation, or conflict, in focus, yet alters its elements and significance to suit the nature of the mediator and the outcome of TRANSFORMATION. [C. Levi-Strauss, *Structural Anthropology*, ch. 11; E. Maranda and P. Maranda, *Structural Models in Folklore and Transformational Essays*]

ECSTASY. In general usage, a transcendent, "standing-outside-of" the ordinary limits of reality under the impetus of a benevolent spiritual presence. This usage is intended here, except where the term is combined with "mundane." Then it denotes a "standing-outside-of" simultaneous with a "standing-more-deeply-within" the everyday, or the two-dimensional reality. In mundane ecstasy, therefore, ordinary existence can be perceived four-dimensionally [S. Kierkegaard, *Fear and Trembling*; P. Tillich, *Systematic Theology Vol. III*]. *See also* QUESTION OF REALITY.

EIKONIC ECLIPSE. A THEORY OF ERROR in which rationalistic assumptions about truth cut off reason from its generative sources in personal knowledge and the imagination. *See also* RATIONALISTIC REDUCTION.

EMPIRICAL KNOWING. The process of acquiring knowledge through the investigation of empirical evidence, experimentation, and inference. Use of this term here stresses Francis Bacon's critique and revision of Aristotle's approach to knowledge. Bacon's *Novum Organon Scientiarum* stressed experimentation and demonstration in revision of Aristotle's philosophical realism in *Organon*. *See also* SCIENTIFIC METHOD.

EUCHARIST. The sacrament of the Lord's Supper and its larger context of meaning. The Greek word *charis*, which stands at the center of this term, implies grace, gratitude, and joy. *Eucharist*, then, is a heightened form of these terms: the Presence of Christ in the Eucharist is both His grace toward us and a cause for our gratitude and joy. In all that it implies, the sacrament is a definitive locus for interpreting Christocentric transformations, none of which is without SACRAMENTAL nature. [G. Kittel, *Theological Dictionary of the New Testament Vol. IX*]

EVENT. *See* CHRIST EVENT; KNOWING EVENT.

EXTREMITY/EXTREMITIES. Boundaries or limits of existence implied in dichotomies such as those between life and death, Divine and human, SELF and others, etc.

FALSIFICATION. In contrast to VERIFICATION, the use of proximate or elementary norms to demonstrate error. Overcoming such demonstration is necessary, but not sufficient, to verify a truth claim.

FIGURE-GROUND SHIFT/REVERSAL. A concept basic to Gestalt psychology which claims that all perception is bifocal: centrally on a figure, and tacitly or peripherally on the background, against which the figure stands out. A shift that reverses figure and ground often produces insight as the tacit dimension becomes the figure and supplies new sources of knowledge. A shift in perception may be reversed again to the original perceptual set. However, an analogous shift in the nature of human existence cannot be reversed again to the original nature. The original condition can be recalled, but not recovered. [M Polanyi, *The Tacit Dimension*]

GNOSIS. The Greek word for knowing, which may refer to human knowledge, knowledge of God, or God's knowledge of us. In the New Testament the proper object of *gnosis* is *aletheia*, or truth. Taken together, *gnosis* and *aletheia* imply a mutual INDWELLING of the knower and the known. [G. Kittel, "gnosis" and "aletheia" in *Theological Dictionary of the New Testament Vol. I*]

HOLY, THE. The Hebrew word for Holy, *qadosh*, implies the separateness of the Holy from all that is worldly, human, or profane. Rudolph Otto (*The Idea of the Holy*) emphasizes the quality of the Holy to fascinate and draw at the same time that it terrifies and repels. Thus he uses the phrase *mysterium tremendum fascinans* to refer to the Holy. In this study The Holy is capitalized, constituting a fourth dimension of existence which has, by the power of the Holy Spirit, the capacity to transform the other three DIMENSIONS.

IMAGINATIVE CONSTRUCT. The use of imagination to create truths which have been unavailable to rational reflection or empirical description; in contrast to imaginary constructs, which are fantastic and inherently fictional. The imaginative construct is the outcome of a CONSTRUCTIVE ACT OF IMAGINATION. [B. Lonergan, *Insight*]

IMAGINATIVE LEAP. The DISCONTINUITY characterizing TRANSFORMATIONAL LOGIC at the point of insight. Because it is imaginative (see IMAGINATIVE CONSTRUCT for imaginative vs. imaginary), it contributes to the completion of the transformational pattern, not disrupting the INTENTION inherent in TRANSFORMATION.

INDUCTIVE THINKING. The rational process by which one reaches general conclusions from particular instances; in contrast to deductive thinking, wherein one reaches conclusions regarding a particular instance by reasoning from general principles. Systematic thinking involves both modes, but a given thinker may stress one mode more than the other.

INDWELLING. A term used by M. Polanyi (*Personal Knowledge*) to indicate the phase of knowing in which the knower moves into deep personal interaction with the known. To indwell a situation, object, or person is to allow its features and essential nature to impress themselves upon the knower, and to establish therefore in terms of its own intelligibility the conditions under which it may be known.

INTELLECTUALIZATION. The truncation of the process of INDWELLING and the premature placing of what is to be learned in terms suitable to intellectual presuppositions than to the intrinsic nature of what is to be known. In extreme instances this is a defense mechanism of the ego, but more commonly it can be viewed an as epistemological error in which the knower is striving for pure OBJECTIVITY [M. Polanyi, *Personal Knowledge*]. *See also* THEORY OF ERROR.

INTELLIGIBILITY. The correspondence and reciprocity between the structures and activity of human intelligence and the structures and activity of the physical universe. Raised to the level of "higher intelligibility," this refers to the *logos* of God's self-revelation in Jesus Christ, the God-man. [T. F. Torrance, *Divine and Contingent Order; Space, Time and Resurrection*]

INTENTION. The innate human tendency to strive for completion of the transforming event, which necessarily involves a dynamic interaction between conscious and unconscious. This is distinct from intentionality as used in phenomenology, since the latter is confined to consciousness, which always intends an object. Here it may be helpful to relate *intention* to the tension experienced in the self as one stretches toward a goal through the tenses of time (from the past through the present toward the future).

INTERDICTION. Authoritative prohibition, as when a parent prohibits a child from potentially harmful activity.

INTERLUDE FOR SCANNING. The second step in the LOGIC OF TRANSFORMATION. During this phase the CONFLICT is for a time put out of one's conscious attention; the creative unconscious then has opportunity to search beneath the surface of awareness for prototypes and patterns that allow the reenvisioning and resolution of the conflict. *See also* PERSONAL PROTOTYPES.

INTERPRETATION. The fifth step in the LOGIC OF TRANSFORMATION whereby the insight, which one has felt with intuitive force to be true, is critically examined by applying both the principles of CONGRUENCE and CORRESPONDENCE. *See also* MEDIATING IMAGE.

KNOWING EVENT. "Event" is described by the basic five steps in TRANSFORMATIONAL LOGIC. As *knowing* event, stress is placed on the power of the insight to generate new knowledge from reality beyond the immediate boundaries of consciousness.

KOINONIA. A New Testament term for fellowship, used here to refer to the unique quality of Christian fellowship which Paul Lehmann has defined as "the fellowship-creating reality of Jesus Christ." This rightly shifts the emphasis from the primacy of interpersonal interaction to the primacy of the reality of Christ's Spiritual Presence by which all interpersonal interactions are to be governed. [P. Lehmann, *Ethics in a Christian Context*]

LOGIC OF TRANSFORMATION. *See* TRANSFORMATIONAL LOGIC.

MEDIATING IMAGE. The specific content of the insight, vision, or intuition as constructed by the creative imagination in the process of TRANSFORMATION. The image mediates when it simultaneously negates the NEGATION of the original CONFLICT and supplies the positive alternative by which the original situation may undergo transformation (see fn 1 on pages 159-60). *See also* CONSTRUCTIVE ACT OF IMAGINATION; DOUBLE NEGATION; SPONTANEOUS IMAGE.

METANOIA. In the New Testament this term means basically "to change one's mind," "to convert," or "conversion." In Jewish piety it tended to focus on remorse for wrong; in Jesus' usage, however, the emphasis shifts to the positive, to the coming Kingdom of God already present in his person as mediator. In this book, TRANSFORMATION especially in relation to the CHRIST EVENT includes what is meant by metanoia in the New Testament. [G. Kittel, *Theological Dictionary of the New Testament Vol. IV*]

MOMENT. As used here the term owes a good deal to Kierkegaard's discussion of Parmenides and the Greek term *metabole*, "the sudden," or its synonym, *exaiphanes*, "suddenly." The latter is used in the New Testament in relation to the annunciation, the TRANSFIGURATION, the descent of the Spirit at Pentecost, and the CONVERSION of St. Paul. As H.-G. Gadamer once put it, " . . . this blow-like occurrence opens a new dimension of time which in the later terminology of the New Testament is called 'eschatological time.'" For many theologians and philosophers—such as Tillich, Heidegger, and Bultmann—the moment is decisive, but as Gadamer points out it is uniquely Kierkegaard who combines the Judeo-Christian understanding with the Platonic-Parmenidean dialectic. For Kierkegaard this is most decisively the moment when eternity and time are joined in the God-man, and, by the happy passion of faith in response to this grace, the existing individual is transformed. [S. Kierkegaard, *Concept of Dread* and *Philosophical Fragments*; F. Lawrence, ed., *The Beginning and the Beyond*]

MOMENTS OF ENLARGEMENT. A phrase used by poet Wallace Stevens to describe the disclosures of reality that characterize much of his poetry. Specifically, this phrase is used here to describe the vivifying movement of consciousness from a specific or local focus of attention to an awareness of the ultimate immensity within which one's being may be apprehended. These are not rare moments, but they are often quickly dismissed and insufficiently appreciated. [A. McGill, *A Celebration of the Flesh*] MUNDANE ECSTASY. *See* ECSTASY.

MYSTERIUM TREMENDUM FASCINANS. *See* HOLY, THE.

NEGATION. As a fundamentally derivative notion, negation must always be understood as negation of something. The nullifications which this term describes can be classified according to what is being negated. Since the general notion admits of many variants—such as limitation, refutation, CONTRADICTION, denial, perversion, annihilation, and the like—four basic types can be described as follows [general reference: M. Heidegger, *Being and Time*; J. P. Sartre, *Being and Nothingness*]: (1) *Calculative*. Preserves objectivity; refers primarily to the negation of subjective or egocentric distortions of presumably objective or universal truths. Positivistic science, e.g., exercises calculative negation *in extremis* [M. Heidegger, *What Is Metaphysics?*; J. Macquarrie, *Principles of Christian Theology*]. (2) *Functional*. Negation in and of psychological functions including both intrapsychic and interpersonal relationships. E.g. shame is the functional negation of autonomy [E. Erikson, *Childhood and Society*]. (3) *Existential*. The negation of one's being; e.g. an experience of near-death which forcibly confronts one with finitude and imminent non-being [M. Heidegger, *Being and Time*; J. P. Sartre, *Being and Nothingness*]. (4) *Transformational*. The negation of negation via a mediator such that a new integration emerges, establishing a gain over the original negated state. For examples refer to pages 160-61. *See also* DOUBLE NEGATION.

NORMALITY. Healthy ego functioning, which constitutes two-dimensional "normality." Under the impact or influence of TRANSFORMATION by the mediation of Christ, the ego continues normal functioning but in a de-centered, yet enhanced, fashion. This allows ego defenses and reality testing to be reversed and reevaluated in light of the Spiritual Presence of Christ [S. Freud, *The Ego and the Id*]. *See also* QUESTION OF REALITY; REVERSIBILITY.

OBJECTIVITY. In its purest form, the impossible goal of positivistic science to eliminate all personal factors, including the knower, from the knowing situation. Thus objectivity in this sense is not neutrality. The nihilistic potential of pure objectivity is described and illustrated on pages 31-33. Objectivity of a higher order can be affirmed with the recognition that it is a distinct category alongside, but finally inseparable from, SUBJECTIVITY within a comprehensive realm of knowledge necessarily including the knower [M. Polanyi, *Personal Knowledge*; *The Tacit Dimension*]. *See also* INTELLECTUALIZATION.

ONTOGENESIS. The development of the individual member of the species in interaction with its environment, in contrast to phylogenesis, the development of the species. This is an important pair of concepts in Piaget's genetic epistemology. [J. Piaget, *The Psychology of the Child*; *Genetic Epistemology*]

ONTOLOGICAL. The study of the nature of being as presupposed by and undergirding the development of a particular being (ONTOGENESIS). The latter is more functional; the former, existential. *See also* NEGATION.

ORDER OF BEING. The ONTOLOGICAL status of an entity and the essential nature of its being; in contrast to the order of knowing, which is the epistemological basis for any claim about the being of an entity. Although they are always related, one order cannot be reduced to the other. [J. Macquarrie, *Principles of Christian Theology*]

ORTHOGENESIS. This term was first taken from biology and applied to human development by Heinz Werner (*Comparative Psychology of Mental Development*). It can be described as a four-phase process of development (genesis) that tends to unfold in a straight (ortho-) line or invariant sequence. The four phases are: (1) global state; (2) differentiation; (3) specialization of differentiated aspects; (4) integration of the differentiated and specialized aspects of the global state into a higher or more complex unity. (See page 127, fn 4.)

PARTICULARITY. Philosophically this term implies a contrast to universality. This classical ONTOLOGICAL distinction underlies a more functional usage in which the term designates the personal uniqueness of a given individual as distinct from others with whom (s)he might be classified and compared.

PERSONAL PROTOTYPES. Patterns or models derived from personal experience, then used as a basis for creating new objects, ideas, or actions. *See also* INTERLUDE FOR SCANNING.

QUESTION OF REALITY. Psychologically, reality consists in the psyche's efforts to balance internal reality (affect, fantasy, bodily sensations) over against external reality (object, person, situation). The balance achieved is called the "reality principle," which governs the "normal" functioning of the ego. This reality is called into question when the third and fourth DIMENSIONS of human existence impinge upon the reality principle with such force that its balance proves intrinsically insufficient to deal with the intractable power and magnitude of human existence. Where, then, is the reality that meets the human need for an ego balance and at the same time embraces the full four-dimensionality of human existence? This question leads into a reexamination of reality and to the nature of Jesus Christ, the God-man in whom these conditions are met and fulfilled. *See also* NORMALITY.

RATIONALISTIC REDUCTION. This phrase includes objectivism (see OBJECTIVITY), EIKONIC ECLIPSE, and other epistemological distortions which in the apparent service of reason systematically exclude the knower from the process of knowing. *See also* INTELLECTUALIZATION.

RELEASE AND OPENNESS. The fourth step in TRANSFORMATIONAL LOGIC, in which the energy bound up with the CONFLICT is released, and a new openness to the surrounding environment—social, cultural, personal, and physical—ensues. The continuing presence of unresolved conflict constricts perception and interactions with the environment, but release opens perception to the world and spontaneously enriches interaction. All this plays into the gain implicit in the TRANSFORMATION of the original conflict-in-context.

REVERSIBILITY. In therapeutic context, this term has two closely related meanings: (1) the meaning of past experiences and of inevitable future experiences, such as death, may be automatically or subliminally altered; (2) one's self-consciousness is liberated to revisit the past or anticipate the future with increased flexibility, illumination, and freedom. Thus, defensive constriction upon the ego can be transformed from rigid to flexible—or become reversible in the sense that one is increasingly able to choose for or against patterns of psychological defense. God's action in effecting both forms of reversibility is decisive.

RITUALS OF DENIAL. Denial is a basic mechanism of ego defense in which fantasies, words, and actions are utilized by the psyche spontaneously—i.e. without conscious choice—to exclude from awareness the reality of an unbearable threat. Rituals of denial are repeated actions over an extended period of time designed to prevent the person from seeing that a threat exists. In usage here, both the VOID and the HOLY may constitute such a threat to the ego. [A. Freud, *The Ego and the Mechanisms of Defense*]

SACRAMENTAL. In a broad, thematic sense, visible forms of invisible and spiritual truth which "prepare the way of the LORD" (Isa. 40:3). Thus, as the various TRANSPOSITIONS of TRANSFORMATION participate in the logos, the ultimate order of all things become flesh in Jesus Christ, they have a sacramental quality [J. Macquarrie, *Principles of Christian Theology*]. *See also* EUCHARIST.

SCIENTIFIC METHOD. In a less than adequate sense, this category in epistemology has been described by John Dewey (*How We Think*) and his tendency toward INTELLECTUALIZATION in the process of scientific knowing. As such this method stresses INDUCTIVE THINKING and OBJECTIVITY in order to arrive at truths of empirical and pragmatic significance. In a more adequate sense, the scientific method is developed in full by M. Polanyi (*Personal Knowledge*). *See also* EMPIRICAL KNOWING; INDWELLING.

SELF. This inherently relational notion has three aspects: (1) *Reflective self-awareness* whereby, in reflection, one ascertains inwardly that agency which is the source of freedom, choice, and belief. (2) *Conscience* in the generic sense of knowing within and together with oneself. This stresses the self as an internal relationship in which the quality of the relationship is decisive; this may be felt as integrity of selfhood. (3) *Self as spirit*, in which the relationship of integrity is grounded transparently in the Spiritual Presence of Christ, "the power that posits the self," as a positive relationship (S. Kierkegaard, *Sickness unto Death*). It is argued here in agreement with Kierkegaard that integrity of self is intrinsically impossible without such a transparent grounding. *See also* SOURCE (OF THE SELF), TRANSPARENCY.

SELF-TRANSCENDENCE. This term may refer to any one of the three aspects of the SELF, but fundamentally it refers to the first aspect, in which one is given freedom to choose for or against a given situation. In different ways the other two aspects transcend the first and fundamental meaning of self-transcendence; the one in the direction of internal relatedness, the other in the direction of Divine groundedness.

SIGNIFICATION. The power of an insight to point beyond itself toward a wider horizon of meaning. Thus the solution provided by special and general relativity to problems in classical physics may *signify* the contingency of all creation upon a higher INTEL-LIGIBILITY. In this study, the ultimate horizon of signification is given in the logos become flesh: the God-man, Jesus Christ. [T. F. Torrance, *Divine and Contingent Order*]

SOURCE (OF THE SELF). Refers in immediate experience to the Spiritual Presence of Christ, in Kierkegaard's usage the "ground of the self." However, it implies further that when the SELF is "transparently grounded" it is fulfilling the intention of God that human nature be conformed to God's image. *See also* TRANSPARENCY.

SPIRITUS CREATOR. A classical way to designate the nature and mission of the Holy Spirit, the third person of the Holy Trinity. The Creator Spirit is most obviously at work in the creation of the world, of new being, and of the people of God in and for the ultimate redemption or re-creaction of all things. [R. Prenter, *Spiritus Creator*]

SPONTANEOUS IMAGE. The emergence of insight in the third step of TRANSFORMA-TIONAL LOGIC; it emphasizes the unpredictability and imaginative qualities of insight in effecting TRANSFORMATION. *See also* CONSTRUCTIVE ACT OF IMAGINA-TION; MEDIATING IMAGE.

SUBJECTIVITY, IMAGINATIVE. The generative, often unconscious, contribution that subjective life makes to the creation of new knowledge. It stresses that subjectivity is not ipso facto solipsistic but may indeed (as imaginative) generate new knowledge of wide objective or public significance. *See also* IMAGINATIVE CONSTRUCT.

THEOLOGICAL SYMBOL. *Symbol* may be understood initially in the Tillichian sense. That is, as distinct from sign, which is arbitrary in relation to what it signifies, the symbol participates in the reality of that which it symbolizes. However, as distinct from Tillichian usage, participation here means that the four-dimensionality of human existence is basic to the reality represented in theological symbols by their very structure. [P. Tillich, *Systematic Theology Vol. I*]

THEORY OF ERROR. An epistemological basis for distinguishing between truth and deviations therefrom. The tests of CONGRUENCE and CORRESPONDENCE have been applied here as bases for distinguishing between truth and error in TRANSFORMA-TIONAL LOGIC. Implied in both, however, is the potential—if not necessary—truth-bearing value of the imaginative insight.

TRANSFIGURATION. The illumination and divination of an otherwise unenlightened or mundane phenomenon. The implication is that the phenomenon as transfigured is the fundamental reality; the darkened version is its common appearance. The paradigm case of Jesus' transfiguration (Mt. 17:2, Mk. 9:2) reveals proleptically the es-chatological reality of his resurrection and glorification in the commonplace context of our humanity. In contrast to TRANSFORMATION, which as a process (though not in its outcome) may be largely invisible, transfiguration is a visible change of essential form (morphe). [G. Kittel, *Theological Dictionary of the New Testament Vol. IV*]

TRANSFORMATION. This key term does not merely refer to change in a positive direction, as common usage would suggest. Rather, transformation occurs whenever, within a given frame of reference or experience, hidden orders of coherence and meaning emerge to replace or alter the axioms of the given frame and reorder its elements accordingly. See pages 63-65 for some significant examples of this term used in this sense.

TRANSFORMATION IN KNOWING. A given frame of knowledge constitutes the context within which a CONFLICT resides; each conflict is defined as such in terms of its contextual frame of reference. Thus, a conflict might be solved within its given frame of reference as one solves a problem in three-dimensional geometry according to Euclid's principles. However, when the conflict requires a solution that challenges the frame of reference itself, TRANSFORMATION may occur. Thus, G. F. B. Reimann transformed geometry: moving it into four dimensions, he helped pave the way for Einstein's theory of relativity. Closer to immediate experience are the transformations described by Piaget whereby the developing child's use of language becomes grammatical and use of thought and idea become logically operational. In each case, the frame of reference (language or thought) is itself altered by transformation. [T. F. Torrance, *Transformation and Convergence in the Frame of Knowledge*]

TRANSFORMATION IN NEGATION. In formal terms, the order of negative assumptions in each of these three types of NEGATION — calculative, functional, existential — constitutes the frame of reference and experience in relation to which new, hidden insight or patterns of meaning emerge. These emergent phenomena then negate the original order of negative assumptions, which thereby undergoes transformation via the mediation of the emergent phenomena. In actual terms, transformations may be content-specific yet have a transformative effect on the frame of reference with respect to which they occur. The cases recorded in Chapter 6 best illustrate this point. *See also* DOUBLE NEGATION.

TRANSFORMATIONAL LOGIC. A patterned process that consists of the systematic inter-connectedness of the following five steps: (1) CONFLICT-in-context; (2) INTERLUDE FOR SCANNING; (3) insight felt with intuitive force; (4) RELEASE and repatterning; (5) interpretation and VERIFICATION. *See also* CONSTRUCTIVE ACT OF IMAGINATION; IMAGINATIVE CONSTRUCT; MEDIATING IMAGE; SPONTANEOUS IMAGE.

TRANSFORMING MOMENT. *See* MOMENT; TRANSFORMATION; CONVICTIONAL EXPERIENCE.

TRANSPARENCY. In Kierkegaardian literature, a direct knowledge of God without intervening persons, images, or symbols. Although Kierkegaard was not a mystic, his understanding was that if the self was to be free of despair it had to be transparently grounded in the Spiritual Presence of Christ. Although sometimes equated with love, this transparency must also be understood as basic to the whole range of Christian experience, including faith and hope. [S. Kierkegaard, *Sickness unto Death*]

TRANSPOSITION. The spontaneous appearance and recognition of a patterned unit of behavior in a variety of different contexts. Specifically the patterned process of TRANSFORMATIONAL LOGIC appears in psychological behavior, social organization, and cultural phenomena. Recognizing the pattern in different positions across disciplinary lines, unfolding in a fashion thoroughly indigenous to the context in which it is embedded, is referred to here as *transposition*. In contrast to imposition, this concept suggests that each context yields up the pattern in its own ways. The task of recognition is to see and describe what is happening. (This is distinct from C. S. Lewis' use of the term in his sermon "Transposition," in which two distinct orders of meaning or being exchange positions — see FIGURE-GROUND SHIFT/REVERSAL).

VALIDATION. The act by which an EVENT, truth statement, or experience is shown or declared to be in fact what it claims to be. As distinct from VERIFICATION, the establishment of truth here is not necessarily by a further gathering of evidence but by AUTHORIZATION, and by any way in which the authorizing one may place a stamp of truth upon the matter in question.

VERIFICATION. The establishment of a truth claim by evidence, and by logical and/or empirical demonstration; as distinct from FALSIFICATION. In contrast to VALIDATION, verification requires rational inquiry, experimental demonstration, inductive and deductive processes, and in the final analysis recognizes that truth will always exceed the proof. *See also* EMPIRICAL KNOWING; INDUCTIVE THINKING.

VOID. The third of the basic four DIMENSIONS of human existence: namely, human existence is destined to annihiliation and the ultimate absence of being. This irrevocable drift toward utter emptiness and nothingness which accompanies human existence from the time of birth has many faces — such as loneliness, depression, and death. [M. Heidegger, *Being and Time*]

WORLD, THE LIVED. Derived from Merleau-Ponty's *Phenomenology of Perception*, this phrase refers to the second major DIMENSION of human existence; it designates the universal human tendency to create and compose the external realities of one's existence — other selves, social and institutional realities, symbolic constructions of culture, and the physical order, including one's body — into a coherent, workable, and livable whole. Since these factors do not spontaneously generate such a coherent whole, the SELF — out of, and in interaction with, its physical, psychological, social, and cultural resources — constructs and maintains a world. In the absence or collapse of the horizon of one's world, pathological behavior may result.

INDEX